C

Down

to Specifics

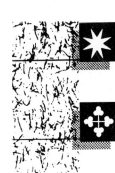

Getting

Down

to Specifics

James Hawley

Rio Hondo College

Charles Tilghman

Cerritos College

HarperCollins*Publishers*

Sponsoring Editor: Jane Kinney
Project Editor: Ellen MacElree
Design Supervisor: Mary Archondes
Text Design: Brand X Studio/Robin Hoffmann
Cover Design: Brand X Studio/Robin Hoffmann
Production Administrator: Paula Keller
Compositor: Circle Graphics Typographers
Printer and Binder: R. R. Donnelley & Sons Company

Library of Congress Cataloging-in-Publication Data

Hawley, James.
    Getting down to specifics / James Hawley, Charles Tilghman.
      p.   cm.
    ISBN 0-06-042712-4
    1. English language—Rhetoric.   2. English language—Grammar—1950–
3. College readers.   I. Tilghman, Charles.
II. Title.
PE1408.H4175   1991   91-10849
808'.0427—dc20   CIP

91 92 93 94 9 8 7 6 5 4 3 2 1

Contents

PART 2 THE ESSAY 119

Chapter 8 The Essay 121

Structure of the Essay 121

The Body 122
Basic Organization 122
Introductions 123
The Thesis Statement 123
Types of Introductions 124
Conclusions 128
Types of Conclusions 128

Chapter 9 Prewriting for the Essay 135

Brainstorming Ideas 135

Outlining Ideas 136

Informal Outline 136
Formal Outline 136

Writing the First Draft 138

Reading and Revising 139

Writing the Second Draft 139

Preface

Getting Down to Specifics uses a whole-language approach to teaching writing skills that integrates reading, writing, and discussion. This book also incorporates a process approach with methods for facilitating writing. In addition, it explains writing structure and mechanics so that students can gain a comprehensive understanding of all the principles involved in writing.

VARIETY IN TEACHING METHODS

We have included many diverse teaching methods in order to reach all types of learners and have used numerous discussion exercises that develop critical thinking and communication skills, as well as elicit ideas for the writing assignments that accompany each exercise. This process provides the students with a wide variety of ideas that enable them to begin writing immediately. We have included a variety of affective exercises because they appeal to a wide range of learning styles and develop writing-related skills. Collaborative learning in group discussions also allows students to share the knowledge they already have and extend it through the problem-solving process and comparing differing points of view.

VERSATILITY

Overall, we have provided far more exercises than can be used in one semester so that teachers can choose those that seem most appropriate for their students. This feature allows the teacher to alter the content of the course to the specific needs of a class; it also permits a teacher to use the book in different ways from semester to semester in order to maintain interest and variation in teaching the course.

COLLABORATIVE WRITING

Collaborative writing exercises also allow students to work through the process of writing with a partner and thereby gain further insight into the uses of different writing methods by discussing their effects and experimenting with them.

PEER EVALUATION

Exercises that involve critiquing in collaboration offer students experience in reading and evaluating the writing of other students, a practice that helps them gain a greater comprehension of reading and revising skills and how to apply them to their own writing. In addition, critiquing other students' writing gives individuals a sense of the needs of an audience and how to meet those needs.

WRITING STRUCTURE

Along with the process approach to writing, we have explained paragraph and essay structure in Chapters 3 and 8 with three purposes in mind. Understanding structure helps students see how to develop paragraphs and essays so that they become comprehensive and understandable to the reader. Understanding writing structure and implementing it in their writing prepares students for the kind of writing they will have to produce for other classes and in their professions. Finally, this approach to understanding writing parallels what students have learned from reading classes where writing structure is taught in order to increase comprehension. From our experience, many students have not been taught structure from the standpont of writing; this knowledge helps them to write effectively.

READING SELECTIONS

The reading selections in Part 4 provide relevant models for writing and topics for discussion and the questions accompanying each essay should further develop critical thinking, critiquing, and communication skills. The essays have been grouped by theme so that they can be compared in order to evaluate how writing techniques affect readers and how students can take advantage of those techniques. Each of these groups of essays develops ideas for student essays.

WRITING MECHANICS

The review of writing mechanics, Part 5, is intended to supplement the content of the course and is set up so that students can be referred by the teacher to specific problems that arise in their writing. Students can then quickly review a particular aspect of writing in order to overcome a deficiency that makes their writing less effective.

Students can, of course, refer to the review on their own to learn or relearn some of the fundamentals of writing they feel unsure of, and this can lead to a greater sense of confidence in writing. The review serves as an overall source of information.

This book has been developed over the last twelve years based on the needs and responses of students who have used it in their classes and have been kind enough to offer their criticism and suggestions. A number of reviewers have provided helpful critiques that we used in revising the text, and we wish to express our appreciation to all these people. They include Mary S. Barrett, Edgecombe Community College; Irene Clark, University of Southern California; J. C. Condravy, Slippery Rock University; Toni Empringham, El Camino College; Diane Jordan, Eastfield College; Joyce Kesser, Case Western Reserve University; Reba Kochesperger, North Harris County School; Wanda Kock, Watterson College; Gretchen Niva, Western Kentucky University; and Patricia Skipper, Trident Technical College.

Finally, we would like to thank the following people for their help in developing the book: Volza Arnold, Robert Chester, Ray Esquivel, LaVonne Moore, Kathy Paulsen, Cindy Reuben, and Kathy Solberg.

James Hawley
Charles Tilghman

P A R T 1

The

Process

of Writing

1 The Writing

Process

From previous experience you may have found that writing well is difficult; however, you may also have discovered that it can be rewarding in a way all its own. Writing can be hard because it involves a complex process of thinking, composing, and revising—a time-consuming task that may seem impossible at times. It is rewarding, for you can learn more about yourself and a subject from writing than from any other learning process. This is because you have to think about what you understand and express it so that a reader can appreciate what you have learned. Often this is not easy, but several techniques can make the process of writing less painful and help you save time. By following these techniques, you can avoid some of the frustration associated with writing and produce work of a higher quality.

BRAINSTORMING

Brainstorming is usually thought of as a group exercise, but you can use it by yourself. Brainstorming involves writing a list of all the ideas that come to mind for a period of ten to fifteen minutes. You may consider every possible topic that seems interesting or important to you, or you can concentrate on a specific subject. During this time you should write down each idea regardless of how good or bad it seems. You need not write in complete sentences; instead, you can jot down phrases and key words to keep up with your train of thought. This technique uses thought association as a means of generating a variety of ideas without interrupting the process by judging their merit. You may begin by listing topics, or, if you already have a topic, by writing down as many attitudes or opinions about that topic as you can. You may list reasons or qualities associated with these opinions; you may also think of advantages and disadvantages and causes and effects. In addition, you could write down examples or experiences. This process allows you to see the different possibilities available. Although a brainstorming session usually lasts ten to fifteen minutes, ideas will come to you afterwards that you should add to your list. When you are ready to start writing, you can look at your list and cross off those ideas that do not sound very good. Then, circle or underline the ones that appear the most interesting or relevant and pick the best reason or quality for each.

Consider the following example of brainstorming and the paragraph that was written using one of the ideas.

Topic: Living together before marriage

Advantages	*Disadvantages*
Get to know the person	Family difficulties
Real-life situation	Lack of commitment
Share responsibilities	Lack of respect
Compatibility	It's expensive
Habits	Cost of setting up household
Get a start on joint finances	Social acceptance
Companionship	Against religious beliefs
Avoid legal complications of divorce	Could be disinherited
	Get a bad reputation

The following paragraph was written after brainstorming this topic. I believe that couples should live together before marriage. Living together allows you to get to know the person's strengths and weaknesses, and know if he or she is responsible and dependable. By living together, you can decide if that indeed is the person with whom you want to spend the rest of your life. I learned this from an experience I had two years ago when I was in love with my boyfriend Manny. We had been going out for a year and a half, and I thought I wanted to marry him because we got along so well. He seemed to be so understanding, but I wanted to be sure, so we rented an apartment and started living together. At first it seemed like an ideal relationship, but after awhile things started to change. We had agreed to share the housework because both of us were working and going to college, but he would make excuses why he didn't have time to take care of his chores, and I would have to do them instead. At other times he would forget that we had planned to go out to dinner and go out with his friends without even leaving a note. After about three months I felt that I couldn't depend on him at all, so I moved out. By living with Manny, I was able to see that I didn't want to marry him.

Raquel Orozco, student

MAPPING

Mapping is a variation of brainstorming. It involves setting out ideas as they relate to a central idea in a form similar to the spokes of a wheel. This approach has the advantage of being more visual than brainstorming, and enables you to organize your ideas easily. Consider this example.

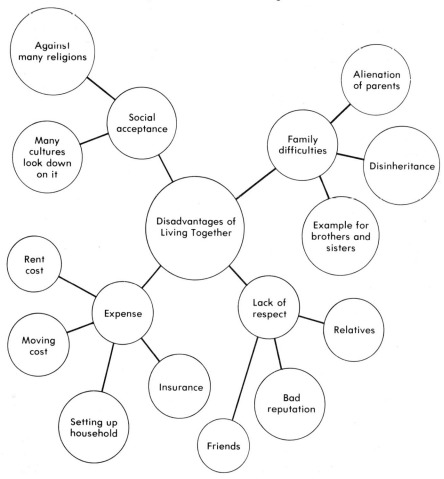

FREEWRITING

Freewriting is closely related to brainstorming and becomes quite useful when you do not know what you want to say until you begin writing. In this case you write out your ideas in sentences so that you capture the complete thought; however, at times you may also use phrases. Because this process helps focus your attention and use your power of concentration, it can generate a variety of ideas that may not occur to you otherwise. In addition, as with all other skills, practicing is important to developing ability. Freewriting gives you practice that should improve the quality of your writing.

With freewriting, you write as automatically as possible without evaluating how good or relevant each idea is. You are using writing to see where ideas lead; if you pause to evaluate an idea, you will interrupt your flow of thought. Therefore, do not stop to correct punctuation, spelling, grammar, or anything else while you are writing, for you will slow down the writing process. You may write out a number of related or unrelated ideas, expressing your thoughts about them. You may write about one idea in detail, developing your reasoning fully. When a new idea strikes, write it down too. You may use this technique for ten to thirty minutes or longer if you are still generating ideas. One of this technique's biggest advantages is that you will have written down several ideas. In many cases, you will have more than you can use, so you will then be able to choose the best ideas and develop them formally.

Occasionally, you will not write anything useful, but this is still not a waste of time. By sitting down and writing, you can start the creative process, part of which involves letting go of the problem when you are stuck and allowing your subconscious mind to work on it. Often, later that night or the next day, a series of thoughts will come to you that sound much better. When this happens, write them down so that you can remember exactly what they were and how you expressed them. If this kind of breakthrough does not occur, you can try the freewriting process again and see what develops.

The next two paragraphs show a sample of a freewriting exercise and then the paragraph written from it.

I learned the hard way that in order to pass a test you have to study and do well on tests. If you want something done well, you have to do it yourself. Whenever I had a test I told myself that I should study. For all of 10 minutes in developing your skills as a writer. I would be determined to study but soon I would be distracted and I would give up. Later on I would reprimand myself and I would swear that next time I would do it. It was just a cycle. I would study, I would give up, and I would fail. Usually my grades weren't that bad but they could have been better especially in math. I knew that I wasn't achieving my full potential. I wasn't really worried about my grade but when I saw the results of my tests I would get mad at myself. My lack of focus made me very angry. I knew that I could do it but I was just lazy. It has always bothered me because I don't know why I don't have the will to stick to it. These days things are a little better. I am able to study if I really will myself; occasionally I will become lazy but for the most part it's going well. I've learned that I have to have more control over myself. I need to focus myself so that I can do what I set out to do. If I am able to do that, then I will be able to study. I need to become more serious about my studies. It's just that I have this restless feeling inside myself. I have so many conflicting aspects inside of me. I don't know who I am or what I am supposed to do with my life. I believe that these feelings are part of why I am not serious about my studies. I need to understand why I don't take my studies seriously before I can solve my problem.

I learned the hard way that in order to pass a test I have to study. I also learned that I had to have more control over myself. I needed to focus my thoughts so that I could do whatever I set out to do. If I was able to do that, then I would be able to study. Whenever I had a test I told myself that I should study. For all of ten minutes I would be determined to study, but soon I would be distracted, and I would give up. Later on I would reprimand myself, and I would swear that next time I would study harder. It was just a vicious cycle. I would study. I would give up, and I would fail. Usually all of my grades were not that bad, but I knew that they could be better. I knew that I was not achieving my full potential. I was never really worried about my grades until I saw them, and then I would get mad at myself. One example was when I was taking history in the eleventh grade. I had a major test coming up, and I knew that I had to pass it. As usual I didn't really study because I couldn't concentrate. When the results came back, I had gotten an F. It really upset me, but I knew that I was the one to blame. I knew that if I wanted good grades, I had to develop better study habits. I was aware that I could do it, but I was lazy, and I had to overcome my laziness. After that I made more of an effort to concentrate when I was studying, and these days things are better. Occasionally, I become lazy, but most of the time when I study, I can focus my attention on what I am doing, and as a result my grades have improved.

Alma Nunez, student

CONCENTRATED THINKING

Using time to think about a writing project can be useful. In contrast to brainstorming and freewriting, you devote more attention to your thoughts, concentrating on possible topics, opinions, points of view, approaches, experiences, examples, and so on. By reflecting on your project, you can let your mind search out all the alternatives open to you. You can consider how your ideas compare and contrast with the opinions of others. To do this you may want to get away and think by yourself; however, you can use a group-think approach and evaluate ideas with others. Furthermore, you will need a place where there are relatively few distractions so that your concentration will not be interrupted.

OUTLINING

The outline is another way of writing out your ideas for a paragraph or essay. You write down the main idea of each paragraph in a complete sentence, along with the reasoning you will use to develop your opinion and the details you need to support each paragraph. Outlining is a useful means of planning what you want to write, seeing if you have enough material to work with, and organizing your ideas and paragraphs effectively. Although most people think of outlines in the formal sense, using Roman numerals, numbers, and letters for each part, you can quickly make an informal "scratch" outline of ideas without bothering with complete sentences. The chapters on the paragraph and the essay contain more information about outlines.

WRITING IN COLLABORATION

You have undoubtedly used this method before, working on a writing assignment with a relative, friend, teacher, or tutor. Writing with another person gives you the opportunity to exchange ideas from two different points of view. This enables you to build on each other's thoughts and consider various topics and approaches. When you work with someone else, you can usually discover more alternatives in a shorter amount of time than when you work by yourself. That way, you overcome some of the frustration associated with writing. Working with another can also give you a more objective view of your ideas. Most of us are far more critical of ourselves than others and we come to the conclusion that none of our writing is any good. Another person can offer a more realistic perspective, so you can better see the strengths and weaknesses of your writing and how to improve it. Furthermore, when you work with a partner, you can divide any research that needs to be done; the workload for each person is cut in half. You can work together to brainstorm ideas for topics, choose a subject that is appropriate and workable, write paragraphs and compose sentences, and evaluate and revise them—thus hastening the process of writing.

Since so much depends on your writing partner, try to find someone you can work with well, who can fairly and intelligently critique your ideas and writing. This may seem obvious, but it is essential. Your writing partner will greatly affect how useful this technique can be. Members of your class should be reliable since they are learning the same methods of writing. If you are working with someone outside of class, be sure to check her or his background in writing.

TALKING OUT IDEAS

A variation of concentrated thinking is talking out ideas. Talking to yourself is, of course, considered a sign of insanity, but that is not always the case. Many writers often verbalize ideas because this is an easy way to compose. It can help you hear more clearly how your writing sounds and enable you to rephrase sentences to express your ideas most effectively. If you get stuck trying to write out your ideas, this technique will hasten the process of writing. You can rephrase an explanation three or four ways out loud much faster than writing each of them out.

Because formal writing is more concise and detailed than conversation, you must talk out your ideas as you want them to sound in writing. If this technique works for you, you can use it to compose or revise sentences or dictate the first drafts of paragraphs and essays. A tape recorder can be useful in talking out ideas, especially if any length of time is involved. Being able to remember exactly how you stated an idea can be difficult, and a tape recorder serves as a memory aid.

THE EXERCISES

Each of the chapters in this book contains exercises that will give you the opportunity to evaluate a topic or situation and discuss your reactions. The exercises allow you to express a variety of ideas and also develop critical thinking skills that are important to writing well. Ideally, you will be exchanging different points of view rather than arguing about them, and you will learn from the experience.

These exercises lead to writing exercises, so you will be able to use the information gained from them in your writing. You will be writing paragraphs and essays, and the paragraphs should resemble the paragraphs in the body of an essay that express one main idea. These writing exercises will enable you to try out the writing techniques discussed in the chapter, and each assignment will suggest a particular method so that you can see how it works for you.

Exercise
Sentence Completion

This exercise gives you a chance to talk out ideas before you write and hear how other students express their ideas on the same topics. The class is to form two concentric circles with the students in the inside circle facing outward and those in the outside facing inward. Pair up with another person and sit facing her or him. The person on the outside will begin by completing the first sentence in as much detail as possible. You will have two minutes to do this, so you will want to explain your opinion in general and then give an example. After two minutes your partner will complete the *same* sentence. While you are the "listener," try to ask leading questions if your partner runs out of things to say before the time is up. After both partners have completed the first sentence, the students in the outside circle will move one place to the left so that everyone has a new partner and then continue with the second sentence.

1. The job I would like to have is. . . .

2. What I remember the most about the English classes (grammar and writing) I have taken is. . . .

3. When I work (on the job, at school, at home), I'm best at. . . .

4. The worst English teacher I ever had was. . . .

5. The best English teacher I ever had was. . . .

6. The most troublesome writing experience I had was. . . .

7. My most successful writing experience was. . . .

8. When I'm approaching a deadline, I. . . .

9. When I think about responsibilities, I think. . . .

10. If I could just learn how to. . . .

Writing Exercise
Sentence Completion

Look through the list of ideas and choose two statements that you found interesting. Develop each into a paragraph.

Prewriting

Use the technique of brainstorming and write down some of the things you said to your partner during the exercise and make notes on any of the examples you used. In addition, write down any ideas that came to mind after the exercise or while you were writing your list. Remember to jot down the ideas without evaluating them.

Writing

Write out each of your paragraphs automatically without stopping to analyze what you are writing. Use as many of the statements and examples that you wrote on your brainstorming list as possible, and try to explain each idea in as much detail as you feel is necessary.

Reading and Revising

After you have finished writing both paragraphs, put them away for awhile (at least two hours but preferably overnight) so you can be more objective in your critique. Then, proofread each paragraph out loud to hear how it sounds. Keep in mind the purpose of your writing and the audience for which it is intended. Check your explanation to see that the main idea of each paragraph is stated clearly, and take out any ideas not directly related to that main idea. Afterwards, check your examples, making sure they illustrate and support your opinion. As you read and critique your paragraphs, make notes in the margins for the changes you feel are necessary; then, rewrite your paragraphs, including the necessary improvements.

THE AUDIENCE

Keeping your audience in mind is essential for good writing. By knowing the level of your readers, you can adjust the sophistication of your writing so that it is appropriate. You will have a clear idea of how complex your topic must be, how much explanation you should include, and the amount and type of detail needed to support and illustrate your opinions. Knowing your audience can help you to choose the proper tone, informal or formal, and the correct level of language. It can also aid in making your writing more interesting and convincing for your readers, for you will be able to meet their needs more successfully.

Unfortunately, keeping your audience in mind could create an obstacle if you picture a highly critical reader. A form of stage fright can result that will prevent you from producing your best writing. Considering an English teacher as your audience could cause anxiety and apprehension that can lead to a complete writer's block. If you find this happening, broaden your perception of your audience. Rather than restricting it to an English teacher, include other teachers, perhaps your favorite ones, or other educated people. By this means you may be able to overcome the sometimes constricting effect of imagining your audience.

WRITING THE FIRST DRAFT

Before you begin to write the first draft, it is a good idea to go back to the prewriting exercise (brainstorming, free writing, concentrated thinking, or outlining) and circle or underline the ideas and details you want to include. Then, make an outline of your paragraph to see how you will organize it. Use the approach explained in freewriting and write as automatically as you can. Do not interrupt the process to check punctuation, spelling, or grammar, or you will stop the flow of ideas, slowing down the process of writing. The main point in writing the first draft is to get all your ideas on paper in complete sentences.

REVISING

Few substantial pieces of writing come out excellently the first time and professional writers usually make three or four revisions before their writing seems satisfactory. Revising is a method of reworking your writing so that it is more complete. This involves critically reading and evaluating what you have written, looking for the strengths and weaknesses and ways to improve, and then doing the necessary rewriting. Be sure to have a clear idea of your audience and focus on the purpose of your writing and what you want to accomplish. If you are writing an essay, you may need to reorganize paragraphs so that the order is more logical. You may also have to delete paragraphs that are weak or off the subject. When revising individual paragraphs, you may want to rephrase sentences to express your ideas more effectively. Unrelated or repetitious sentences can be deleted or condensed and combined to reduce wordiness. If your explanation is too short, you can elaborate on it so that it becomes more understandable and persuasive. You may replace the details you are using for support if they are ineffective, or you may develop them more completely if they are too sketchy. In some cases, revising can involve scrapping everything and starting over with a better idea or approach.

Letting Time Elapse

It is essential to let some time pass before you read your first draft since you are likely to be more objective in your evaluation. Ideally, you should allow it to sit overnight and read it the next day when you are in a different frame of mind.

When you read your writing immediately, you rarely see strengths and weaknesses because you are in the same mind-set as when you wrote it. You should start by reading your writing out loud; this slows you down and enables you to hear your writing more like a member of your audience. As you are doing this, make notes in the margins pointing out strong and weak sections, questions that come to mind, and changes to be made. You can check your paragraph against your outline to see that you have included everything and not added any ideas not related to the main idea. Finally, you can rewrite each paragraph, making necessary improvements to develop it completely.

Revising in Collaboration

As with writing, you can revise by yourself or in collaboration, but revising in collaboration has the advantage of accelerating the process. It also gives you feedback from a member of your audience so that you can better understand how effective your writing is and how to improve it. To use this approach, you must be able to accept criticism objectively and listen to someone else's opinion of your writing that points out its good and bad aspects. Most of us consider our writing very personal, and giving it to another person to criticize can make us feel quite uncomfortable. But if you overcome this feeling, you can give yourself the opportunity to learn from the reactions of another. You must be careful, though, to choose someone who can offer constructive criticism, rather than destructive or strictly negative criticism. In addition, you should work with a person who can describe why something is good or bad—"It's wonderful!" does not tell you anything useful.

WRITING THE SECOND DRAFT

A second draft of a paragraph or essay is always necessary. Use the notes on the margins of your first draft to develop each part. Add whatever explanation and details will make your writing more effective for the reader. The main focus of the second draft is to develop the strengths of your first draft and eliminate its weaknesses.

EDITING

Editing is often confused with revising. Editing is the last part of the writing process and involves reading and correcting sentence mechanics, spelling, and grammar. In this stage of writing you concentrate on finding and eliminating mechanical errors. Here it helps to slow down and read your writing carefully since finding mistakes in your own work can be difficult. It is usually much easier to spot the mistakes someone else makes and, for this reason, you need to take your time when you edit. Editing is explained further in the review of writing mechanics at the back of the book.

HINTS AND TIPS

Your attitude has a tremendous effect on the process of writing. It can turn it into an enjoyable and insightful learning experience, or it can make it pure torture. If you have a positive attitude about your writing, you will get more involved, and this involvement will create better writing because of the time and effort you put into it. It will also result in personal and intellectual growth that should make the process even more rewarding. To keep a positive attitude, keep in mind what you have to gain from writing and how improving your writing will benefit you overall. You also need to remember that you have the ability to write and to learn through the process.

Your level of interest will have a direct effect on the quality of your writing. It is almost impossible to write something good if you are not involved with your topic, so be sure to find something interesting. You may approach it from an unusual or controversial point of view, or you may look for what is most significant to you personally or for others. The key is in manipulating the subject so that you spark your interest.

There are peak times for writing, and you should take advantage of them. At certain unpredictable moments, a series of ideas will come to you that sound excellent. When this happens, stop whatever you are doing and write them down. The quality of your writing at that time will usually be quite high, so you will want to put your ideas down on paper immediately. If you wait, it may be impossible to recapture the ideas or the way you expressed them. You will also discover predictable peak times during the day to write. Some people like to write in the morning when they have the most energy. Others prefer to write at night when there are fewer distractions. Try writing at different times, and then use the time when you are most in the mood to write. Finally, ideas will come to you while you are falling asleep, so keep a pen and paper by your bed and write them down. The ideas you have then can be well worth saving, but they are likely to have vanished if you wait until morning.

Most people have a particular place where they feel most productive as a writer. Some of the most common are the bedroom, kitchen, living room, library, park, friend's house, classroom, and so on. Experiment at finding a place where you work well and use it. Creating an atmosphere conducive to writing can also benefit you. Good lighting, a comfortable chair, and music can aid the process of writing. It also helps to make sure when you begin that you have everything you need in order to use your time efficiently. You can lose your train of thought and waste a great deal of time if you have to get up and look for more paper, a pen, a dictionary, or the like.

Techniques

You may also try one or more of the following techniques:

Take periodic breaks (every 30 to 45 minutes) while you write. Do something else for ten to twenty minutes and then return to writing. This will give you a rest that can improve your concentration.

Schedule your writing so that you have plenty of time. Start doing the preliminary work as soon as you get the assignment, and then work at it on a regular basis, rather than waiting until the last minute.

If you become overwhelmed by the size of the project, break it down into individual parts and work on them one at a time.

Keep your writing together. Use a notebook, clipboard, or a place where you keep all of your writing so as not to misplace it.

Approaches

If you experience writer's block, try one of the following approaches:

Write in a different place or at a different time.

Try a different method of writing. If you usually write in longhand, use a typewriter or word processor.

Use a different technique such as brainstorming, freewriting, concentrated thinking, writing in collaboration, talking out ideas, working with a tutor, meeting with the teacher.

Change the atmosphere where you are writing.

Get rid of distractions.

These techniques can accelerate the process of writing and make it less frustrating. The writing exercises in this book will give you practice, and the discussion exercises will allow you to express your feelings and opinions, compare them with those of others, and work together to develop problem-solving and communication skills that will further enhance your ability to write.

CRITIQUING IN COLLABORATION

Some exercises in this book will include reading your writing in small groups and receiving feedback from fellow students so that you get a more concrete idea of how a reader would respond. Be as objective as you can. You should not take the criticism as judgment of you as a person—remember that it is only an evaluation of something you have written. Hearing the reactions of your classmates should speed up the process of revising, for you will be able to understand what needs to be done.

You will also be giving your classmates constructive criticism of their writing, noting both the strengths and weaknesses. In pointing out strengths, you should identify effective sentences, ones that have a definite impact on you, and that explain an idea well. This can be easily done by underlining those sentences. Regarding weaknesses, you need to indicate where ideas or explanations are too general. You can show where details are weak or do not relate directly to the main idea of the paragraph or where problems in punctuation or sentence structure occur. You may also write out questions that come to mind that the writer should address. Finally, you can make suggestions for improvements.

In order to hasten the process of critiquing, your teacher may provide a copy of the Worksheet for Critiquing in Collaboration. The first worksheet is quite simple with headings for strengths, weaknesses, questions, and suggestions. The second is a checklist for paragraph structure wherein you can identify specific strengths and weaknesses quickly.

 Exercise

Success Sharing

This exercise allows you to talk out ideas before writing and share experiences to see how they can help generate additional ideas. It also gives you the opportunity to recall experiences that occurred some years ago and use them in your writing.

I. Divide your life into three stages and think of a success for each. For example, if you are eighteen, you would divide your life into one to six years, six to twelve years, and twelve to eighteen years. You may want to write down more than one success for each period; then, pick three successes and visualize what happened in each situation. What were the circumstances that led up to this event? What occurred during the actual event? Who was there and what part did they play in your success? Finally, how did you feel about yourself at the time? How do you feel now looking back on these experiences?

II. In groups of three or four, one at a time, tell your partners in as much detail as you can the story behind each of the three successes. Be sure to cover each of the questions in the first paragraph. If the person talking seems to be leaving out significant details, ask leading questions to gain more information.

When all have told their stories, consider the following questions:

1. What different kinds of stories did people tell?
2. How did these experiences make you feel at the time they occurred?
3. How do you feel now, recalling them?
4. How can you use such experiences to continue to benefit you?

 Writing Exercise
Success Sharing

Choose two stories you told in class and develop each into a paragraph. Explain the sequence of events leading up to each experience and relate exactly what happened during the experience itself. Use quotations, if you can, to recreate the dialogue between the people involved and describe your feelings both during and afterward. In addition, employ as much visual description as necessary to enable your readers to see what happened.

Prewriting

Use the technique of freewriting and write as automatically as you can without stopping to make any corrections. Revisualize the experience while you write and include any ideas and details you used when you told your story in class.

Writing

Circle or underline the best sentences in your freewriting paragraphs and cross out those that are off the subject. Then use this rough draft for reference in writing your first formal draft. Again, write automatically without judging your writing.

Reading and Revising

Allow some time to elapse before you read your paragraphs; then read them out loud to hear how they sound. Keep in mind the needs of your audience and the purpose of each paragraph, and make notes on the changes that come to mind as you read. You may want to read each paragraph two or three times to see how it stands up. This practice can expose weaknesses more easily so that you can overcome them in the second draft.

Exercise

Risk Taking

This exercise lets you evaluate the risks associated with school and writing; you also will have a chance to compare ideas and see the different perceptions that people have.

I. Before you form groups, read the following statements and rate them with regard to how much risk you feel would be involved in each behavior. Use the class as a reference, writing the appropriate number from the scale below in front of each statement.

Would be no risk for me	Would be a small risk for me	Would be some risk for me	Would be a high risk for me
0	1	2	3

____ 1. Disclosing certain negative feelings about myself to others

____ 2. Revealing certain things about my past to others

____ 3. Asking for help with my problems from others

____ 4. Expressing anger toward someone in class

____ 5. Receiving praise on my writing in class

____ 6. Receiving constructive negative criticism of my writing in class

____ 7. Expressing constructive negative criticism about someone's writing in class

____ 8. Asking for feedback on my writing from a significant member of the class

____ 9. Expressing affection toward someone in class

____10. Receiving affection from someone in the class

____11. Making a statement that might anger someone in class

____12. Being the center of attention in class

____13. Expressing anger or dissatisfaction with the teacher

____14. Admitting I was wrong about someone or something in class

____15. Sharing a fantasy I have had

II. In small groups you are to do some amateur statistics to discover which statements ranked highest within your group. Go through each statement and add the total without discussion. Then, list the top eight statements, organizing them by order of importance. If you finish before the other groups, go back and discuss the risks involved with each of the top statements and make notes about them.

Writing Exercise
Risk Taking

Writing in Collaboration

You are to write one paragraph for this assignment. You may develop any statement from the previous questionnaire; for example, "Being the center of attention is a risk for some people because . . . " or "Some people feel that asking for help is a risk because. . . . " Limit your paragraph to one reason, explain it in detail, and give examples to illustrate what you are saying in general. In addition, you may write on the following topics:

1. A major risk associated with going to college

2. One way some people react to risks or a specific risk

3. An effect the element of risk has on your education

4. A major risk associated with writing and its effect

5. One way a person can overcome one risk in particular

Prewriting

You are to write this paragraph in collaboration, so find someone you would like to work with. Begin by discussing which topics are most appealing to you; then choose one of the prewriting techniques (brainstorming, freewriting, outlining) to start the assignment. Work together exchanging ideas and composing sentences, and share the task of writing.

Writing

Work together to author a first draft of your paragraph. Talk out your ideas and write them down automatically. Put most of your emphasis on generating ideas rather than criticizing them. Explain these ideas in depth and use supporting details.

Reading and Revising

Read your paragraph out loud and evaluate its strengths and weaknesses. Note these in the margin along with ideas on how to improve it where necessary. Talk out any of the ideas you have for writing the second draft, making notes of these as well. Then, work together to write a second draft of your paragraph.

Critiquing in Collaboration

When you have completed your second draft, get together in groups of four. First, read the paragraph out loud. Then, pass a copy to your new partners of your paragraph and the Worksheet for Critiquing in Collaboration. Read the paragraph silently, and work as a team to critique it. Underline the best sentences in the paragraph, those that made the strongest impact on you. Make specific references to strengths and weaknesses so that the writers can find them easily.

 Alternate Writing Exercise
Risk Taking

Choose one of the ideas from the risk-taking questionnaire or the five options on the previous page and write a paragraph by yourself. This time try using the technique of composing your ideas out loud before you write them. Combine this technique with freewriting and write everything that comes to mind without criticizing your ideas. Once you have written a first draft, follow the previous instructions for reading and revising, and compose a second draft of this paragraph.

Chapter

2 Using

The Senses

VISUALIZATION

One of the most useful devices for writers is visualization. You have undoubtedly read stories that came alive in your imagination much the same as when
seeing a movie. Such stories are interesting because they let the reader take an
active part, and since the reader can see what is going on, it becomes easy to
follow the action.

By creating a vivid mental picture of your subject, you can write a description that will create this same picture for your reader more efficiently than if you
tried to write it with a blank mind. You can use this technique before you write
by visualizing your subject and getting an overall concept of the details you
want to include. Then, while writing, you can keep a visual image in mind and
describe its most significant features. You may be able to do this with your eyes
open while you are writing; if you cannot, stop writing from time to time and
close your eyes to produce a strong mental picture.

The more visual your writing, the more accessible your mental picture will
be for the reader. Anytime you express an opinion and explain it in general, you
take the chance of someone's misinterpreting it. Because pictures are concrete
and exact, they are less likely to be misunderstood. As a result they can clarify
and support the opinion you are expressing. When we talk in conversation, we
tend to use generalizations to conserve time, and we take for granted that our
listener understands exactly what we mean. Often, however, this leads to
miscommunication, and what the speaker means is not what the listener

understands. By using visualization in your writing, you can avoid this kind of miscommunication.

To create a visual image for the reader, you need only present the most important objects or details and describe them—it is not necessary to describe everything. While you are writing, be sure to include all the significant features and provide enough detail to create a complete picture.

Note the author's use of visualization in the following paragraph.

It was a beautiful college. The buildings were old and covered with vines and the roads gracefully winding, lined with hedges and wild roses that dazzled the eyes in the summer sun. Honey suckle and purple wisteria hung heavy from the trees and white magnolias mixed with their scents in the bee-humming air. I've recalled it often, here in my hole: How the grass turned green in the springtime and how the mocking birds fluttered their tails and sang, how the moon shone down on the buildings, how the bell in the chapel tower rang out the precious short-lived hours; how the girls in bright summer dresses promenaded the grassy lawn. Many times here at night, I've closed my eyes and walked along the forbidden road that winds past the girls' dormitories, past the hall with the clock in the tower, its windows warmly aglow, on down past the small white Home Economics practice cottage, whiter still in the moonlight, and on down the road with its sloping and turning, paralleling the black powerhouse with its engines droning earth-shaking rhythms in the dark, its windows red from the glow of the furnace, on to where the road became a bridge over a dry riverbed, tangled with brush and clinging vines; the bridge of rustic logs, made for trysting, but virginal and untested by lovers; on up the road, past the buildings, with the southern verandas, half-a-city-block long. to the sudden forking barren of buildings, birds, or grass, where the road turned off to the insane asylum.

Ralph Ellison, Invisible Man

USING THE OTHER SENSES

For those of us who can see, the sense of sight seems to dominate our other senses, but hearing, touch, taste, and smell are also important senses in achieving a complete description. In depicting a certain place, the senses of hearing and smell add depth to the image you are developing in the reader's mind. These senses should convey more of the impression of being in the place you are describing, since they often remind the reader of similar experiences. The sense of touch can be used to enhance an image by particularizing the elements, such as air, sun, wind, rain, or snow; it can also depict how something feels. The sense of taste adds more specific detail to the experience of eating or sampling something, and this sense, like the others, can recall memories that will accentuate your description.

Notice how Margaret Atwood uses the senses of sight, sound, and touch in the following paragraph to make the experience come alive.

> The beach was dusty and hot, with trash from picnickers left here and there about it: paper plates showing half-moons above the sand, dented paper cups, bottles. Part of a hot-dog wiener floated near where we waded in, pallid, greyish-pink, lost-looking. The lake was shallow and weedy, the water the temperature of cooling soup. The bottom was of sand so fine-grained it was almost mud; I expected leeches in it, and clams, which would probably be dead, because of the warmth. I swam out into it anyway. Trish was screaming because she had walked into some water weeds; then she was splashing Charlie. I felt that I ought to be doing these things too, and that Buddy would note the omission. But instead I floated on my back in the lukewarm water, squinting up at the cloudless sky, which was depthless and hot blue and had things like microbes drifting across it, which I knew were the rods and cones in my eyeballs. I had skipped ahead in the health book; I even knew what a zygote was. In a while Buddy swam out to join me and spurted water at me out of his mouth, grinning.
>
> *Margaret Atwood, "Hurricane Hazel"*

 Writing Exercise
Using Visualization

In this exercise you use two photographs as the source for writing two short descriptive paragraphs. These paragraphs require visualization so that the reader can picture what you are seeing. You may use the two photos on the following page (Figures 2-1 and 2-2), or two photographs of your own.

Prewriting

1. Look at the first photograph and, using the techniques of brainstorming, list the most important things you see in the picture (there should be at least ten). You may also write down key adjectives or images that come to mind.

2. Study the second picture carefully; then close your eyes and visualize it in your imagination. Notice the details that stand out the most. Afterwards, look

Figure 2.1

Figure 2.2

at the picture again, noting how accurately you were able to visualize the dominant details. You may want to try this process a few more times until you can visualize the majority of the photograph. Finally, use the technique of freewriting to write a paragraph that conveys a mental picture of the photograph to the reader.

Writing

Use the information from the prewriting exercise as the basis for your first draft and, before you begin to write, revisualize the photograph so that you have a strong mental image of it. Write as automatically as you can, elaborating on the dominant features to create a complete picture for your reader.

Reading and Revising

Read each paragraph out loud to see how strong a mental picture it evokes. After reading each paragraph, compare your mental picture with the photograph, and make notes on which features could be developed in more detail. Also note any major or minor features that may have been left out, and delete any details that seem irrelevant. Finally, write a second draft that develops a full picture for the reader.

Critiquing in Collaboration

In groups of four or five, each person should read his or her paragraph out loud. Then, give the person to your right a copy of your paragraph and the worksheet for critiquing. After you read the paragraph, underline the best sentences and then fill out the worksheet, making specific references to strengths and weaknesses. Be sure to note questions the writer should address and suggestions for improvement. Pass the paragraph to the next person so that each paragraph is read at least twice.

 Exercise
Two Guided Fantasies

Meadow/Hammock

Close your eyes and get into a comfortable position. Your instructor will read the following guided fantasy, and while he or she does, use your ability to visualize a strong mental picture of the fantasy.

Picture yourself in a meadow where bees are humming. As you look around, you notice wild flowers blooming . . . the grass is tall and swaying back and forth in the wind. . . . You can hear the sound of river and feel the warmth of the sun. . . . There are two eucalyptus trees close together . . . and between them is a hammock. . . . You walk over and lie down on the hammock. . . . While you are relaxing, you pick up a glass of homemade lemonade from the table next to you, and sip it as the hammock swings gently. . . . A blackbird lands on your toe and says something to you. . . . Then, the trees disappear. . . . (Allow one to two minutes for students to complete the fantasy.) Now come back to the room.

Questions for Large-Group Discussion

1. How real was the fantasy? How well could you visualize the meadow? How did it feel to lie in the hammock?

2. What did the blackbird say to you? How did you respond?

3. What happened when the trees disappeared?

Skyscraper

Part I

Again close your eyes and get comfortable while your instructor reads the following fantasy.

Imagine yourself walking down the sidewalk in New York City. . . . Notice the sounds and smells that catch your attention . . . and the conversations that you overhear. . . . As you walk along, you look up and realize that you are at the World Trade Towers. . . . These skyscrapers are so high you can barely see the tops of them, so you walk inside and look for the express elevator. . . . When you press the button, the doors open, and you walk inside. . . . You press the button for the top floor, and *Whooooosh* it propels you upwards like a rocket. . . . When the doors open, you see a large lobby and beyond it an outside observation deck. . . . You walk over to it and notice that the deck doesn't have a guard rail . . . but you walk to the edge anyway and stand with your toes dangling over it. . . . Then, you look down to admire the view below you. . . . (Allow one to two minutes for students to complete the fantasy.) Now come back to the classroom.

Questions for Large-Group Discussion

1. How well could you picture being in New York City? In the elevator? On the observation deck?

2. What happened during the fantasy?

3. How did you feel during the exercise?

Part II

Close your eyes again.

Imagine that you have the ability to fly. . . . Test it out by flying out of the classroom. . . . See how it feels to fly as fast as you can. . . . Fly straight up into the sky as far as you can. . . . Then, dive back down at the earth, pulling up just in the nick of time. . . . Do a couple of loop the loops . . . and some of the other things you've wanted to do if you could fly. . . . Now at the speed of light, fly to New York City and land on the sidewalk. As you make your way down the street, you find yourself again in front of the World Trade Towers. . . . You go inside and press the button for the express elevator. When the doors open, you get inside and *Whooosh* you're at the top floor. . . . You walk out to the observation deck and notice again there is no guard rail, but you walk out to the edge anyway and dangle your toes over it. While you do, you admire the view below you. . . . Notice how you feel. . . . Now you leap off the edge and fly through the air. . . . (Allow one to two minutes for the students to complete the fantasy.) Now come back to the classroom.

Questions for Large-Group Discussion

1. How well could you imagine flying?

2. What happened when you went back to New York City?

3. How different was this experience?

4. What does this teach you about how you can use your ability to visualize?

 Writing Exercise
Two Guided Fantasies

Write two paragraphs from this exercise on any of the following topics.

1. Describe what you imagined in the meadow hammock exercise and relate its overall effect on you.

2. Describe what happened while you were going through the skyscraper fantasy and tell how you felt.

3. Explain the difficulty you had in fantasizing and describe what happened.

4. Explain how fantasy or visualization can be useful in writing, giving a long description to illustrate what you are saying in general.

Prewriting

Before you write, try to revisualize what you fantasized during the class exercise. Picture it as clearly as you can, and use your other senses as much as possible to evoke the feeling of being there.

Writing

Write as quickly as you can without making corrections. Keep in mind the picture you have created in the fantasy. Describe the features that made the strongest impression on you, and go into enough detail to recreate these for the reader. You may want to close your eyes periodically to revisualize the experience.

Reading and Revising

Read your paragraphs out loud to see how well the visual imagery creates the picture you have in mind. If parts of your description seem vague, add more details to develop a more effective mental picture for the reader.

Critiquing in Collaboration

In small groups, give the person to your right a copy of your paragraph, so each of you has a paragraph to read and evaluate. Read the paragraph and fill out the Worksheet for Critiquing in Collaboration. Then, pass the paragraph to the person on your right, so he or she can evaluate it. Each paragraph should be evaluated at least twice. Afterwards, give each member of your group the evaluation you wrote for him or her. When everyone has read their evaluations, discuss your reactions to what you have read and written.

 Writing Exercise
Using the Other Senses

Use one of the photographs on the following page (Figures 2-3 and 2-4) and a photograph of your own choice. Write a descriptive paragraph for each photo that presents a visualization of what you see and uses the senses of hearing, smell, touch, and taste to add further detail. You may not be able to use all the senses in each paragraph, but use as many as seem appropriate.

Prewriting

Look closely at the photograph, noting the most important features. Then, close your eyes and, using your ability to fantasize, imagine yourself in that

Figure 2.3

Figure 2.4

setting. Create a vivid mental picture, paying particular attention to the other senses that would be most dominant. Use brainstorming or freewriting to write down your observations.

Writing

Write the first draft of each paragraph quickly, referring to the notes you made in the prewriting exercise. Keep a visual image of the photograph in mind while you write, and elaborate on the details and senses that most affect you.

Reading and Revising

Let your mind go blank, and read your paragraph out loud, observing how complete a picture it creates. Crosscheck the mental picture you get with the photograph itself, and make notes on any details that you should develop more or that you have not included. Delete any sentences that seem repetitious or insignificant, and rephrase those that seem sketchy or awkward. Try talking out any of these that are particularly difficult to compose. Note which sense you have used the most, and see whether you can use any of the others. As a last step, write a second draft of each paragraph.

 Exercise

Blind Walk

This exercise has also been called a trust walk because you will be able to see how well you can trust another person and how well you can be trusted. This exercise also allows the participants to experience nonvisual senses that are usually overshadowed by the sense of sight. If the students wish, they can use a blindfold, but it is usually better to have the person simply close his or her eyes.

1. Look around the room and find someone you feel you can trust.

2. Go to the person and ask if you could trust him or her if you were blind and needed someone to help you get around.

3. After partnering up, decide who will be A and who will be B.

4. B will lead A anywhere on campus, introducing A to new sensations that are *not* visual: taste, touch, smell, and hearing. A's eyes should be closed the entire time. There should be NO *talking* because it detracts from the experience.

5. B leads A for exactly 20 minutes, introducing A to as many different sensory experiences as B can think of. After 20 minutes stop, and A leads B for 20 minutes, winding up in the classroom.

6. You must do nothing at any time on the blind walk to endanger the life of, or embarrass in any way, the person you are leading. You are to merit the trust placed in you. If you come to stairs, you should take extra care. Ask your partner if he or she would prefer to open his or her eyes. If your partner wishes to do this blind also, place his or her hand on the banister for orientation. When you are the blind person, use your feet to feel the stairs so as to gauge where to step. While you are blind, you should hold onto your partner's arm or shoulder for guidance.

7. Do not begin talking when you return until all members of the class have come back to the room.

8. When everyone has returned, As and Bs should converse one at a time in a large group, reporting their feelings of trust and other reactions.

 Writing Exercise
Blind Walk

Give a detailed description of what you experienced and how it felt to be blind. Go into detail about the senses you used the most and describe your sensations. Also, give some examples of the specific things that happened to you involving these senses.

Prewriting

Close your eyes and recall your experience during the blind walk. Make a list of the different situations you encountered and note the things you came in contact with that involved various senses.

Writing

Begin your paragraph with an overall statement about the blind walk that will be developed by the detail in your description. Then compose your paragraph by giving an extended description of the experience. As you are writing, use the senses of sound, touch, smell, and taste so your reader will get a vivid impression of what happened. Also use examples of different experiences that took place during the exercise.

Reading and Revising

Allow at least two hours to pass before proofreading your paragraph. Then read it out loud. Pay close attention to the detail in your paragraph to see if it creates a visual impression as you are reading. Check your depiction to determine where you can add further detail to make it even more effective. Go through and combine shorter sentences, and use the techniques for expanding sentences to add variety to your sentence structure. Write a second draft of your paragraph, and check your punctuation and spelling.

Critiquing in Collaboration

In small groups, give the person to your right a copy of your paragraph so that each of you has a paragraph to read and evaluate. Read the paragraph and fill out the Worksheet for Critiquing in Collaboration. Be specific in noting strengths and weaknesses, and include any pertinent questions that will help the writer develop the paragraph. Continue to circulate the paragraphs until all of them have been evaluated, and afterwards give each member of your group the evaluation you wrote for him or her. When everyone has read the evaluations, discuss your reactions to what you have read and written.

P A R T 2

The

Paragraph

3   The Paragraph

Although you have been writing paragraphs as part of the exercises in the first two chapters, a more complete understanding of paragraph structure can help make your writing more effective. A paragraph is a group of sentences developing one central idea or making a single point. Knowing the origin of the term may aid you in understanding its purpose. When essays were first written, they were not divided into sections as they are now; the columns and pages of the manuscripts flowed unbroken. Scholars would stop reading from time to time and, in the margin, write a brief explanation of the passage to summarize its main idea. These notes came to be called paragraphs ("writing beside") and later, after the invention of printing, essays were divided into groups of related sentences for the sake of clarity. This made it easier for the reader to comprehend and remember the main points. The word "paragraph" was then applied to these groups of sentences.

PARAGRAPH STRUCTURE

Knowing paragraph structure can help you write more effective and convincing paragraphs. There are three essential parts to the paragraph: the topic sentence that states the controlling idea, primary supporting sentences that explain the main idea, and secondary supporting sentences that give details or description to support and clarify the opinion being expressed. It is important to include all three parts so that the main idea is understandable and convincing. The topic sentence makes it possible for the reader to easily grasp the paragraph's overall point. The primary support clarifies what the writer is thinking, and the secondary support illustrates what the writer is saying in general.

The Topic Sentence

Usually a paragraph begins with a topic sentence that functions in much the same way as the ancient scholars' marginal notes. This sentence states the point, the main idea, of the paragraph. In effective writing, all the other sentences in the paragraph serve to explain or support the statement made in the topic sentence. The topic sentence does not have to come at the beginning of the paragraph; it may occur later—even at the end.

A topic sentence makes a value judgment of some kind about the subject; that is, it states an opinion or conclusion. For instance, it may declare that the subject is desirable or undesirable, constructive or destructive, or effective or ineffective, and so on. Another way of viewing the topic sentence is to see that it states a point to be proven or demonstrated. It is not a simple statement of fact: "Geneva is a city in upstate New York" is not a topic sentence because it makes no statement of opinion or judgment; there is nothing to be shown. The heart of a true topic sentence is the controlling idea, so called because it controls the direction the paragraph will take. "Geneva is a friendly city" is a topic sentence because it has the controlling idea "friendly"; what follows in the paragraph will have to support the idea of friendliness. In addition, the opinion expressed should be composed as a general statement and not be an "I" statement.

Limiting the Topic Sentence

A topic sentence must be limited so that the idea can be developed in a single paragraph. If the topic sentence is too broad (not limited), the paragraph is likely to be entirely general in its development. A series of generalizations cannot convince the reader that your idea is true or reasonable, for your reasoning will not have enough detail to make your point clear. The more limited your topic sentence, the more specific and convincing your supporting sentences are. For this reason the topic sentence should be limited to one reason, way (or method), or cause-effect in most paragraphs.

On the other hand, if a topic sentence is too limited, it will not express enough of an idea to be developed into a paragraph. Many times the statement is so restricted that it does not offer an opinion but instead states a fact.

The following sentences are examples of unlimited, limited, and too limited topic sentences.

| (Broad: long essay topic): | Nuclear energy is the most dangerous way to produce electricity. |

(Somewhat limited: short essay):   Waste products from nuclear
                                    plants threaten our environment.

(Limited: paragraph topic):   The disposal of nuclear wastes at
                                    sea is not so safe as it was be-
                                    lieved.

(Too limited): ⟍   states   The Navy disposes of radioactive
                 ⟍ a   ⟶   wastes 25 miles off the coast of
                    fact   southern California.

 Exercise

Identifying Good Topic Sentences

Part I

Read the following topic sentences and decide which ones are too limited, too
broad, or appropriate. Make a notation for each sentence, signifying whether it
is:

A. Appropriate topic sentence

B. Too broad

C. Too limited

   1. Competition in sports builds a person's self-confidence.

   2. Basic English is a requirement at most colleges.

   3. Speaking skillfully can enhance a person's career.

   4. Young harp seals are slaughtered every year for their valuable fur.

   5. Robot technology threatens to increase unemployment by reducing the
      number of factory jobs.

   6. Junk food can drastically affect your personality.

   7. Acid rain is deteriorating the statues in Greece.

   8. Small electric cars will be the main solution to the energy crisis.

   9. Women's liberation has saved men a great deal of money.

  10. Boredom is one of the major problems facing people today.

  11. A successful marriage takes a great deal of work by both the husband and
      wife.

12. Most wars could be avoided if countries would communicate effectively.

13. Spanking children causes more problems than it solves.

14. Knowledge does not always give a person power.

15. The information gained by wiretapping cannot be used in court.

Part II

Choose five of the sentences that were too broad or limited and rewrite them so that they would make good topic sentences.

Primary Supporting Sentences

The primary supporting sentences, usually two to fifteen in number, explain the meaning of the topic sentence. These sentences elaborate on the reasoning involved so that the reader can easily understand what the writer is thinking. Primary support serves to answer any questions about the topic sentence. Because of this, it helps the reader appreciate the significance of your opinion. The complexity of your subject will determine just how much primary support you will need. If your topic is complicated, you will need to explain your reasoning in detail; however, if your idea is fairly simple, you may only require a few sentences. In composing these sentences, you should address every writer's basic questions: when, where, what, why, and how. By answering these questions, your logic will be understandable and convincing.

Secondary Supporting Sentences

The secondary supporting sentences present specific supporting details that serve to prove what you are saying is true or clarify in concrete detail your general explanation. These are the most specific sentences in the paragraph, and they should be the greatest in number; consequently, they may make up the major part of each paragraph. Secondary supporting sentences are composed of facts, statistics, descriptions, examples, and illustrations.

Summary

1. *Topic sentence.* State the controlling idea for the paragraph in one sentence, remembering that everything in that paragraph should develop this idea only. The topic sentence must state an opinion and develop only one *key idea,* so it must be limited to one reason, quality, way (or method), or cause or effect.

2. *Primary supporting sentences.* Write two to fifteen sentences explaining more specifically what your topic sentence means.

These sentences should clarify the statement you are making about your subject in more detail, telling why what you are saying is true or how it happens.

3. *Secondary supporting sentences.*   Use specific supporting details that verify or further clarify the opinion you are expressing in general. These may be facts, statistics, examples, or illustrations.

Consider the following paragraphs and notice how in each the topic sentence seems to summarize all the following material. Primary and secondary supporting sentences are identified for you.

Being placed in a convalescent home can destroy an old person's self-confidence. Many times the workers in the home assume that the old people are senile and treat them as such. This treatment causes old people to feel useless, and they can give up the will to live because they are not allowed to control any part of their lives. My great aunt was in one of these homes. She was old but still capable of doing things for herself. The nurses and attendants would not let her leave her room to go anywhere alone, not even to the commissary. They told her when to go to bed and when to get up. The attendants insisted on choosing my great aunt's reading matter and telling her when she could watch television. One time when I visited her, she was sitting in her room with the television on, watching the C.B.S. Evening News which she always enjoyed. The nurse came in the room and said, "Remember, deary, you're not supposed to turn on the TV unless Bobby or I are in the room with you," and then she changed the channel to Lawrence Welk. My great aunt resented this treatment and changed the channel as soon as the nurse left the room. But eventually she gave up and began to believe she was incompetent. She stopped trying to do things for herself or even thinking for herself; in other words, she had no will to live.

Topic Sentence

Primary Support

Secondary Support (Example)

Carolyn Kunisaki, student

A third factor is *patience.* Again, anyone who ever tried to master an art knows that patience is necessary if you want to achieve anything. If one is after quick results one never learns an art. Yet, for modern man, patience is as difficult to practice as discipline and concentration. Our whole industrial system fosters exactly the opposite: quickness. All our machines are designed for quickness: the car and airplane bring us quickly to our destination—and the quicker the better. The machine which can produce the same quantity in half the time is twice as good as the older and slower one. Of course, there are important economic reasons for this. But, as in so many other aspects, human values have become determined by economic values. What is good for machines must be good for man—so goes the logic. Modern man thinks he loses something—

Topic Sentence

Primary Support

Secondary Support

Primary Support

time—when he does not do things quickly; yet he does not know what to do
with the time he gains—except kill it.

Erich Fromm, *The Art of Loving*

UNITY

The term unity relates to the quality of oneness. When all the supporting
sentences relate directly to the topic, the paragraph is unified—that is, it
develops only one idea. It is easy, however, to include details that relate only
indirectly to the controlling idea. These irrelevant details can confuse the
reader, making the main idea of the paragraph uncertain.

Consider the following paragraph from a student essay.

During my junior high school days, the early Seventies, when hard
rock was getting harder, everybody wore his hair long. The surfed-out
look was "in," and in order to be cool you wore Hang Ten shirts (the
ones with the two little feet sewn on) and Levi's cords, straight-leg or
flared jeans. They had to be Levi's or else you weren't cool. There were
only two kinds of shoes that were cool: deck shoes and Wallabees. Deck
shoes are tennis shoes with cloth uppers, and Wallabees, which were
more popular, were made of suede with rubber soles. If you were
caught wearing anything else, you were instantly teased, made fun of,
and thought to be "weird." It always turned out that the "weird"
people didn't wear cool clothes. Guys wore bead chokers around their
necks, and during summer Hawaiian shirts were "in," with cords and
sandals. Motocross bikes were cool; if you had a regular bike, you were
a "nerd." Skateboards with urethane wheels were definitely cool. Ten-
speeds were cool also, abut not as cool as Motocross bikes.

Lack of unity is the main problem in this paragraph (there are others as
well!). There is no definite topic sentence: certainly the first sentence does not
relate clearly to the implied main idea of "cool" attire. Sentences 6 and 7 seem
out of place. The idea in sentence 6 might be expressed either after the first
sentence (as revised, below) or after sentence 8, as a conclusion. The last three
sentences do not belong in the paragraph.

Here is the paragraph rewritten.

During my junior-high-school days, the early seventies, when hard
rock was getting harder, the cool look was the surfed-out look. Long,

sun-bleached hair was, of course, a part of the look. So were Hang Ten shirts (the ones with the two little feet sewn on) and Levi's cords, straight-legged or flared. During the summer Hawaiian shirts replaced Hang Ten. The jeans, however, always had to be Levi's; otherwise, they weren't cool. There were only two kinds of shoes for the surf set: deck shoes and Wallabees. Deck shoes are tennis shoes with cloth uppers; Wallabees, which were more popular, were made of suede with rubber soles. The really cool guys topped off their outfits with bead chokers. That was the uniform. If you wore anything different, you were "weird."

The paragraph has gained unity through the addition of a topic sentence and the deletion of needless repetitions and material not part of the main idea. Note also that the last two sentences now sum up the details in the paragraph and point back to the topic sentence.

One way to work toward unity is to make the topic sentence the first sentence in the paragraph. Then, as you write succeeding sentences, check each one against the controlling idea. You can also build in unity while planning the paragraph. If you make an outline, or brainstorm a list of details relating to your topic idea, you can check to see if each one supports the topic sentence and cross off those that do not fit. Then, when you begin the actual writing, the only details left will be those supporting the main idea.

COHERENCE

The sentences in a paragraph should not only all relate to the main idea, they should relate closely and logically to each other as well. When they do, and the discussion proceeds in an orderly flow, the paragraph is said to be coherent. Coherence, the quality of sticking together, helps keep the reader oriented and progressing through the paragraph. Lack of coherence often causes confusion and slows down the reading process.

Consider the following paragraph from a student essay.

One reason that students graduate from high school without the ability to read is that some teachers do not want to look bad. Teachers may have in their classes students that cannot read very well. The teacher may appear successful if he has to hold back students for not being able to read. It would be as if they did not do a good job of teaching. Instead of holding back the students, the teacher simply passes them to the next grade, for which they are not prepared. For a student who is slow it can be hard to learn the skills of reading. It can be frustrating not being able to learn. The student may not comprehend that it is not entirely his fault. The student may feel stupid and stop trying altogether.

One is tempted to say that this paragraph is simply not unified. There appears, however, to be a loose relationship between sentences 6 to 9 and the idea in the topic sentence. That relationship must be made definite and clear; what the paragraph lacks is coherence. The unnecessary and confusing shifts in number (from plural to singular, in sentences 2 and 3; from singular to plural in 3 and 4) also detract from coherence. In addition, sentences 3 and 4 say the same thing—a kind of repetition that does not move the discussion along. Here is the paragraph rewritten.

One reason that students graduate from high school without the ability to read is that some teachers do not want to look bad. A teacher may have in his class students who cannot read very well, but be afraid to give them failing grades. His fear is that if he holds back students who cannot read, he will appear unsuccessful as a teacher. Therefore, instead of holding back those students, he simply passes them on to the next grade, for which they are not prepared. In the new class, these students find it even harder to learn the necessary skills; they become frustrated. Not comprehending that their failure is not entirely their own fault, they may feel stupid and stop trying altogether. Still, if they have encountered another insecure teacher, they continue to "progress" until they are awarded diplomas.

In this second version the student achieved greater coherence by showing the relationships between ideas and bringing the discussion to a conclusion.

Coherence is achieved in two basic ways: by the arrangement of sentences and by the use of words and phrases that show the relationship between sentences. You have seen an example in which both methods were used successfully. Now let us take a closer look at achieving coherence by using various words and phrases.

Repetition

One way to keep the reader oriented to the parts of your discussion is to repeat key words and phrases from sentence to sentence. Such repetition can take several forms: the original word itself, a synonym, or a pronoun. The following paragraph, by a professional writer, demonstrates the effective use of repetition.

A simple example of the way in which a child can be seen putting together the rules for his language's grammar is the English word *his,* an "erroneous" form of *himself* which most children use until about the age of four, despite attempts by parents to correct them. So persistent is this "error" that it has been known since the time of Chaucer and it survives in several dialects of English. What is the explanation for its persistence? And why is it constructed by children who usually have never heard it before? The answer is that *himself* strictly follows the rules of English grammar that the child is acquiring. *Hisself* is a reflexive pronoun like *myself, yourself,* and herself—each of which is formed by combining the possessive pronoun him or her with self. The masculine possessive in this set is his and therefore, when combined with *self,* should rightly produce the reflexive *hisself.* But English is inconsistent in this instance, as all languages are in one instance or another, and the preferred form is *himself.* Children, by insisting upon *hisself* until the age when they acquire knowledge about the irregularities of English, show that they have internalized a basic rule of their grammar and follow it for a long time, despite adult attempts to correct them.

Peter Farb, "The-Language of Children," in Word Play: What Happens
When People Talk
(Knopf, 1973)

In this paragraph Peter Farb argues that a child's apparent error is, in fact, a demonstration that the child is learning one of the rules of English grammar. The word used as an example, *hisself,* is introduced in the topic sentence (sentence 1) and repeated in sentences 5,6,7 (twice, counting the division into its parts), and 9. In addition, it is referred to in other sentences by the pronouns it and its and by *this "error"* (sentence 2). These references remind the reader of the word in question while avoiding the excessive repetition of the word itself *(hisself).*

Transitional Devices

Transitional devices can help develop coherence within a paragraph by establishing a connection between statements or elements in a sentence. They thus emphasize the interrelationship of ideas so that the reader can appreciate their relevance. These devices include coordinating and subordinating conjunctions, conjunctive adverbs, and transitional phrases.

Coordinating conjunctions sometimes aid in achieving coherence, especially when the relationship between ideas involves simple addition or contrast. A complete list of these conjunctions can be seen in the comma section of the review of writing mechanics.

"The best car" used to mean different things to different people—the most reliable car, the most comfortable car, the biggest car for the money, the safest car, the car that handled best on the road. *But* as dollar-a-gallon gasoline fades into a fond memory and the price on the pump edges toward $2, "best" for many consumers is becoming synonymous with "most fuel efficient." *And* the question heard in car dealerships around the land is, "What mileage will it get?"

> *"How to Get the Most MPG's."*
> Consumer Reports, *April 1980, p. 228.*

Note that the sentences connected by but are not short, simple sentences but rather complicated ones. These conjunctions link ideas together, adding coherence to the paragraph. You should, however, avoid joining several simple sentences with coordinating conjunctions; the effect is choppy and incoherent—the opposite of what you seek.

Three Additional Transitional Devices

Subordinating conjunctions show a specific relationship between ideas that enhances coherence within a paragraph. These include words such as although, because, if, since, so that, until, when, and so on. Each conjunction links ideas and makes an association between them. A more complete list is included in the review of writing mechanics in the comma section.

Conjunctive adverbs are one of the most useful transitional devices because they indicate the kind of relationship between statements and elements within a statement. These include such words as however, moreover, consequently, and therefore. Again, a more complete list is included in the review of writing mechanics.

Transitional phrases may also be used to develop coherence in a paragraph. Because they indicate a specific relationship between ideas they thereby connect them. These include such phrases as for example, on the other hand, and in addition.

Transitional Words and Phrases

It is especially important to learn the exact meanings of these constructions so that you can use them properly. Some transitional words and phrases are listed below and categorized according to the relationships they indicate.

EXAMPLE	for example, for instance, namely, to cite an example, that is, i.e. (Latin *id est*, "that is"), such as
ADDITION	and, also, besides, furthermore, in addition, moreover, not only that but, next, first, second, etc.
COMPARISON	also, as well, equally, likewise, similarly

CONTRAST	but, however, nevertheless, nonetheless, notwithstanding, still, yet, although
EMPHASIS	to wit, in particular, most important, most of all, indeed, especially
TIME	in the interim, at the same time, subsequently, earlier, later, before, afterward, at last, ultimately, once
PLACE	elsewhere, here, there, above, below, beyond, where, behind,
EFFECT	as a result, consequently, so, therefore, thus, because
CONCLUSION	in conclusion, in other words, in brief, in short, finally, lastly, to conclude

While these transitional expressions can contribute to coherence in a paragraph, be sure not to overuse them. When that happens the effect is a self-conscious, overripe sort of writing that calls attention to itself and away from the content. Employ these devices where necessary, but remember also to work toward coherence by arranging sentences in a logical order, being consistent in verb tense and point of view (no unnecessary shifts in person), and making good use of repetition.

PARAGRAPH OUTLINING

Making an outline for a paragraph, discussed in Chapter 1, enables you to put into writing the entire concept of a paragraph so that you can organize ideas and evaluate whether you have enough information for completing it. If you stop to make a quick scratch outline, you can check that you included all three parts of the paragraph and that these parts develop the same idea. Many people just start writing whatever comes into mind—and they often leave out one of the important paragraph parts.

To make an outline, refer to the information you developed by brainstorming and follow the instructions below. If you find it hard to come up with any part of the paragraph, perhaps you should reevaluate the subject or idea so that you can change it and make it easier to write.

Summary

1. *Topic sentence.* State the controlling idea of the paragraph as a generalization and limit to one reason (or two closely related rea-

sons), one way, a quality, a comparison or contrast, or a cause-effect relationship. This should be general statement about the topic that applies to a variety of similar experiences or situations. Also, it should not be an "I" statement.

2. *Primary support.*   Make notes on the reasoning associated with the opinion you are expressing. These sentences or phrases clarify your main idea and encompass the overall thinking that substantiates your position. They should point out why your opinion is true or important, and/or how it is or can be accomplished.

3. *Secondary support.*   Decide on the type of support that would be the most effective (specific, typical, or hypothetical examples, illustration, description, facts) and note the details you need to verify and illustrate your opinion.

WRITING THE FIRST DRAFT

For your first draft, use one or more of the prewriting methods you have been practicing. When you write the rough draft, use all the ideas that come to you. Do not take time to rephrase sentences if they do not sound exactly right, and try not to get stuck attempting to find the "right" word. If you cannot think of the word, leave a blank or jot down another word, and continue writing.

READING AND REVISING

At this stage, you must consider who you are writing for and what this reader's needs are. Try also to concentrate on the purpose of your writing, and the methods for accomplishing it. To do this, let some time elapse before you read your first draft so that you can view it more objectively. Read the rough draft out loud so that you hear it better. While you are reading, keep in mind the three parts of paragraph structure and be sure you included them; also check that your paragraph is unified and organized. More specifically, be sure that you stated the main idea clearly and that you limited it. Check your explanation to see that is it understandable and convincing. Cross out anything that is unclear or off the main idea, and jot down ideas for improvements. Finally, check your details, making sure they illustrate your point and are developed fully. Remove any vague or repetitious sentences, and note the revisions you want in the second draft.

WRITING THE SECOND DRAFT

With your first draft and revision notes in front of you, write out your second draft, including the changes cited, and develop each part of the paragraph thoroughly. Keep the purpose of the paragraph and the needs of the reader in mind, so you can add the necessary explanation and detail. If you have trouble phrasing a sentence, try composing it out loud.

 Exercise

Proofreading for Paragraph Structure

Part I

Read the following paragraphs and identify their strengths and weaknesses, using the Worksheet for Critiquing in Collaboration. Note which elements of paragraph structure are strong or weak in each: a good topic sentence, unity, coherence, primary supporting sentences, secondary supporting sentences. Compose questions that the writer should answer within the paragraph and make suggestions for improvements. For this exercise, do not concern yourself with such matters as spelling, punctuation, or grammar.

1. Sometimes parents don't like to give advice to their children because they end up getting into arguments with them. One day, for example, I was getting dressed to go out, and I couldn't decide what to wear. I finally narrowed it down to a black dress with black shoes, or a pair of black pants with a gray blouse and black shoes. I wanted someone's opinion on which of the two outfits I should wear, so I modeled them both for my mother and asked what she thought. She said that I looked like I was going to a funeral and I shouldn't wear either one. That remark really made me mad. She then continued to say that I always wear black and that neither one of the outfits looked good. She really made me mad because I was undecided to begin with and she only made things worse. We got into an argument and I ended up wearing all black in spite of her.

2. We left-handers are constantly annoyed in all sorts of little ways by the world's right-handedness. The door to a telephone booth is designed to be opened by a right-handed person and inside is a phone with a receiver to be held by the left hand, freeing the right for depositing coins, dialing and taking notes. Has it ever occurred to you (if you are right-handed) that all wrist watches are made for right-handers? Try winding a wrist watch placed on your right wrist, and you will see how awkwardly the stem is

placed for left-handed winding. As a child, my mother tried to teach me how to crochet. It was very difficult for me, as I had to translate every left into right and every right into left. It all seemed backwards to me and took me several years to master it (well, sort of), whereas my right-handed sisters had no difficulty whatsoever. I felt like a real dummy!

3. Most people assume that all old people are senile, a burden, and just plain useless; however, that is not always true. Some senior citizens are still energetic, cheerful, and willing to give others a helping hand. For example, my father, who will be eighty-eight years old this January, walks six blocks to church every morning, rakes the leaves off the lawn, helps clear the table, and washes the breakfast dishes after the children and I leave for school in the morning. Furthermore, he gets along fine with the neighbors. They visit each other frequently and usually play cards or Parcheesi. Dad, like many other senior citizens, is a human being who has wants and needs just like everyone else. Senior citizens have plenty of love and wisdom and are willing to share it with us if we give them the opportunity.

4. Today, couples have no sense of responsibility towards one another. They live in a dream world promoted by soap operas and warm, passionate love stories. Couples of today have been programmed to escape from the realm of reality by these types of shows. They never take into account the expenditure, sacrifice, consideration, trust, and most important of all the love that must be developed between them. Couples, though they may not be married, must develop a union between themselves while sharing their life, and not live as two separate individuals.

5. Women are usually shown in commercials doing the cooking or cleaning, domestic types of work. It is always the woman doing the shopping in the stores. She spends all her time debating over what cereal or coffee to buy. The woman also talks and dances with the cats and dogs, as in the Purina Cat Chow and dog food commercials.

Part II

Choose one of the paragraphs and revise it so that it becomes fully developed.

UNITY IN ART

The same principles of composition apply to paintings and photographs. Both, when done well, should have a central focus of interest comparable to a paragraph's topic sentence. This focus should command the viewer's attention so that there is no confusion about the subject of the work. In both paintings and photographs, the subject is usually made more obvious by being placed in or near the center.

The subject may also be larger than the other people or things in the composition, thereby attracting more attention. Another technique is to place other people or things in the picture facing or pointing toward the main subject so that the viewer's eye follows them and ultimately ends up at the subject. In some cases the main subject is more detailed or more colorful than anything else.

Photographers, on the other hand, can focus on the main subject and leave everything else out of focus, forcing the viewer to concentrate on only one thing.

In Figure 3-1 the artist Edward Degas used several of these techniques. The woman is obviously the main focus of interest; she is in the center of the picture, and she is taller than the man next to her, so she commands more attention. In addition, the edge of the table where she is sitting points at her, as does the corner of the table in the lower part of the picture. The glass to her left and the bottle on her right "frame in" her body and add emphasis to the woman. Notice, too, how the shadows on the wall "frame" her face.

A photograph or painting, like a paragraph, should make only one state-ment, and everything in the picture must directly relate to and reinforce that statement. If the viewer cannot see a relationship between the component parts of the picture and the main subject, the picture's meaning will be unclear. The degree of unity depends on the care taken by the artist in choosing and placing the details or figures surrounding the subject. Using various shades of the same color throughout can also create a unified mood. In most cases the artist's effectiveness, like a writer's, relies on the unity within the composition. For this reason both need to be sure that everything they include has a specific reason for being there.

 Exercise

Evaluating Art

Study the following paintings (Figures 3-1 to 3-6) and discuss their techniques of composition and unity. Compare them, and decide which are more effective; explain what you feel the artist was trying to express through the painting. Also, you may look back at the pictures in Chapter 2 and discuss the use of unity in them.

Figure 3.1 *The Glass of Absinthe* by Edgar Degas.

Figure 3.2 *Relativity* by M.C. Esher.

Figure 3.3 *Marcelle Lender in the Ballet "CHILPERIC"* by Henri de Toulouse-Lautrec.

Figure 3.4 *The Fall of the Rebel Angels* by Pieter Breughel.

Figure 3.5 *Gin Lane* by William Hogarth.

Figure 3.6 *The Execution of the Rebels on the 3rd May 1808* by Francisco Goya.

Exercise
Making a Collage

A collage is a group of pictures that expresses a statement about a particular subject (see Figure 3-7). Effective collages follow the same principles of unity used in art, photography, and writing. There should be a central focus of attention that orients the viewer to the subject being developed. This center of attention should also relate the statement being made about the subject. The rest of the pictures serve to develop and reinforce that statement. In making collages you can also include short statements or quotations from magazines or newspapers to emphasize the message you are projecting.

In this exercise, make a collage using pictures from magazines, brochures, newspapers, or your own photographs. Pick a subject that interests you and express an opinion about it through the pictures. In composing the pictures you should try to arrange them so that they emphasize or enhance the central focus of attention. So that your collage can be seen and appreciated from a distance, glue your pictures onto a piece of construction board which is about 28 inches by 22 inches. It is also helpful to use a thick enough board so that it can stand up by itself.

Writing Exercise
The Collage

Using the topic of your collage, write a paragraph expressing one opinion about its subject. Limit your opinion to one or two reasons brought out in the collage and be sure the reader can understand how you feel. Use details to develop your paragraph, just as you used pictures in the collage.

Prewriting

Examine your collage and list all the ideas related to its subject. Use brainstorming to write out all the ideas that come to you; also write down some of the reasons associated with each idea. Make notes of the pictures you have used and jot down any other examples you think of.

Allow some time to elapse, and then return to your list, circling the best ideas and crossing off the others. Link related ideas and underline examples that could be used to support your main idea. Finally, choose the best idea and make a paragraph outline for it.

Figure 3.7 Collage.

Writing

Use automatic writing to compose a rough draft of your paragraph. You may want to begin with the statement of your main idea, but you do not have to; you can start by writing the details you feel are important. Do not hold yourself back by rephrasing ideas or trying to choose the right word, just keep writing.

Reading and Revising

Again, wait before you proofread your paragraph. Get a clear idea of your purpose and your audience's specific needs. Then read the paragraph out loud to hear how it sounds. Check to see that you have included a topic sentence stating the main idea of your paragraph, limited to one or two reasons. If you do not find one, write it in the margin or on a separate piece of paper so that you can include it in your second draft. Review your primary supporting sentences for sufficient detail. If you have not developed your reasoning enough, make notes on how you can expand it. Then, look over the details and see if you have developed them fully. Finally, rephrase any sentences that seem awkward and replace any words that do not seem quite right. After this, write a second draft of your paragraph, making the necessary revisions. When you have completed it, let your second draft sit for awhile before proofreading it.

Critiquing in Collaboration

In small groups of three or four, read your paragraphs out loud so that your partners can hear what you have written. Afterwards, pass out a copy of your paragraph and the Worksheet for Critiquing in Collaboration. When giving criticism, note both strengths and weaknesses and give specific references. In addition, write down questions that the writer should answer within the paragraph and make suggestions for improvements.

4   Details

Details provide one of the most useful techniques for developing a paragraph's secondary support. These include illustrations, examples, facts, and statistics, and they serve two purposes. They show the reader what happens under certain circumstances or what has happened at one time in particular. In so doing, they clarify the general explanation in the primary support. They can also prove that what you are saying is true. In using details it is important to explain the situation at length—a short example is not as convincing as a long one. In addition, you must emphasize the significance of your details. It is not enough to tell what has occurred or could occur; you must also explain why it is important so that the reader can understand the relationship. When you use details, consider how arguable your opinion is. If you are stating a controversial idea, use more than one illustration, example, fact, or statistic as proof. If the idea is not controversial, one well-developed example, or other type of detail, will illustrate your point.

Any opinion, even if limited to one reason and explained in general, can be misinterpreted. Details serve to clarify what you are saying and avoid misunderstanding. Concrete, specific details are needed; that is, details relating to the senses (concrete) and referring to particular individuals and events (specific). These details support your ideas, clarify your main idea, and make your writing more interesting.

You may use your own experiences, or you could use situations you have heard or read about from a reliable source. Your own personal experience can illustrate your point as well as provide an example the reader may identify with. Using a reliable source can add credibility to your opinion and make it more convincing to the reader. Consider the following types of details.

USE OF EXAMPLES

One of the most effective ways of expressing and supporting an idea is through the use of examples. Examples depict experiences and show the reader what has happened or may happen. Good examples can demonstrate in detail what you are saying in general, so your main idea becomes more understandable. You may have noticed that when a science instructor is trying to teach a principle, she always gives several examples to make the principle clear and concrete because our brains seem to process specific data more rapidly than abstract ideas. For this reason it is important to use appropriate examples in your writing to clarify and support your generalizations.

There are four types of examples: specific, typical, and hypothetical examples, and illustrations. Illustrations and specific examples are the most convincing because they refer to something that has, in fact, occurred. Often you cannot think of a specific example to demonstrate your idea and in these cases typical or hypothetical examples will help develop your paragraph.

Specific Examples

A specific example refers to an experience that took place at a particular time, and it explains exactly what happened so that the reader gets a clear idea of what occurred. Specific examples show what happened and also substantiate the writer's opinion. By giving a specific example, you prove to your reader that what you have said has, in fact, taken place at least once. You can use different types of specific examples to develop a paragraph: your own personal experience, the personal experience of someone you know, an experience you read about (from a reliable source), an experience you have seen in a documentary film, or specific facts.

When you use specific examples, you must provide enough detail for readers to appreciate the significance of what took place. To do this, you may explain the sequence of events, describe the interaction of people involved, and use dialogue to bring the situation to life. You may also quote or paraphrase an example from a reliable source.

Consider the following paragraphs that employ examples.

Most of us have a certain amount of fear about death. It seems only the very young and the very old who do not fear death. The young don't fear death because they haven't picked up our fears yet. The old don't seem to fear death as much as the rest of us because they may understand it very well and sometimes even welcome it. Maybe they see no need to hold on to past fears. Some seem to be more ready than others. I remember when my grandfather died last year. He knew he was dying, and he waited for all of his children to come to his bedside. As soon as he had seen each one, he died. It seemed as if, to him, it was a long awaited trip. He told me once how he was looking forward to seeing his wife again. That was what death was to him, seeing my grandmother again.

Marlene Sparling, student

Television commercials have a tremendous impact on children because they are very gullible. They believe everything they see and hear to be the absolute truth. They hardly ever question the validity or sincerity. If a commercial for a particular rug shampoo shows a filthy white carpet turn snow white in only minutes, a child really believes it actually will do that no matter what stains are on it. My daughter Jenny, who is five years old, saw me scrubbing spots out of the rug one day. She watched me for a while and then said, "Mommy, why don't you use that spray stuff we saw on TV? It gets the rug clean without any scrubbing. All you have to do is vacuum it. You wouldn't have to work so hard." I tried to explain to her that no rug shampoo works that well, but I could not convince her. As far as she was concerned, the "spray stuff" worked like magic.

Sandi Aldaco, student

Summary: Structure of a Paragraph Developed with Details

A paragraph developed with details must have all three elements: topic sentence, primary supporting sentences, and secondary supporting sentences (the details). The main idea must be stated directly in one sentence and limited in most cases to one reason. That idea must be explained in general with three to five or more sentences depending on how complex the idea is, so the reader knows exactly what the topic sentence means. Details should make up the largest part of the paragraph, ten to twenty or more sentences. When using examples or illustrations, the writer should not only tell what happened or happens but explain the significance of the situation and how it relates to the main idea.

Exercise
Brainstorming Ideas

Each of the statements below is broad enough to be developed into an entire essay. In this exercise you are to work in small groups to brainstorm the reasons, ways, and cause-effects associated with *two* statements. Follow the brainstorming procedure and write out as many as you can without evaluating them. After this, provide at least two specific examples that illustrate each reason, way, and cause-effect.

1. People discriminate against the young (or old).

2. Some advertising is false or misleading.

3. Children are not always a blessing.

4. My experience in high school was (was not) useful.

Exercise
Paragraph Outlining

Using the information from the brainstorming exercise, make an informal paragraph outline for both statements. Limit each statement to one of the reasons, ways, or cause-effects that you brainstormed. Then, make notes on your reasoning and the specific example you will use to develop your paragraph.

You may use the following format:

1. Topic sentence.

2. Notes on reasoning.

3. Notes on important details in the example.

Writing Exercise
Using Specific Examples

For this writing assignment, choose one of the statements and write a paragraph, limiting it to one of the reasons, ways, or cause-effects your group produced. Use primary supporting sentences to explain why the statement is true and/or how it occurs; then, give a specific example to illustrate your opinion.

Writing

Choose the most interesting idea and use freewriting to create a rough draft of your paragraph. Write as quickly as you can, including all the ideas or details that come to you. Follow each thought completely to see where it leads you without evaluating it. Try not to slow yourself down by phrasing each sentence perfectly. In using a typical example, go into enough detail so that the reader understands exactly what happens under the circumstances associated with the topic.

Reading and Revising

Proofread your first draft out loud to hear how it sounds, checking to see that your paragraph is unified and develops one major idea. Make sure you have included enough primary supporting sentences to explain your reasoning and that your example works effectively to demonstrate the main idea. Is it developed fully and convincing to other people? Afterwards, write a second draft, making the improvements you feel are necessary.

Critiquing in Collaboration

In small groups of three or four, read your paragraph out loud so that your partners can hear it. Then, give one of them the copy of your paragraph and the Worksheet for Critiquing in Collaboration. When offering criticism, comment on the strengths and weaknesses in the paragraph, referring to specific places. Write out questions the writers should answer and suggest ways to develop their paragraph. Make sure that each paragraph is read at least twice.

Typical Examples

Typical examples explain what happens under the same conditions over and over again. Composed of information gathered over a period of time, they do not refer to one specific incident. They may relate the sequence of events that take place under the right circumstances, or they may list typical kinds of behavior or effects. These examples illustrate what you have said in general, so the reader cannot misinterpret your point. You may use typical examples when you want to clarify how something happens but cannot think of a particular experience to support your paragraph. If you were defining *courtesy* in a paragraph, you might mention such examples as giving up one's bus seat for an elderly person, returning phone calls, and expressing thanks.

The following two paragraphs illustrate the use of typical examples. Although quoted statements appear in the second paragraph, these are not the words of an actual speaker, but probable responses. The first paragraph contains one fairly detailed example, the one about "Kitty's meow," but no specific cat is mentioned. The remaining examples are clearly general.

> Cats really know how to keep you guessing. Sometimes a cat will pester you for affection; then, when you feel like petting him, the animal doesn't want to be bothered. Maybe you think you've mastered all the various shades of meaning in Kitty's "meow," and that this particular one means he wants to go outside. You rush to open the door, and Kitty just stands there surveying the scene until you lose all patience and nudge him outside with your foot. Perhaps you think of your cat while shopping for groceries, and you buy him a toy. You bring it home, and it just lies on the living room floor for weeks. The day you decide to throw it into the trash, what does the beast do? Right. Suddenly it's his favorite thing. You can't win.
>
> *Sylvester Green, student*

> I would like to propose, as an hypothesis for consideration, that the major barrier to mutual interpersonal communication is our very natural tendency to judge, to evaluate, to approve or disapprove, the statement of the other person, or the other group. Let me illustrate my meaning with some very simple examples. As you leave the meeting tonight, one of the statements you are likely to hear is, "I didn't like that man's talk." Now what do you respond? Almost invariably your reply will be either approval or disapproval of the attitude expressed. Either you respond, "I didn't either. I thought it was terrible," or else you tend to reply, "Oh, I thought it was really good." In other words, your primary reaction is to evaluate what has just been said to you, to evaluate it from point of view, your own frame of reference.
>
> *Excerpt from "Dealing with Breakdowns in Communication"*
> *by Carl Rogers*

The choice of typical or specific examples depends on the how much space you wish to devote to it. In an essay there are both major and minor points; more emphasis, more detail, should be given to the major points. If you are trying to prove or demonstrate that an opinion is generally true, you will need to cite a number of specific experiences, occasions, or situations that verify your statement; otherwise, all you will have shown is that your statement is true in one isolated instance. That will not be convincing, especially to someone who does not already agree with you. Also, when you are considering which type of example to use, keep in mind that the more you rely on specific examples, the more believable your statements will be. Specific examples are more indisputable than typical ones.

Hypothetical Examples

Even when you are not writing from personal experience, you can support your ideas and enliven your writing with detailed examples. You can create examples from your general knowledge of the subject—hypothetical examples. (You probably know the word "hypothesis" from a science or history course; here, "hypothetical" means something like "imaginary.") Hypothetical examples project what will occur under certain conditions. They speculate on future experiences on the basis of past events. You can also use hypothetical examples when you want the reader to consider a possible situation and its likely results.

The following two paragraphs use hypothetical examples. In the first, note that although Bill and Vic are imaginary people, the events described correspond with our perception of reality; the specific details (estimates, most likely) seem reasonable. In the second paragraph, two hypothetical examples are included.

> Bill Burglar breaks into Vic Victim's house and steals a $500 television set. Bill is arrested, tried, found guilty and sentenced to the median term of four years in prison. During that time, the state of California will spend about $20,000 a year to punish Bill for stealing Vic's television set. Vic has nothing to show for his ordeal except an insurance report—and a paycheck stub showing three days lost in court. Later, Bill will emerge from prison a hardened criminal, likely to commit many more crimes against other innocent people.
>
> *From "Restitution as 'Punishment' for Crime," by Laurance S. Smith*

> Women are unpredictable because they can get away with it. It is widely accepted by both sexes that it is a woman's "right" to change her mind. Because men believe that women are born with unpredictableness, women take advantage of this belief and keep up the myth. For example, if a woman breaks a wedding engagement, she is considered fickle at the worst. It is normally accepted by all to be her right to change her mind about her fiance. However, if the man breaks off the engagement, he is the bad guy, the woman is jilted and he is considered the scum of the earth for leading her on. A woman may buy an outrageous amount of clothes one day and send most of them back to the store the next day. The store just takes it in stride, and the woman's husband may just shrug his shoulders as if that is to be expected. As

long as men are dumb enough to believe it, women will continue to exercise their "right" to be unpredictable.

Cathy Blackmon, student

 Writing Exercise
Using Typical or Hypothetical Examples

Writing in Collaboration

Choose one of the statements below and develop it into a complete paragraph by limiting it to one reason. Explain your reasoning at length so that it is clear to a reader who holds the opposite opinion and give a typical or hypothetical example to support and clarify your opinion.

Prewriting: Brainstorming

Each statement expresses a broad opinion. Choose two and brainstorm specific reasons, ways, qualities, and cause-effects to limit the statements. Then, brainstorm some of the reasoning behind the opinion being expressed. Finally, brainstorm typical or hypothetical examples (situations) that could be used to illustrate each opinion, and note the elements involved in each example that make it significant.

1. Staying married is growing more difficult.

2. Some women are (are not) unpredictable.

3. Some men are (are not) logical.

4. A person should (should not) live with a prospective mate before getting married.

5. Parents should (should not) give advice.

Writing

Pair up with a partner and choose one of the ideas you outlined as the topic of your paragraph. Review the notes you made during the brainstorming exercise and work together to write a paragraph. Talk out your ideas and write them down as automatically as you can. Be sure to explain your reasoning in detail and use at least one example to develop your paragraph.

Reading and Revising

Read your paragraph out loud, deleting the parts that do not seem relevant or important. Make notes on ideas for improvements that occur to you. Check your example to see that it is typical or hypothetical, that you have used enough detail, and that it relates directly to the topic. Then, write a second draft of your paragraph, making the necessary improvements.

Illustrations

Illustration is essentially a single, long example that might occupy an entire paragraph. It is usually a specific anecdote (story) that supports the idea in the topic sentence. An illustration differs from other examples because of its length and the amount of detail used. In the following example paragraphs, note the length of each illustration; you will get an idea of the detail needed. Use an illustration to clarify a complex idea that would not be fully explained by a shorter example. You may also use an illustration when you want the reader to know the importance of the opinion you are expressing. The added details in the illustration should help establish the significance of your main idea. Let's say your topic sentence is this: Honesty is not always the best policy. The remainder of your paragraph might relate a personal experience that demonstrates the truth of the topic sentence. The experience would constitute an illustration.

The first paragraph below uses a story to illustrate its main idea (expressed in the first sentence). The second paragraph uses a personal experience for illustration.

A tradition can be changed and weakened to the point where only a hint of the original idea remains; as time passes, parts of the tradition are lost until the tradition doesn't mean the same thing at all. Many people feel that Christmas is such a tradition; that the giving associated with Christ's birth has given way to over-eating, secular amusements, and the greedy exchange of presents. Another example of a faded tradition is shown in the film *The Lottery*. The film is about a traditional lottery, held once a year, in which the "winner" is stoned to death. The viewer knows that the lottery is traditional because it takes place on a fixed date each year and has gone on for many generations. There are traditional procedures involved in the lottery: the gathering of stones beforehand, the roll call to make certain that everyone participates, the use of the black box from which the slips of paper are drawn, and so on. But there are also signs that this is a weakening tradition. Several members of the community state that the lottery is being discontinued in other towns. Further, not all the community members are as blood-thirsty as they apparently have been in the past. When one girl hopes aloud that Nancy Hutchinson isn't chosen, Old Man Warner states grouchily that things "ain't the way they used to be." The most important and most chilling sign of all is that hardly anyone remembers why the lottery takes place. Only Old Man Warner, lucky veteran of 77 lotteries, recalls an old saying: "Lottery in June, corn be heavy soon." At some time in the dim past, this was a human sacrifice for good crops. Now that purpose is all but forgotten. Still, as with a number of other traditions, the townspeople persist in this observance, which ends with one of their number dead and a family in grief. Christmas may be a tradition whose true meaning is lost for many people, but at least its observance is still characterized by giving, and it does not involve the spilling of blood.

Josette Arellano, student

Writing a letter of complaint to a large corporation is often a waste of time. Although these companies have customer relations departments, they generally respond to letters of complaint with a form letter that disclaims their responsibility. Any further correspondence by the consumer rarely gets any personal consideration by a representative. They generally respond to such inquiries by restating the limitations of the company's liability. An experience I had recently serves well to illustrate this. I purchased a Subaru station wagon new in June 1979. At 8,000 miles while the car was under warranty, I took it to the dealer and complained that the engine was "pinging" a great deal while accelerating or climbing a hill. The service manager had the engine "scoped" but explained that the Subarus tended to ping because they needed more octane than was in unleaded gasoline. The mechanic could find nothing wrong with the engine, but at 37,000 when I returned to the dealership because the car was getting poor gas mileage and was losing power, I was told that the engine needed a valve job because there was no compression in the number one cylinder. The total bill came to $385.00; consequently, I noticed while driving the car afterwards, it no longer pinged while accelerating. I tested it further by driving up a hill, and the car had more power than it did new. From this I had to surmise that the original pinging problem was due to the valves in the number one cylinder not functioning properly, so I wrote a letter to the customer relations department of Subaru explaining the situation. I received a letter from one of their representatives which said, "Our experience indicates that had a manufacturing defect been in existence to cause the needed repairs, it would have presented itself at a much earlier time" (less than 37,000 miles). "Therefore, we regret that we cannot be of any financial assistance in this matter." I wrote the representative back to remind him that I had explained that the problem had "presented itself at a much earlier time," at 8,000 miles while the car was under warranty. I received a brief response to this letter which said, "the life expectancy of mechanical devices is subject to many considerations . . . the performance or lifetime of one vehicle cannot be directly related to that of another." This was supposed to explain why it was understandable for my car to need a valve job when most cars don't need one until 80,000–100,000 miles. I was rather displeased with this response, so I wrote the representative back to explain just how dissatisfied I was with his response, and I also wrote to the head office of Subaru in Japan hoping they would be more responsive, but their representative simply forwarded my letter back to the same customer relations department which I had been writing to before. This time the senior customer relations representative wrote back to me to explain that she had read all of my correspondence, but Subaru's position remained unchanged. Still unhappy with this decision, I wrote back to the manager in Japan asking him to review the situation personally, but he again forwarded my letter back to the same office, refusing to intervene. After writing six letters, I've received nothing but a great deal of frustration and a cancelled check for $385.

James Blake, student

Writing Exercise
Learning the Hard Way, Using an Illustration

Everyone learns at least one thing the hard way. This usually involves doing something wrong, ignoring the advice of others, and suffering the consequences. Many people take this approach to learn how to drive safely. They may have been told how to drive safely repeatedly but paid no attention. As a result, they may be involved in several accidents or receive numerous tickets before they change how they drive. Think of something you have learned the hard way, and write a paragraph about this experience. In some cases learning the hard way may involve a number of minor events finalized by a major one. If your experience was like this, you may use shorter specific or typical examples for the minor events and an illustration for the major one. In this illustration, go into a great deal of detail to show what happened so that you establish the incident's significance. If by chance you have not learned anything the hard way and are still repeating the same bad habits, you can write about something you should have learned the hard way.

Prewriting

First, think of as many things as you can that you have learned the hard way. Make a list, and choose one that made the greatest impression on you. Then, recall the events involved, and make notes on what happened. Finally, think of what you learned overall from this experience and write out a statement summarizing it.

Writing

Write your illustration as automatically as you can, including everything that comes to mind. Visualize the events so that you can include enough detail for the reader to appreciate what you experienced. Try not to get stuck choosing words or phrasing your sentences perfectly. Instead, concentrate on writing ideas as they come to you, knowing that you can revise later. After you have completed your illustration, write out a topic sentence, and explain its significance in general.

Reading and Revising

Read your paragraph aloud after you have let it sit for a while. See that your topic sentence is broad enough to make a general point about learning and check your primary supporting sentences to be sure you have explained the importance of your controlling idea. Then, review your illustration, making sure you have included enough detail to develop your paragraph completely. Make marginal notes of strengths and weaknesses that you notice. Rephrase any weaker sentences, and delete those that are repetitious or off the subject. Also, add sentences that will help clarify your point.

Critiquing in Collaboration

In small groups of three or four, read your paragraph out loud. Then, give a copy of it and the Worksheet for Critiquing in Collaboration to the person to your right. Makes notes on all four sections of the Worksheet, referring to specific places in the paragraph. If you find weaknesses in grammar, spelling, and punctuation, you can make notes in the margin so that the writer can spot them easily.

 Exercise

Aims of Education

This exercise explores your attitudes about education and compares them with the opinions of others. In small groups, rank the following statements in order of preference from one to eight, with one being the most important. First, read through the statements to see which ones seem most important to you. You may want to give each a value while you do this. Then, begin a group discussion by telling how you interpret each statement and explaining the reasons why each is important. As you discuss them, make notes on the reasons expressed so that you may use them later in the writing assignment. Reach a consensus by comparing reasons and evaluating the impact or significance of each statement. As you are doing this, take into consideration your own concerns and the overall needs of society. Remember: the purpose of this exercise is to exchange points of view rather than argue about them.

A. (_____) Society is held together by proper behavior. Education should teach people to be good, honest, upright human beings.

B. (_____) People are happiest when they know they have done a skillful job. Therefore, they should be taught things that will help them do their work better.

C. (_____) Knowledge should be valued for its own sake because in knowledge there is power; knowledge can build a person's character and sense of self-worth for in knowledge there is wisdom.

D. (_____) The family is most important. Education should teach one to be a more able parent and responsible family member.

E. (_____) In these times when we must all work together to build our country, education must first teach us to be informed, reliable, and cooperative citizens.

F. (_____) It is natural for people to want a reasonably comfortable way of life and a share in the good things of life. Education should primarily teach people how to attain money and success.

G. (_____) If our nation is to go forward, our people must know and understand their own historical and cultural roots. Education should teach us about our past and how it can help or hinder us today.

H. (_____) Freedom means choice. An uneducated person may believe all or nothing of what he hears or reads. Education should teach people how to make intelligent choices in all areas of their lives.

Writing Exercise
Aims of Education

For this exercise consider as your audience the president of the college who is making a survey of student opinions in order to reevaluate the goals of the college. The purpose of this assignment is to inform the president what you consider the most important aim of education. Choose the statement from the

Aims of Education Worksheet that you feel expresses the most important function of education. Do not copy it verbatim, but instead state the idea in your own words, and use it as the topic sentence for your paragraph, limiting it to one quality, reason, or way. Explain your reasoning in general, and then give one long, detailed example or a number of short examples to support your opinion.

Prewriting

After you have chosen one of the statements, compose a topic sentence that expresses the same opinion in your own words. Make a list of your reasons for this attitude and choose the best one. Similarly, list some examples that support this reason. If you have trouble thinking of a good example, try another reason and write a list of examples for it. Then, you may make an outline for your paragraph so that you can see how you will organize it.

Writing

Use your outline to guide your writing, and write your ideas without critiquing. If any related ideas come to mind, write them out to see if they might be better than your original ones. With this topic, be sure to explain your reasoning at length because of its complexity, and use as much detail as you can. You will want to develop your example(s) in the same manner so that they work effectively for the reader.

Reading and Revising

In addition to the standard practices of reading and revising, pay particular attention to the primary and secondary supporting sentences. Read your explanation carefully, rephrasing any sentences that seem awkward or vague. Elaborate on your reasoning so that the reader cannot misunderstand what you mean. Give this same critical attention to your example(s), taking out any sentences that seem repetitious and adding details that will help clarify the situations you are discussing.

Facts and Statistics

Television detective Sgt. Joe Friday ("Dragnet") was famous for one line: "Nothing but the facts, ma'am." This often-repeated reply was an admonition to the witness that interpretation was not wanted. In criminal investigations, as in many other important situations, only verifiable facts and figures are acceptable; conjecture, opinion, emotional reaction—these do not prove anything. The writing that you are called on to do in college (and elsewhere) often requires "nothing but the facts" to support or prove a point.

One source of factual information is your own research. Let's suppose that you live in a quiet, residential neighborhood containing a large, attractive park, and you want to complain to the city council about some uses of the park. You would, of course, express your own observations and opinions; but to get serious attention at City Hall, you also need facts and statistics. It would be useful to canvass the neighbors on your block—ask them specific questions— and tabulate the results of your poll. You might also, with their permission, include their names and addresses.

If your own observations have been accurate, the neighbors' responses might provide something like these hypothetical facts:

1. During and shortly after the recent "Peace Sunday" celebration, seven households reported burglaries.

2. Late in the evening the music was so loud that you and three neighbors were unable to sleep.

3. Immediately before and after the event, the neighborhood streets were impassable because of the celebrants' automobiles.

4. Visitors to houses on your block were unable to park on the street.

5. The neighbors unanimously disapprove of the music and some of the language heard over loudspeakers during the celebration.

Armed with such facts, you can now write a strong letter to the city council demanding that events like "Peace Sunday" be banned in the future. Of course, you cannot always conduct your own research when you need facts and statistics. When thinking and writing about topics of broader interest than, for example, a problem in your own neighborhood, you will have to rely on *secondary* research—the written results of other people's research. Two of the easiest sources are newspapers and news magazines such as *Time, Newsweek,* and *U.S. News and World Report.* However, if you wish to use surveys and scientific tests, you need to research professional journals and books. These can supply information on in-depth studies and investigations that can verify your conclusions. Because you are depending on the credibility of your sources, you must choose them carefully. The reputations of the journal and the author are important factors in establishing the reliability of your information.

Some factual information will be found in practically every periodical you encounter during a given week. Such facts can be considered general knowledge, and you are free to incorporate them in your writing with an introductory phrase such as, "As reported in the press. . . . " This procedure should be used only in connection with generally known facts such as the recent passage of a law, a rise or decline in interest rates, and the like. When you use detailed information from a printed source, however, you must give credit to the source. This is true whether you quote the facts verbatim (with quotation marks) or summarize the information in your own words. Failure to do so constitutes *plagiarism*, a kind of fraud in which you give the impression that someone else's ideas or words are your own.

The following passage is the lead paragraph from a newspaper article.

> In the months immediately before Japan's attack on Pearl Harbor, the FBI shared with military intelligence a double-agent's information disclosing that the Japanese had sought the assistance of Nazi Germany to learn about U.S. defenses in Hawaii, newly declassified documents showed Thursday.

You might use this information in a written discussion about this country's state of preparedness at the time of World War II, or to support your argument that the U.S. military could have prevented the Japanese attack.

Here are a couple of ways in which you might use the information and avoid plagiarism.

> PARAPHRASE: According to the Los Angeles *Times* (April 1, 1983), American military intelligence agents knew that Japan was studying U.S. defenses in Hawaii.

> QUOTATION: When American military personnel found out that Japan "had sought the assistance of Nazi Germany to learn about U.S. defenses in Hawaii," they should have moved to prevent a possible attack. (Los Angeles *Times*, April 1, 1983)

In a formal research paper, you would follow standard procedure for documenting your source, but the citation illustrated above should suffice for less formal paragraphs and essays. For more detailed instructions on secondary research materials, you can refer to Chapter 10 or consult a college librarian who will probably have helpful handouts on the use of the library. For now, note that the author of the news article based the statement on specific documents (identified later in the article) and that the two sample references above give credit to the source of the information.

Writing Exercise
Using Facts and Statistics

Choose one of the topics listed below and write a paragraph in which you use secondary research materials. Devise your own topic sentence and primary supporting sentences so that you are expressing a definite opinion; it is not enough simply to link a series of facts and figures borrowed from a printed source. Each topic has suggestions for finding the information you need.

1. A specific need of the students at your college. Most colleges publish, through the registrar's office or admissions and records office, a "student profile" or demographic breakdown of the student population. This information is available to anyone. You may also contact individual programs or departments on campus that can give you data they have collected.

2. An important development in industry. You may be able to find an article on this topic in *Time* or *Newsweek*. You may also check some of the business magazines or technical journals in your library. If you do not find anything in these, you may use the *Reader's Guide to Periodical Literature;* also, your instructor or a librarian can give you some helpful hints.

3. The overall critical appraisal of a recent play or motion picture. Usually, the large daily newspapers and the weekly news magazines review a motion picture within a week of each other; tabulation and comparison of critics' views should be fairly simple.

4. Public sentiment concerning a current social or political issue. Two of the best sources are, of course, the letters-to-the-editor column and the opinion section of the newspaper. You can also find articles and essays in news magazines.

Prewriting

For this kind of assignment, you must first find sources for your information before you can begin to write because you may not be able to obtain enough information to support your opinion, or the information you find may change your opinion. Depending on the topic, go to the library to check for references, or call or visit offices, departments, or institutions that can provide you with the necessary information. Once you gather this information, select the parts of it you wish to use.

Writing

It is usually easiest to begin your paragraph with a topic sentence stating the controlling idea followed by a general explanation of your reasoning, but you may organize your paragraph in any manner that is logical. In using facts and statistics, quote the most significant passages or data. You may also paraphrase ideas to develop your paragraph, but be sure to cite your sources.

Reading and Revising

You should follow the same general techniques for reading and revising. In this case, be sure that you have quoted your sources accurately and have included enough information to convince your reader.

Chapter

5 Description

USING DESCRIPTION

You have used description as part of the examples in previous writing exercises; in the chapter on visual details, you used it to evoke a sensory impression. This kind of description can make up the main body of a paragraph or an essay. The purpose of description is to create a complete mental picture for the reader and thereby establish the significance of what you are saying. There are two basic types of description: objective description, which chiefly provides information about the subject, and interpretive description, which expresses your attitude or reaction. In both cases you are developing a single idea about the subject that must be stated in the topic sentence of the paragraph (or thesis of the essay).

An important part of writing description is organizing the details in a coherent, logical pattern. This aids you in thinking about the topic, and allows the reader to follow your discussion. There are numerous ways of organizing descriptive details; the choice depends somewhat on the topic. If you are describing a place, you may present the overall scene and then focus on specific details; you may proceed from the farthest to the nearest features, or vice versa. In dealing with a well-defined area, you may describe it from left to right, right to left, top to bottom, bottom to top—whichever seems most appropriate and will allow you to finish with an important detail (beginnings and endings are positions of greatest emphasis). Physically describing a person, you may proceed from top to toe, or the opposite. Your primary consideration is having a definite pattern of organization and following it consistently.

Objective Description

Informative or objective description gives only factual details—the writer makes no interpretation but simply describes what has been observed. In this type of description, detail that will create a picture for the reader is essential. You will need to visualize your subject, the place, and situation as clearly as you can while writing so that you can include the necessary details to convey the same impression to the reader. In describing a person, place, or object, you must present specific sensory details that provide an unbiased understanding of the subject. To do this, you would describe the subject's features—dimensions, shape, color, parts, function.

Describing an event can be complicated. It may involve locale, people, any apparatus involved, the people's actions—any sights, sounds, and activities. Suppose you are describing a concert you attended. For a short paper you would first have to limit the topic to one aspect of the event. You might focus on the building or arena itself, the general appearance or behavior of the audience, the actions of a few people you encountered, the stage manner of the performers, the style of the music, and so on; each of these topic limitations would produce a substantial paragraph. Let us say you have decided to focus on the audience. You could begin by describing the spectators' overall appearance and average age. You could depict the dominant impression they made (keeping in mind that this is an objective description, and your impression should be one an average reader would agree with, given the details you present). The impression might concern the apparent mood of the crowd, their general behavior, their style of dress. To do this, you would describe in detail several representative individuals. If the people were unruly, you could relate the actions of several individuals or groups. Maybe it was an occasion when a number of concertgoers rushed to congregate in front of the stage, blocking the view of others. To make this situation come alive for the reader, you might tell of several people's vain attempts to see over the group.

Interpretive Description

In the kind of description just explained, details are presented as objectively as possible; the description is not interpretive or judgmental. The other type of description, interpretive, allows the writer to express reactions and attitudes even while presenting specific details. The purpose of such writing is to make the reader share your reactions. Your appeal is to her or his emotions, not just the person's senses. To do this, you describe the subject, or one aspect of it, and the effect it had on you or others. Describing the audience at the same concert, you might now conclude that they behaved *immaturely*, for example. In using interpretive description, you proceed in the same basic way as in objective description: an overall view of the crowd, then descriptions of specific individuals, groups, and actions that led you to your attitude. The chief difference is *how* you describe them. In this case you may "color" your details, that is, use words that express judgments. For example, when you describe an individual who shoved a couple of people while trying to get closer to the stage, you could state that he *rudely muscled his way* to the front.

The following two paragraphs make extensive use of description in their development.

> When I arrived at the ball park, most of our players were there watching a game which had already started. As I was walking over to where we were supposed to meet, I walked by four Greyhound buses, which were marked "chartered." I really didn't think much about it then; I just said to myself, "Wonder what all these buses are doing here." Continuing toward the ball field, I noticed a ball team warming up on the sidelines. There must have been at least 30 ball players, all wearing beautiful brown and gold uniforms. As I approached them, I could make out the writing on the uniforms (Carpetbaggers, Las Vegas, Nevada). It suddenly dawned on me why the buses were there. I remember saying to myself, "What have we gotten ourselves into?" Then I noticed another team warming up on the other side of the field, dressed in beautiful blue and white uniforms; they were from Colorado. As I continued walking toward our players, the ball field came into view. It was a beautifully manicured field, not anything like the fields we were used to playing on. Our players were sitting around under a large oak tree in the usual multicolored jerseys and Levi's or cut-offs, looking at each other in total amazement as to the present surroundings. Apparently, they had just come down the same path I had. We just didn't know what to think.
>
> *Michael Mize, student*

> Laurie has a petite, svelte frame measuring five feet, four inches tall and weighing 115 pounds, making her the envy of many women. Her light brown hair, combed softly away from her face and falling wistfully on her neck, flatters her oval face tremendously. Her hazel green eyes, slightly almond shaped, are always lively and sparkly, that complements her medium-sized, triangular nose that is minimally pointed at the end. Laurie's most attractive feature is her mouth, with a heart-shaped upper lip and full, red bottom lip that spread widely when she smiles, showing straight, white, perfect teeth. Amidst her rosy and creamy smooth complexion are small, faded brown freckles, giving her whole face a country-fresh look. Continuing down from her thin neck is her slender torso, containing a flat middle, 23-inch waist, well rounded chest, small back and curved shoulders holding firm, hairless

arms ending with tiny, feminine hands. Her full, yet tight, muscular buttocks join her strong, willowy legs, that give her an extra added womanliness that her figure naturally carries. Laurie wears her neatly pressed red and white pin-striped blouse and blue, freshly ironed jeans with a great amount of ease. She chooses brown leather sport shoes to match her comfortable wardrobe. Laurie's young figure and taste in clothes make her easily eligible to be in the pages of *Seventeen* magazine.

Denise Sandoval, student

Summary: Structure of a Paragraph Developed by Description

A paragraph developed through description follows the same basic structure as other paragraphs. The writer must include a topic sentence that expresses the controlling idea. This is important so that readers will understand the point of the description; without it the description serves no apparent purpose. The primary supporting sentences are usually limited to three to five, explaining in general the opinion stated in the topic sentence. The secondary supporting sentences, the detailed description, should make up the largest part of the paragraph, fifteen to thirty or more sentences. You must not only describe each of the features or parts but elaborate on each to create a complete mental picture for the reader.

Exercise
Drawing a Face

This exercise focuses your attention on details you might otherwise overlook. Pair up with another student and sit opposite one another. You will need at least four sheets of paper ($8^{1}/_{2} \times 11$), crayons, pencils, and an eraser since you will be making four drawings. Be sure to make your drawings as large as possible.

Part I

A. Looking at your partner, draw a detailed picture of his or her face. If you do not feel that confident as an artist, use a pencil and eraser to make a sketch. When your pencil sketch is finished, use your crayons to add color. Since this is not an art class, you will not be graded on the quality of your picture.

B. When you have finished your first sketch, take out another piece of paper, and *make a second drawing of your partner focusing only on your partner's face and not looking at the paper.* This time use a crayon instead of a pencil, and be sure to create your drawing *without looking at what you are drawing* to see how it is coming out.

Part II

A. Think about your own face. You have seen it hundreds of times, so use your pencil to sketch a self-portrait. You may use a mirror or photograph if you wish. Go into as much detail as you can in completing your picture, and finish it off by coloring it in with crayons.

B. After this, take out another piece of paper for a second self-portrait; this time use a crayon and *make your picture while staring off into space and not looking at the piece of paper while you are drawing.* Try to put as much detail into this picture as you can.

    Writing Exercise
Describing a Face

Write two paragraphs, one describing your partner's face and one describing your own. Since your description must develop a controlling idea in your paragraph, include an opinion somewhere in the paragraph. Because you are using description as a method of development, you should depict the other person's and your own face in as much detail as possible.

Prewriting

Using the technique of brainstorming, refer to the pictures you drew in class and list the dominant features of your partner's face. Write out some elaboration on each feature to bring out a visual impression. You may stop from time to time and try to visualize the person's face in order to obtain more detail. After this, order the features in a logical sequence. Then do the same for your own face. As a final step you may write an outline for each paragraph.

Writing

Write out the description of your partner's face following the outline you made. Use as much detail as you can, elaborating on each feature so that the reader gets a clear mental picture of the person. Write a separate sentence for each feature, using both objective and interpretive description; in addition, describe as many features as you can: facial shape, hair, eyes, cheeks, nose, mouth, teeth, chin, ears, forehead, dimples, complexion, and so on. For instance, you can describe how a person's eyes look objectively and the impression they make or the attitude they express. You may also describe the general expression on the person's face and how that enhances what the eyes express. Be sure to include a topic sentence and primary support somewhere in your paragraph; it is easy to overlook them. Follow the same process for the description of your own face.

Reading and Revising

Read your paragraph out loud, checking to see that you developed your description with enough detail to create a picture for the reader. Be sure the dominating features of the face are included and that you have elaborated on each. At the same time, guard against exaggerating a feature, making it sound out of proportion. If you find that you have left out necessary features, or lumped two or three together in one sentence, make the necessary changes. Pay close attention to the organization of your description so that it has a definite logic the reader can follow. Finally, check to see that you are making a definite statement about your and your partner's face and that you explain this in general terms.

 Writing Exercise

Describing the Entire Person

For this exercise you are to write two descriptive paragraphs, one about a woman and one about a man in your class. In each paragraph, describe the entire person. So that you can make the necessary observations, the class may sit in a large circle. Since you are using description as the major part of your paragraph, you will want to create a vivid mental picture of the person for your reader. To complete your paragraph, you will need to express an opinion based on your description and explain it to some extent.

Prewriting

Look around the room and choose someone of the opposite sex whom you would like to describe. If you wish, you may use an outline to organize your paragraph, or you may simply list the features you want to include. Since you will be modeling as well as writing, be sure to look up periodically, so people can see your face.

Writing

Write your paragraph as automatically as you can, following your train of thought thoroughly. Use objective description to create a picture for the reader and use interpretive description to convey the impression the person makes on you. Since the person is fairly idle, you may refer to his or her general behavior and personality to develop your interpretive description. As you write about each feature, elaborate enough so that it establishes a strong image for the reader.

Reading and Revising

Read the first draft of your paragraphs aloud, checking to see that you have described each feature in sufficient detail. Whenever you find you have been sketchy, make notes on how you could expand your description. See if you have explained the effect certain features have on you and others. Also, check that you have described the person's personality. Write a second draft of your paragraphs, making the necessary additions.

Critiquing in Collaboration

In groups of four or five, read your paragraphs out loud. Then give your paragraph and a copy of the Worksheet for Critiquing in Collaboration to the person next to you. Be sure to fill out all parts of the Worksheet, making specific references to aid the writer. Each paragraph should be read at least twice.

 Exercise
Being Friendly to Strangers

For this exercise you should pair up with one other person. Go out on campus and act more friendly and outgoing to people than you normally would. You should stop and strike up conversations with people waiting outside classes, sitting on the lawn, or eating in the cafeteria. Try to act as though this is nothing out of the ordinary, and do not let them know that this is part of a classroom exercise. Be as personable as you can, and observe the reactions you get. Notice the facial expressions, the body language, and the amount of space between you.

You may strike up a conversation by asking people if they can recommend a class or a teacher for a certain class; you might say you are new to the campus and ask them for other information. You could also say that you are looking for a good book for a reading class and inquire if they can recommend one. If you meet someone who is in the middle of doing something, you could ask them to tell you about it. Before the class goes out, you can brainstorm some other approaches that may work better for you.

When you leave the room, be sure to go to different parts of the campus, so everyone does not end up in one place.

 Writing Exercise

Being Friendly to Strangers

Writing in Collaboration

Choose two or three people with whom you came into contact, and describe their reaction to you during the exercise. You should relate the different things these people did while you were talking to them. These descriptions will make up the majority of the paragraph, but you may want to use some dialogue within them; however, the main emphasis should be on describing the people and their reaction to you. As in other paragraphs, you will need to include a sentence that states an overall opinion about some people, derived from the exercise; then explain your opinion in general somewhere within the paragraph.

Prewriting

Working with your partner, begin by making notes describing the reactions you received. Describe the people's facial expressions, the way they talked or reacted to you, and their body language. You can also describe their general appearance. In addition, you may record some of the dialogue that took place between you. After you have done this, you may write down a general opinion based on this experience.

Writing

Before you begin writing, decide where you would like to start—with a topic sentence and primary support or the description. Share the process of composing. Talk out your ideas and combine them to add content to your paragraph. Use the notes you made during the prewriting exercise and include all the characteristics that were important. If you have trouble describing an individual, close your eyes and try to visualize the person and the interaction. Use both objective and interpretive description to bring the experience to life for the reader.

Reading and Revising

One of you should read your paragraph out loud to hear how it sounds altogether. In evaluating your description, note the parts that are most effective. Then, consider those parts that may be weaker, and work together to develop these. If you have trouble writing your revisions, try composing out loud. Finally, be sure that you have included a topic sentence that expresses a definite opinion and that you have explained its significance.

Critiquing in Collaboration

In small groups of four or six, read your paragraphs out loud. Afterwards, exchange your paragraphs and fill out the Worksheet for Critiquing in Collaboration. When you are completing it, make specific references for the writers. After the paragraphs have been critiqued, discuss what you noticed about the paragraphs overall and the use of description.

 Exercise

Paradise Fantasy

This exercise allows you to explore the qualities that people associate with the concept of a paradise. Most everyone has a paradise fantasy of an ideal place. This may be a favorite vacation spot or a place you have never been. In this exercise you are to imagine what for you would be a paradise.

Part I

Take five minutes to think about the following questions. It is usually best to close your eyes while you imagine what your paradise would be like.

What would your paradise look like?

Where would it be?

Who would be in it?

What would be the essential ingredients of your paradise?

How would you survive in this paradise?

Part II

Draw a picture of your paradise, so your partners can see how you visualize it. Make a sketch that includes its major and minor features. While you are drawing, consider the following questions:

What would your average day be like?

How would you spend your weekends?

What would you need if you spent a year there?

Part III

Get into groups of no more than five, and individually show your pictures. While displaying your picture, describe your fantasy of what it would be like, what you would do with your time, and how you would feel living there. Go into as much detail as you can.

Part IV

Pause to consider what people have said and ask yourself what this experience meant to you. Then discuss the following questions:

1.   What common qualities did the paradises have? How similar or different were the fantasies?

2.   What qualities did the pictures and stories bring out about the members of your group?

3.   In what ways would your life be different? In what ways would it be the same?

4.   How can you create more of a paradise where you are?

5.   What did you learn or relearn about yourself and others?

 Writing Exercise
Paradise Fantasy

A travel magazine is publishing a series on readers' ideal vacation spots. Write a descriptive paragraph about your paradise for submission to the editor. Use as much visual detail as necessary for the reader to imagine it and explain why it would be a paradise for you.

Prewriting

Go back in your imagination and revisualize the paradise you created during the exercise in class. Picture it clearly in your mind and add any other aspects that you have thought about since then. After you have done this, you may list those features you want to emphasize in your paragraph.

Writing

Using freewriting, write your description as automatically as you can. From time to time, you may want to close your eyes and revisualize your fantasy so that you select the details that made the greatest impression. Elaborate on them so that the reader can see the picture you have in mind. Do not worry about the organization of details at this point. Instead, let your mind make associations that seem natural as you are writing.

Reading and Revising

Read your paragraph out loud to see if it creates a complete picture. If any features seem vague, try to describe them in more concrete detail. Then read your paragraph again, paying close attention to the organization of your description. Keep in mind the needs of your reader for a logical order to the features you are describing. If you find that you are jumping from one feature to another in a way that might lose the reader, reorganize your paragraph. Also, check to see that you have explained why this would be a paradise for you. As a last step, make a second draft of your paragraph.

6 Comparison

and Contrast

USING COMPARISON AND CONTRAST

Comparison and contrast are two techniques of paragraph development that can help make your opinion more understandable and convincing for your reader. With comparison, you can show how two things are similar. With contrast, you can demonstrate how they differ. Both involve a common process of thinking that enables a person to learn new concepts easily, make decisions, and understand information, as well as communicate ideas.

You can use comparison to demonstrate how two things, people, or ideas are alike and thereby how one is equally as desirable or undesirable as the other. You may compare something unfamiliar with something more widely known to take advantage of an established reputation or information already possessed by the reader. For instance, if you wanted to show how sophisticated an educational program is at your college, you could compare it to one at Stanford or Harvard. If you wanted to depict how serious the situation is at a local dump site, you could compare it with Love Canal. In other cases you may compare two well-known things to substantiate the significance of one or both. For example, if you wanted to show what a great leader Archbishop Desmond Tutu is, you could compare him with Martin Luther King or Ghandi. If you wanted to demonstrate how challenging mountain climbing is in the Tetons, you could compare them with the Alps.

You can use contrast to show how two concepts, people, or things are different and, therefore, how one is preferable to the other. If you wanted to convince your reader that composing on a computer was less time consuming than other methods of writing, you could contrast making revisions on the computer with using a typewriter. You can also use contrast to illustrate how something has changed. For example, you could contrast yourself at your present age with what you were like when you were fourteen in order to reveal how much your attitude toward education has improved.

A comparison or contrast paragraph may show either one way or several in which two items are alike or different. When limited to one way, you can go into more detail in explaining the similarity or difference. In addition, you can provide a specific example or detailed description of each item. Comparing two things in several ways has the advantage of showing the depth or extent of similarity or difference. For the sake of clarity, a writer should use either comparison or contrast to develop a paragraph. You would not usually combine the two techniques, for you would not be able to develop either in enough detail to explain the significance of the relationship. Generally speaking, these techniques are used in one or two paragraphs—never for an entire essay.

Here are two examples of development by comparison and contrast.

Although Ken and Beverly seem to be coping well with their unhappy experiences as children, Beverly seems the more affected. Both she and Ken were raised by fathers who gave them no positive support whatsoever and who browbeat them through a mute childhood where they were not allowed to communicate any ideas or feelings of their own. Neither of them could live up to their fathers' expectations, and they both lived with daily downgrading remarks and daily abuse which gave them no sense of self-worth as they were growing up. Beverly is the more shy probably because her mother gave her no support either and at times showed a great deal of resentment towards her if she sided with her father. Her parents had a long stormy marriage, and she found herself as a much-used buffer between them. From this she has become quiet and self-conscious. Ken, on the other hand, looked to his mother for support, and although she had plenty of opportunities, she did not turn him against his father; instead, she found reasons for the father's ill behavior and taught Ken how to try to cope with each situation making it a learning experience. Because of this Ken is far more confident and outspoken.

Coty Younger, student

The Volkswagen station wagon is a better buy than a Mazda RX-3 station wagon because of the engine. The Volkswagen has an opposed, four-cylinder engine similar in design to the original Volkswagen "Bug" engine which was known for its reliability. Because of this the VW has been rated as having a much better than average (top rating) overall record according to the *Consumer Report Buying Guide Issue 1980.* In addition, the Volkswagen gets 23 miles per gallon in the city and 28 miles per gallon on the highway. The Mazda, on the other hand, has a rotary engine which has a poor repair record. The engine seals have a tendency to become defective, causing the combustion chamber to become warped. According to an article in the *Los Angeles Times* in October 1979, the problem generally occurs some time after the warranty has expired. The only way to correct the problem is to replace the engine, which costs the owner approximately $900. Furthermore, the Mazda gets only 18 miles per gallon in the city and 22 on the highway.

James Blake, student

Summary: Structure of a Paragraph Developed by Comparison/Contrast

The structure of a paragraph developed through comparison or contrast must have all three essential parts: the topic sentence stating the main idea, the primary supporting sentence explaining the basis of the comparison or contrast of *both* subjects, and specific details showing the reader the similarity or difference involved. It is essential to state the comparison or contrast directly in one sentence and limit it, in most cases, to one quality or way so that the reader knows exactly what the point of the paragraph is. It is also important to include primary supporting sentences so the reader understands how the two items compare or contrast. In addition, it is necessary to include specific details, examples, or descriptions of both items in order for the reader to appreciate the similarity or difference involved. In this kind of paragraph, the primary support should amount to three to five sentences; the secondary support, the two comparative examples or descriptions, may be twenty to forty sentences in length.

 Writing Exercise
Contrasting Advantages and Disadvantages

Writing in Collaboration

Most situations have advantages as well as disadvantages. Choose one of the following pairs of ideas, and write one paragraph in which you contrast the subject to show how it is better in *one* way. Then write one paragraph in which you show how it is worse in *one* way. In each paragraph start with the topic sentence and limit it to one reason. Using primary supporting sentences, explain in general terms why what you are saying is true; then give a specific example of each of the two things being contrasted. Remember, to show how different two things are, you must provide an example of both.

1. Living at home (or owning your own home) is better than living in your own apartment . . .
   Living at home (or owning your own home) is worse than living in your own apartment . . .

2. Going to college is better than going to high school . . .

   Going to college is worse than going to high school . . .

3. Attending a community college is better than going to a university . . .
   Attending a community college is worse than going to a university . . .

4. Make up contrasting statements of your own.

Prewriting

Working together, choose two statements that are most interesting to you (or make up your own), and brainstorm as many reasons as you can for each. Try to come up with as many as possible, so you have several alternatives. Then, make a list of possible examples illustrating each reason to see which would be the best to use. Be sure to have examples for both things being contrasted in each paragraph. As a final step, outline your paragraphs before you begin writing.

Writing

Follow your outline and share the process of composing your paragraphs. Talk out your thoughts, so you can build from each other's best ideas. In this kind of paragraph, include description and details for the two things being contrasted. You also want to develop both to a similar extent.

Reading and Revising

Follow the regular method of reading and revising. Make it a point to see that your primary supporting sentences explain your idea thoroughly and that your secondary supporting sentences give examples and/or description for both things being contrasted. Again, make sure you have used the same amount of detail for both, so the reader can see exactly how these two things contrast.

Critiquing in Collaboration

In groups of four or six, read your paragraphs aloud. Then give a copy of your paragraph and the Worksheet for Critiquing in Collaboration to your partners. Fill out the Worksheet, making specific references to strengths and weaknesses. At times you may make notes in the margins of the paragraph. When each paragraph has been read, discuss your reactions and suggestions.

Writing Exercise
Comparison and Contrast

For this exercise you are to write two paragraphs.

Part I   Comparison

Compare a first impression of someone to a later impression that confirmed the first impression, for example, a friend, doctor, teacher, classmate, coworker, and so on. Describe in detail what your first impression was (good or bad), and give some examples of the person's behavior that made this impression. Then use comparative examples to show how this first impression was confirmed.

Part II   Contrast

Contrast your first impression of someone who later turned out to be quite the opposite. Describe the impression, and provide supporting examples. Then explain how this first impression was inaccurate, and give contrasting examples to show how different this person turned out to be.

Prewriting

Compose two lists of people who would fit in either category, and choose the best person for each paragraph. Make notes on examples that show this comparison or contrast most effectively. You may also make notes on descriptions that would help develop your paragraphs. While doing this, you might try closing your eyes and visualizing the person and the situations with which you associate him or her. As a last step you can compose a topic sentence that states the comparison or contrast completely, and then, if you wish, you may make an outline for each paragraph.

Writing

Use freewriting to write out the examples and/or description you need for developing your paragraphs. Go into enough detail for the reader to appreciate the different impressions these people made on you. Follow your outline loosely, allowing yourself to explore any new ideas or examples that occur to you as you are writing.

Reading and Revising

In addition to the usual procedure of reading and revising, check your paragraphs to see that you have developed both impressions to the same extent so that the reader receives a clear idea of what your first and later impressions of the person were. Also, be sure that you have explained the comparison and contrast in general, so your reader understands the significance of the details you are giving.

Writing Exercise
Contrast

Every once in a while, we go through an experience that seems at the time to be one of the worst in our lives. This may involve getting an "F" in a class, losing a job, breaking up with a girl or boy friend, or something similar. However, after time goes by, this seemingly tragic experience leads to an even greater opportunity that we otherwise would have missed.

Assume that your old high school newspaper is running a series of inspirational articles by graduates, and you have been asked to write one. In a single paragraph, contrast a bad experience with the opportunity that resulted. Explain why you thought this experience was so negative, how you felt at the time, and how it turned out to be positive for you. Use contrasting examples or descriptions to illustrate what happened.

Prewriting

Think of as many experiences as you can that fall into this category, and choose the best one for this exercise. Using brainstorming, make notes on the original experience and the opportunity that resulted, focusing on the most significant details. Afterwards, compose a topic sentence that expresses what you learned overall from this experience.

Writing

Using the technique of freewriting, write out an explanation of why the experience at first seemed so bad. Go into detail, including typical or specific examples that will help establish why this seemed such a tragic event. Then, use the same kind of detail to explain the opportunity that resulted so that the reader can appreciate the contrast. Follow your outline loosely, allowing yourself to include any new ideas or details that come to mind while you are writing.

Reading and Revising

Read your writing out loud, paying particular attention to the detail you have used in the description and examples in the secondary support. Remove any details that seem unnecessary or repetitious, and add detail where you are bringing up an idea that needs to be developed more. After checking your use of detail, look at the organization, taking into consideration how it will affect the reader. Then, make sure you have included a general explanation that summarizes what you learned from this experience and the impact it had on you. Finally, check that you have written a topic sentence for your paragraph.

Critiquing in Collaboration

In small groups of four or five, read your paragraphs out loud. Afterwards, pass your paragraph to one of your partners and fill out a copy of the Worksheet for Critiquing in Collaboration. Be as specific as you can in making comments. When each paragraph has been read three times, discuss your reactions, the questions that came to mind, and the suggestions you can make. Then, use this information to write a final draft of your paragraph.

Exercise
The Party

Part I

You are giving a hypothetical party for some of the people you most admire, so you must make a list of five public figures (politicians, entertainers, scientists, writers, etc.), living or dead, whom you would definitely want at such a party. After each person's name write an adjective that best describes the quality you admire about the person. Next, list five people you definitely would not want to attend this party. Again these people should be public figures whom most people could be expected to recognize. For each of these people you should also write an adjective that best describes the quality you dislike.

Part II

When everyone has finished making up the lists, each student should read both lists to the class, including the adjective for each public figure. After everyone has read his or her list, the class may discuss the qualities that were most admired and those most disliked.

Writing Exercise
Comparison and Contrast

Part I   Comparison

The purpose of this exercise is to compare yourself with a public figure to show how you are alike and contrast yourself with another public figure to demonstrate how you differ. Pick one of the five people you wanted at the party, and write a paragraph comparing yourself to that person. Explain in detail how you are similar in *one specific way*. Then describe the public figure in detail and/or give an example of what that person is like. After this provide a comparative description of yourself and/or an example of what you are like to show how the two of you are similar. *Do not explain why you would invite this person to the party,* but rather express in a topic sentence how you are similar.

Part II   Contrast

Choose one of the people you would definitely not want at your party, and write a paragraph contrasting yourself with this person. Explain how you differ in one particular way, and use specific examples to illustrate the quality each of you has.

Prewriting

Choose one or two people from each list and write out several qualities for each. Make notes on any examples that reveal how each person has demonstrated a particular quality. Try to think up both typical and specific examples, and if you have difficulty, you may need to pick another person. After this, write out some explanation of how you demonstrate the same quality and list a few examples.

Writing

Choose one person for each paragraph and limit it to one quality. You may begin with a statement comparing or contrasting yourself with the public figure and include a general explanation of how you are similar or dissimilar before you go into detail. Then, give examples or description of you and this public figure to illustrate what you are saying in general. Or you may start by writing out your examples and description, provide a general explanation, and at the end make an overall statement of the comparison or contrast.

Reading and Revising

Follow the normal procedure of reading and revising, checking your topic sentence to see that it is confined to one quality. Make sure that you have explained the comparison or contrast at some length, so the reader understands your reasoning. Then, read your examples and description to see that both you and the public figure are portrayed in detail. In this type of paragraph it is easy to emphasize one person more than the other; try to develop them with the same amount of detail, so the comparison or contrast is clear to the reader.

C h a p t e r

7   Analysis

USING ANALYSIS

The best way to understand and explain a complex subject is to analyze it; that is, break it down into its component parts and then consider those parts separately. You will then be better able to convince the reader of your opinion because the reader—and you—will see the relationships between your ideas. Suppose, for example, you wish to write a piece on the topic of airline safety and your opinion is that flying is becoming increasingly dangerous. Part of your task in the brainstorming stage will be to *analyze* the idea "dangerous." Perhaps you determine that the danger consists of three components:

1. Old planes

2. Substandard engine parts

3. The threat of terrorism

These three ideas—the result of your analysis—are probably more than enough for a one-paragraph paper; the paragraph could only be developed in general terms. Otherwise, it could serve as the introduction in an essay or present a minor point in a discussion of the problems associated with flying.

A paragraph in the body of an essay, on the other hand, should consider just one of the dangers listed above in order to develop the idea with explanation and examples. Most problems, situations, causes, or effects that you write about in college involve complex relationships, and you will need to explain those relationships in detail to be convincing. Compared to the other techniques of paragraph development, analysis involves a more extensive explanation of the reasoning associated with the opinion expressed. In addition, you must give at least one example or illustration to clarify and support your opinion.

The type of analysis demonstrated in the list of dangers is sometimes called *classification* because it begins in the brainstorming process with the grouping together of related details. There are several other types of analysis that will help you in your writing.

Cause and Effect

Another major type of analysis involves the explanation of cause-effect relationships. Such analysis may focus on causes, explaining why something happens or has happened, or on effects, describing what will result or has resulted. Often when we seek to establish a solution to a problem, we begin by identifying its major causes. On the other hand, if we wish to continue or repeat something that has been successful in the past, we must discover the causes that have led to this success. A cause-effect analysis seeks to answer questions like these:

Why has *The Phantom of the Opera* become one of the most successful musicals of all time?

What led to the apparent break-up of the communist bloc in Eastern Europe?

What would happen if abortion were declared illegal throughout the United States?

Pitfalls

Causal analysis involves some pitfalls that must be avoided. One is oversimplification, which usually happens when the writer attributes one or two causes for a certain situation that actually has several interrelated causes. For instance, in many recent magazine articles about the decline in reading skills among American youth, the single cause cited has been television although experts have recognized a number of other equally important contributing causes. It is important to keep in mind the complexity of most cause-effect relationships and account for all major causes.

Another common error in thinking about causal relationships is to assume that because event B follows event A, it is caused by A. This is referred to as the *post hoc ergo proptor hoc* fallacy ("After this, therefore because of this"). A typical example is this: A man is seen running from a bank after a burglar alarm has sounded. It is assumed that he held up the bank when, on the contrary, he might be chasing the robber.

There may be many causes or effects of a given situation. In developing a paragraph, however, it is preferable to limit the discussion to a single cause or effect so that you can explain the relationship in detail. If you write only a topic sentence and a brief explanation or example, you are relying on the reader to agree with you on the basis of scant proof. Because most cause-effect relationships are fairly complex, the primary support in your paragraph should be extensive enough to explain the concept completely. Use specific details and examples as evidence for your explanation.

The following paragraphs are examples of cause-effect analysis.

One of the major effects of the energy problem is the rise in inflation. As the supply of oil becomes limited and the demand increases, the price continues to rise. In addition, O.P.E.C., the oil exporting cartel, has maintained a monopolistic control over the price of crude oil and has raised the price dramatically to reduce the demand and increase profits. This spirals inflation because almost all products on the market are shipped by truck, and the increased cost of shipping is added to the purchase price paid by the customer. The cost of manufacturing items is further increased since most electricity is generated by oil, and most factory machinery is powered by electricity. This operating expense is also added to the total price. Moreover, certain products such as plastics are made from petroleum, so their cost is directly related to the increase in the price of crude oil. A good example of this is the cost of record albums. Because records are a petroleum product, their cost increases directly with the rise in the price of oil and indirectly with the added cost of electricity and shipping. As a result, an album which cost $3.50 in 1973, cost $5.25 in 1979 and $7.89 in 1983.

James Blake, student

One of the largest problems today is apathy toward our fellow man. I feel that a majority of the problems we face today all stem from apathy. We have become indifferent to the chaos around us. I think the reason for this indifference is due to the overwhelming enormity of our problems. People who have tried to alleviate the problems of the world have become discouraged and given up. They feel as though they have tried and failed; therefore, they see the problems as unsolvable. For example, men went to Viet Nam to fight a war. They felt they were doing a brave and noble act for the people of the U.S. and Viet Nam. Yet when they came back, the citizens of the U.S. shunned them as murderers and the people of Viet Nam were no better than before the war. The veterans felt as though they were failures. They felt as though they fought a war, lost their friends and youth for nothing. A lot of these men withdrew both physically and emotionally. Some gave up; why should they put themselves out again when they tried and "failed"? They feel used and now indifferent toward the people who asked them for help and then spit in their faces.

Linda Stewart, student

Yet, despite all this interest it remains true that it is very difficult for most of us to talk about death. There are at least two reasons for this. One of them is primarily psychological and cultural: The subject of death is taboo. We feel, perhaps only subconsciously, that to be in contact with death in any way, even indirectly, somehow confronts us with the prospect of our own deaths, draws our own deaths closer and makes them more real and thinkable. For example, most medical students, myself included, have found that even the remote encounter with death which occurs upon one's first visit to the anatomical laboratories when entering medical school can evoke strong feelings of uneasiness. In my own case, the reason for this response now seems quite obvious. It has occurred to me in retrospect that it wasn't entirely concern for the person whose remains I saw there, although that feeling certainly figured, too. What I was seeing on that table was a symbol of my own mortality. In some way, if only preconsciously, the thought must have been in my mind, "That will happen to me, too."

From "Life After Life," by Raymond A. Moody, Jr., M.D.

You can turn stressful situations around 180 degrees. You can turn these situations into situations that build your personal character and make you feel good about yourself and help you acknowledge the fact that you are indeed progressing forward. Instead of becoming angry or depressed, you can focus your attention on what you have accomplished and how much you have learned. By this means you turn each problem into a challenge, not an impossible situation, so you can use your capabilities to find a workable solution. Take for instance one situation in which you have one problem complicated by another. You realize the fact that you are dealing with more than one problem; then, you figure priorities of the problems. You finally solve one of the problems. After this you should take the time to realize that you have solved one problem, and give yourself credit for it. Instead of saying "I have another problem to contend with," tell yourself you have conquered one problem; you are progressing, so you feel more confident to take on and tackle another. You will build your confidence and know that stress will come along, and you will deal with it accordingly and overcome it. Where would we be if humanity had stopped trying to fly or if Henry Miller had stopped writing because he felt his writing wasn't good enough?

Lou Pedroza, student

Process

Process analysis explains how to do something or how it is or was done. When giving this kind of explanation, you describe the step-by-step procedure necessary for accomplishing it. If you have purchased any sound equipment, you have seen this technique used in the instruction book that detailed the process of installation. Another example is the common cookbook that describes the steps involved in preparing food.

When you explain how something is or was done, the order of events leading up to a specific situation or end product is given. You are not necessarily telling the reader how to accomplish something but, instead, how it happens or has happened. For instance, you might explain the sequence of events by which crude oil is processed into gasoline. History books use this technique to chronicle the events leading to the Civil War.

In both kinds of process analysis, it is important to include all the major steps in proper chronological order so that the reader will not get confused or obtain a distorted view of the process. When telling how to do something, it's also wise to point out any special precautions for the reader as they come up. You do not want to wait until the end of the essay to tell readers to be sure to turn off the electricity before removing any circuit boards from a television, or they may never get to read the instructions.

The following are two good examples of process analysis. Note that in the first piece the author explains all the steps involved and, in addition, cautions the reader about movements to be avoided.

While knives don't rank as appliances, they're mighty important tools around the kitchen, and they're a real nuisance if they're not sharp. The best way to sharpen them these days is with an electric knife sharpener, if you're lucky enough to have one. But even then there's a trick to getting the best results. First, push the button that starts the sharpener. Then lower the handle end of the blade into the knife slot (some sharpeners also have a scissors slot) until it comes into contact with the grinding wheel or wheels gently. As soon as the blade touches the grinding element, draw the blade through the slot at an even speed and at a gentle and even pressure. Don't bear down enough to slow the grinder. And be sure to tip the knife handle upward as the tip of the blade reaches the grinder, so you sharpen the curved end of the cutting edge. You use this part of the blade in much of your carving. The number of times you pass the blade through the sharpener depends on the dullness of the blade. If the edge is so badly dulled that it's actually visible as a rounded surface, keep at the job until you can see it's ground to a cutting edge. This may take half a dozen passes or more. People who know how to test the sharpness slide a fingertip across the cutting edge. *Never*—repeat—*never* slide your finger along the edge lengthwise. A really keen blade can give you a serious cut this way before you even know it happened. If you want to play it safe (and why not?), try the blade on a piece of meat. That's what you'll use it on anyway. But wipe it with a sponge before you test it. This removes any minute metal or abrasive particles that may be on it.

From The Awful Handyman's Book, *by George Daniels, p. 65–66*

The next example presents a different kind of process. The author's tone is ironic; he explains how to create an *undesirable* effect.

Everywhere you look the trend is toward more and more people paid just enough to get them out of bed in the morning—otherwise known as the Motor Vehicle Bureau Syndrome. Here is how you create that kind of organization.

Start with, say ten thousand employees. Put them all in one building and divide them into departments. When communication breaks down, develop inter- and intra-office memo forms, job descriptions, and a police manual. When expenses begin to get out of hand, develop rigid salary limits and layers of salary committees. Develop purchasing forms and procedures so that it takes six months to get a desk lamp. When the best people get frustrated and leave, the salary limits will ensure that each will be replaced by a warm body. At this point, Leo Rosten's Law (second-rate people hire third-rate people) will take over. Soon you'll have sixteen thousand sullen timeservers, each bitterly resentful of customer intrusions, and bent on getting even with the company any way they can.

Robert Townsend, "Bigness in Business Petrie's Law," Horizon, XV
(Winter, 1973), p. 37.

Summary: Structure of a Paragraph Developed by Analysis

A paragraph that emphasizes analysis must include all three essential parts. The topic sentence states an opinion directly and is limited to one reason, cause, or effect. Primary supporting sentences that explain the main idea must be developed in detail to make the reasoning clear and understandable. This may amount to five to fifteen or more sentences depending on how complex the idea is. Secondary supporting sentences are developed extensively with substantial explanation of details, examples, or descriptions and how they demonstrate the opinion expressed in the paragraph. Ten to twenty or more sentences will be needed for the paragraph to be effective.

 Exercise

An Essay and Transcript on the Effects of Unemployment

The following two pieces of writing analyze the effects of unemployment. Read them and then discuss them in groups.

New Health Hazard: Being Out of Work

Abigail Trafford

FAMILY DISCORD, ALCHOLISM, HIGH BLOOD PRESSURE, AND STOMACH AILMENTS—THESE AND A HOST OF OTHER PROBLEMS TEND TO RISE HAND IN HAND WITH JOBLESSNESS.

WARNING: UNEMPLOYMENT MAY BE HAZARDOUS TO YOUR HEALTH.

It's not a sign that appears in doctors' offices, but as the recession deepens health authorities see indications of increased emotional and physical illness in communities hard hit by layoffs and plant closings.

Many mental-health clinics and hospitals are linking the loss of jobs to increases in family disturbances, child abuse, alcoholism, behavioral disorders, stomach ailments, diarrhea, colds, sleep problems and other stress-related diseases.

"There's a powerful and direct connection between unemployment and physical and mental health," says Dr. Elliot Liebow, Chief of the Center for Work and Mental Health at the National Institute of Mental Health. "People react to stress in different ways. Some have stomach pains or hypertension. Others suffer depression, drink too much or become violent."

Unemployment in May rose to 9.5 percent of the work force—the highest rate since 1941—which meant that 10.5 million people who sought jobs couldn't find them. Most of the jobless weather their plight without significant health problems. Others are not so fortunate. For an idea of how some of these jobless workers have been affected—

In Alabama, with 16 percent unemployment, state mental-health clinics are swamped with cases of stress because one or both family breadwinners are unemployed. In Selma, the welfare office reports a sharp rise in child-neglect cases among out-of-work families. At the Mental Health Center in Mobile, Director William H. Simpson says, "We're seeing an increase in patients, an increase in depression and an increase in domestic problems. I've been in this business for 30 years, and I've never seen so many economy related cases."

At the Midwest Health Center in the Detroit suburb of Dearborn, prescriptions for antidepressants and anti-anxiety drugs are up 25 percent over last year. The number of patients requiring psychiatric counseling has risen 15 to 20 percent in the past six months. "We're seeing a slight increase in ulcers and inflammation of the stomach as well," says the center's gastroenterologist, Dr. Freddy Sosa.

In Hartford, Conn., 1 of every 2 workers laid off by the Pratt & Whitney aircraft plant reported difficulty sleeping. One out of 3 complained of stomach upsets and headaches, and one out of 8 had problems with alcohol abuse.

In Pittsburgh, doctors found increased family tension, more depression and apathy, higher blood pressures, increased cigarette smoking and child abuse in a survey of 250 laid-off steelworkers. "These are normal people," says Dr. Ruth Kane, Chief of Children's and Adolescent-Mental-Health Services, at St Francis General Hospital. "They are not sickies or goofies. These are working people who would have carried on their lives if they hadn't lost their jobs."

Research on previous recessions underscores the medical impact of economic hard times.

Sociologist Harvey Brenner, of Johns Hopkins University, calculates that for each rise of 1 percent in the unemployment rate, 4 percent more people wind up in state prisons, 5.7 percent more are murdered, 4.1 percent more commit suicide, 4.3 percent more men and 2.3 percent more women are admitted to state mental institutions for the first time, and 1.9 percent more people complain of heart disease, cirrhosis of the liver and other ailments.

"Right now, we are seeing increases in disturbed behavior," says Brenner. "I think the impact of this recession on death rates and illness will be more serious than what we've experienced in the last two decades."

"Pink-slip syndrome." For the person who is laid off, unemployment represents more than the loss of a paycheck. "These people experience loss of self-esteem and loss of pride," explains psychiatrist

Raymond Mercier at the Midwest Health Center in Dearborn. "There's also the loss of social contact and support."

Experts are identifying a pattern to the emotional effects of unemployment, and they've even given it a name—the "pink-slip syndrome." For the first few weeks, laid-off workers may experience relief. The tension of wondering when the ax would fall is broken and there is hope of finding a new job. If a person finds comparable work soon, health impact is negligible.

From three to six months of unemployment is a period of intense anger and family trauma. The worker tends to blame the company and other family members. The nonworking spouse may look for a job, and teenage children drop out of school to work.

"Six months seems to be the critical breaking point," says sociologist Paula Bayman of Brandeis University, who conducted the Hartford Project study of Pratt & Whitney layoffs. "Unemployment benefits usually stop, and workers are thrust into an economic nowhere land. Depression replaces anger. After a year, the unemployed person is so isolated and frustrated he or she may not go looking for work any more."

Researchers caution that just finding another job is not always a solution. In many instances, the new job involves lower status, less pay, fewer benefits and no long-term security.

To Louis A. Ferman, Research Director of the Institute of Labor and Industrial Relations at the University of Michigan, the worst cases of physical and mental illness are found in workers who go through cycles of employment and unemployment.

"These are the two and three-time losers who get on the roller coaster of career instability," says Ferman, whose study of 446 jobless workers in Detroit suggests that these workers were also more likely to be pack-a-day smokers, to drink regularly and be overweight.

A study of the closing of a Virginia soda-ash plant showed that subsequent jobs for many workers were continuous steps backward. Said one laboratory technician who held a series of low-paying jobs after 25 years at the plant: "I thought I was successful at one time in my life. Since the plant closed, I've been a failure. I've tried, but so far I've failed." He began drinking heavily, developed an ulcer and suffered a stroke.

Loss of medical benefits. For many, the critical issue is health insurance. Most laid-off workers eventually lose their coverage. Buying individual insurance is usually too expensive. A worker laid off by Ford Motor Company, for example, might spend two thirds of his unemployment payments to buy similar medical coverage.

At the same time, as the federal government tries to cut back health programs, unemployed people find it difficult to qualify for Medicaid or Medicare. In Wyandotte, near Detroit, an emergency hot line has been established to refer the jobless without coverage to a range of services from marriage counseling to resuscitation after a heart attack. In the last year, the hot-line calls have tripled.

Explains Nancy Nagle, supervisor of the hot line: "It's a gray area in which a lot of people who can't afford to continue their medical insurance also find that they're ineligible for public assistance because they have assets such as a home or car."

Roberta Wood of Chicago, for example, feels that she and her husband are caught in the health-insurance gap. Both are jobless, and their unemployment benefits run out soon.

"We really have to have medical insurance, but I don't know how we can pay for it," she says. "It would cost almost $200 a month. We can't even pay our house payment. I'm trying to balance priorities—food, utilities, car insurance, medical insurance. You add up all those priorities and you don't have enough money."

As the recession widens, a number of doctors and hospitals are providing care at reduced charges.

In Detroit, Project Health Care has been set up to make sure the recently unemployed have access to service. Many doctors and hospitals have agreed to treat the jobless who have no health coverage on an ability-to-pay basis.

Similar free-care programs are under way in at least four more states for people who have lost their medical insurance or have been forced off medicaid and medicare rolls.

Some people make do by seeing doctors less often for routine care. Physicians in Detroit report declines of as much as 50 percent in office visits by patients. Dr. Kenneth Ray, past president of the Wayne County Medical Society, reports he is seeing 30 to 40 percent fewer patients than two years ago. "There's no questions that people are deferring medical care," he says. "A lot of people with chronic illness such as diabetes and hypertension are not coming in as frequently even though they know they could be treated for free. They're too proud."

At the same time, public hospitals note a dramatic rise in the number of patients with no coverage, bringing many of these hospitals close to bankruptcy. If the present trend continues, Boston City Hospital, for example, will be 53 million dollars in debt by 1983. Leaders of the National Association of Public Hospitals have appealed for emergency legislation that would set up a special federal fund for medical coverage for the unemployed.

But that is not an option the Reagan administration is exploring. Says Dr. Edward N. Brandt, Jr., assistant secretary for health: "The real solution is to get the economy on its feet."

Exercise

Discussion Questions

In small groups of three to five, answer the following questions.

1. What, according to this essay, are the major effects of unemployment?

2. How well are the cause-effect relations explained in the essay? Cite at least three examples.

3. What writing techniques does the author use? How effective are they? Explain.

4. The author quotes a statement at the end of the essay that the real solution to this problem is to get the economy on its feet. Do you agree or disagree? Explain your reasoning.

5. What inferences (conclusions made in addition to what the author states directly) can you make based on this essay?

Why Work?

Bill Moyers

(AN EXCERPT FROM *BILL MOYERS' JOURNAL*)

MOYERS: Work is the force that creates, empowers and enlarges human society. But from the beginning of the Industrial Revolution there had been too few jobs for those seeking work.

Mass unemployment began in the 16th century in England as peasants were driven off their farms to make way for sheep raising.

Woolen cloth was becoming the base of Britain's burgeoning work trade. But there weren't enough jobs for all the dispossessed in the growing towns. Ever since it has been the demands of the market place that dictate who shall work at what and when. Many see the history of nations as the on-going struggle over markets and materials. And the history of a single society is a chronicle of how its work and wealth are managed.

Since the 19th century Europe has been questioning the capitalist system and experimenting with new forms, as the working class has demanded more from the economy.

Today, everywhere, people are questioning the ups and downs of the profit system resisting its boom-bust rhythm, and insisting that human need must become the "Why" of work.

In the United States these days, with as many as 10 million people out of work, there's little talk of alternative economic strategies; we're urged to accommodate. We tolerate a much higher rate of unemployment than Europe, although in a very literal sense unemployment is devastating to the health of the body politic. The dollars and cents cost of 10 million unemployed people can be computed. But there's a higher cost that has to be calculated. Medical sociologists and biologists say that unemployment is a killer. Being out of work puts stress on the mind and body which causes physical damage; this can shorten the life span. If our economy is, indeed, under anybody's control then those in command are dooming many of the unemployed to die before their time.

(At an unemployment office)

MAN: It affects me in this manner. You know some nights I go to bed early, it's hard for me to go to sleep, I'll be lyin' in bed thinkin' what's gonna happen for me tomorrow, you know, and sometime I get up and I pray and ask the Lord could he help me some kind of a way to make life a little bit more better for me, you know, because things is kind a rough. Sometime I feel like I'm gonna go in the hospital you know, try to get myself together. But I'm just holdin' on with the prayers and the help of the Lord. It's rough out there.

MAN B: Can't pay your bills, you have to work . . . make you sick and everything else.

WOMAN: I don't know like some of my morals have just evaporated. I don't know. It's just depressing at times.

WOMAN B: Well, I just got depressed for a moment I felt like, you know, I didn't care. I let the home go, I let everything else go . . . even a time I thought about suicide, you know, because I thought there was no way out, and that's when I started seein' my psychiatrist, you know. And things are better for work.

WOMAN C: You come back on the 28th at 11 o'clock, line 8 for your pay.

MOYERS: Psychologist say that being unemployed robs people of the identity and purpose that work gives. That the jobless lose their sense of achievement and self-propriety. They're thrown into a kind of limbo that oppresses the mind, and eventually the body.

Joseph Ire, a biologist and authority on vital statistics.

IRE: In one study they followed people through a closing of a plant. Started off measuring their blood pressure before the announcement of the plant closing, followed them right through the experience of unemployment and then into the period when they got a job again. And you found that their blood pressure went up dramatically with the announcement of the possibility of plant closing, remained high through the whole unemployment period, and didn't come down again until they were stably integrated into a new job. Since blood pressure is a significant risk factor for heart disease, it's one of the main ones, you'd expect that there would be a correlation between unemployment and heart attacks. And, indeed, one or two or three years after a peak in unemployment, you regularly find a peak in the heart attack death rate, implying that there is a direct relationship which takes some time to develop, between the experience of unemployment and a heart attack. Another way of indicating the health risk associated with unemployment is to talk about the suicide rate, mental hospital admissions, alcoholism, general depression, which can be reflected in a number of those things. With every business cycle recession when unemployment goes up, the mental hospital admission rate goes up; alcoholism rates go up, and it's not uncommon to have a doubling or a tripling of the suicide rate during this period of time. You can sum up a lot of the things about unemployment by comparing general death rates. Long-term unemployed people have twice the death rate during the adult life span compared with people who are employed.

 Exercise

Discussion Questions

1. What, according to this transcript, are the effects of unemployment?

2. How does this transcript compare to the essay "New Health Hazard: Being Out Of Work?"

    A. What writing techniques does each use?

    B. Which is the more effective piece of writing? Why?

    C. What does this tell you about your own writing?

3. Why, in your opinion, does unemployment affect people so severely?

Additional Questions

1. What is your own attitude toward work?

2. Considering the people you know, how happy are most of them with their jobs? Why?

3. Where do people get their negative attitudes about work?

4. What experiences did you have with work when you were a child? How did these serve to develop your present attitude?

5. Since education is a form of work, what is your attitude toward going to school? Is learning fun or just work?

6. How do people obtain a negative attitude concerning school?

7. Writing is also a form of work. What is your attitude about writing? Is it always work, or is it ever enjoyable? What makes the difference?

8. What causes negative attitudes about writing?

9. How does a person's attitude about work, school, and writing affect his or her performance?

10. How much control do you take over your attitude toward these things? What effect can this have?

11. Given the reaction people have to unemployment, how would you expect people to respond to retirement?

12. What effect would you imagine living on welfare has on people? How does this compare with the attitude many people have about those who are on welfare?

 ## Writing Exercise
Attitudes About Work

The purpose of this exercise is to analyze your attitude about one aspect of work. Using one of the topics brought up in the discussion, write a paragraph that expresses an attitude about a specific aspect of work. Limit your opinion to one reason, and develop your paragraph by using analysis to explain your reasoning in detail so that the reader can comprehend what you mean. Use at least one well-developed example, illustration, or description to support and clarify what you are saying in general.

Prewriting

Consider at least two topics from the discussion and, by brainstorming, make a list of opinions related to them. Try to come up with as many different opinions as you can. After ten to fifteen minutes, look them over and write down reasons, ways, or qualities for each. Again, brainstorm as many as possible. When you have completed this, go back and choose the best reason and think of specific examples for each reason if you can. If not, think up typical examples. As you are doing this, cross off any opinions or reasons for which you cannot find examples. Finally, select the opinion that is the most interesting or important and for which you have a good reason and example.

Writing

Use the technique of freewriting and begin your paragraph wherever you feel comfortable. Write as quickly as you can, including all the ideas that occur to you. Allow yourself to write out new ideas to see where they lead. Since you are using analysis to develop this paragraph, go into detail explaining your reasoning and example, illustration, or description.

Reading and Revising

Follow the usual process of reading and revising, paying particular attention to the explanation and details or description you are using. As you read, cross out any vague or repetitious sentences. Make notes on how to elaborate on ideas or details that are not developed enough. Rephrase any sentences that seem awkward or wordy. Also, make sure that you have included a topic sentence. As a last step, write a second draft of your paragraph, including the necessary improvements.

Critiquing in Collaboration

In small groups of four or five, read your paragraphs aloud. Then, circulate paragraphs and Worksheets for Critiquing in Collaboration as usual. When you are giving criticism, write down specific strengths and weaknesses and share any ideas you have on ways to make improvements. Be sure also to include questions that the writer should answer in the paragraph.

 Exercise
Top Problems

This exercise evaluates the importance of major problems facing our country and the world. By working together, you can pool the information you have to gain a greater overall understanding of these problems.

Form small groups and rank these problems in order of importance starting with number one as the most important. Work as a group and discuss the individual reasons for your choices. You may add any other problems you feel are important.

____A. Low productivity standards

____B. Pollution of air and water

____C. Overpopulation

____D. Unemployment

____E. Drug addiction

____F. Disease and poor health conditions

____G. The threat of nuclear war

____H. Crime and lack of respect for the law

____I. Energy

____J. Racial prejudice

____K. The need for government reform

____L. Inadequate housing

____M. Inflation

____N. Low educational standards and achievement

____O. Apathy

____P. Hunger

____Q. Disposal of nuclear waste

____R. AIDS

____S. The homeless

Exercise
Causes and Effects

Choose two problems from the Top Problem worksheet and, as a group, compose a list of the four major causes and effects of each problem. Make notes on your reasoning and cite examples.

Problem: _____

Causes	Reasoning	Examples
1.	1.	1.
2.	2.	2.

Causes	Reasoning	Examples
3.	3.	3.
4.	4.	4.

Effects	Reasoning	Examples
1.	1.	1.
2.	2.	2.
3.	3.	3.
4.	4.	4.

Problem: _____

Causes	Reasoning	Examples
1.	1.	1.
2.	2.	2.
3.	3.	3.
4.	4.	4.

Effects	Reasoning	Examples
1.	1.	1.
2.	2.	2.
3.	3.	3.
4.	4.	4.

Writing Exercise
One Top Problem

For this exercise write a letter to the editor of your local paper. Choose one problem from the Top Problems list and what you feel are its major cause and effect. Then, write one paragraph on the cause of the problem and one on the effect. The body of each paragraph should include a detailed explanation of how and why the cause-effect relationship works. Give one or two specific examples as evidence of what you have stated; be sure to use well-developed examples that contain as many details as you can think of.

Prewriting

Choose one problem that you worked on in the previous exercise and add to your list any other causes, effects, or examples that come to mind. Select the best cause and effect and talk out the reasoning involved in each relationship so that you understand it thoroughly. If you have difficulty in explaining one of them, choose a different cause or effect (or problem), and talk out this one to see that you can explain how the cause-effect relationship works. When you have done this for both, go through the same process with the examples to see that you can come up with enough detail to develop them in writing. If you have difficulty talking out an example, find a different one, and go through the same process with it.

Writing

Concentrate on explaining your reasoning in detail and use a similar amount of detail in your example, illustration, or description. As always, if a new or more important cause, effect, example, or description emerges, write it out and consider it later. As a last step, make sure that you have included a topic sentence stating the cause-effect relationship.

Reading and Revising

Read your paragraphs out loud, listening to how you have explained your analysis of the cause-effect relationship. Note the places where your explanation is strong and weak. Wherever it is weak, rephrase the idea so that it becomes more concise or understandable. If you have used any new, unrelated ideas, evaluate them and decide whether they should replace the original idea. If any parts duplicate what you have already said and do not add clarification, remove them. Read your example the same way and make the necessary changes to make it more effective. Check the overall paragraph organization to see that it is understandable and easy for the reader to follow. As a final step write a second draft of your paragraph.

Critiquing in Collaboration

Use the same format for critiquing. Read your paragraphs out loud and pass a copy of them along with the Worksheet for Critiquing in Collaboration. Provide specific references for each comment. Make notes about spelling, grammar, or word usage on the paragraph so that the writer can find them easily.

 Exercise
Brainstorming Causes and Effects

In small groups choose two of the following topics and brainstorm as many causes and effects as you can. When you have finished, think up as many specific examples for each and write them down, making notes on some of the details involved.

1. Gang violence

2. High self-esteem

3. Cheating in school (or business)

4. Success in college

5. A successful marriage

6. Divorce

7. A close and lasting friendship

8. A fulfilling career

9. A topic of your choice

 Writing Exercise
Cause-Effect Relationships

In this exercise, select one of the above topics and write two paragraphs. The first paragraph should explain the major cause, and the second should explain the major effect. In each paragraph limit your topic sentence to one cause or effect; then explain the cause-effect relationship in detail. After your explanation, give one specific example to support what you are saying.

Writing

Pick the topic that is most interesting to you and choose the cause, effect, and specific examples about which you have the most information. Write out each of your paragraphs as automatically as you can. As in the previous writing exercise, go into detail in your explanation and example since you are using analysis to develop your paragraph. Keep your reader in mind so that you explain your reasoning thoroughly.

Reading and Revising

Use the same approach to reading and revising as you did in the last exercise. Read your paragraphs carefully, paying close attention to primary and secondary support. Identify the strengths and weaknesses, and revise the weaker parts of your paragraphs.

 Writing Exercise
What Should Be Legal: Writing from the Opposite point of view

Writing in Collaboration

From the list below choose the statement that you *disagree* with the most. Then, find one other person who has chosen the same subject and together write one paragraph expressing the best reason *for* legalization. For example, if you disagreed the most with the legalization of prostitution, you would write a paragraph presenting what you feel is the strongest argument for legalizing it. When people write, they often express one point of view and disregard any other. By writing from the opposite point of view, you should be able to discover and consider arguments that you might otherwise overlook.

Develop your paragraph using primary supporting sentences to explain your topic sentence in general. Then, with one or more techniques of paragraph development, add specific detail to illustrate your statements. If you choose the subject of drugs, limit your paragraph to one type of drug such as heroin, cocaine, or marijuana. You may, if you wish, confine the topic of gambling to one type, such as horse racing, poker, lotteries, and so on.

1. Gambling should be legalized.

2. Prostitution should be legalized.

3. Drugs should be legalized.

4. Abortion should remain legalized.

Prewriting

Work together with your partner in choosing a topic; then brainstorm several reasons for the legalization of this activity. Since you are writing from the opposite point of view, try to put yourself in someone else's position, and see the problem from a different perspective. Afterwards, think up as many specific or typical examples that illustrate the point.

Writing

Share the process of writing and compose your sentences out loud so that you can play off each other's ideas. Explain your reasoning at length, clarifying the logic involved in the opinion you are expressing. In this kind of paragraph, you might use comparative examples to show the difference in the situation should the activity become legalized. In the case of abortion, you could give an example of the problems that occurred when abortion was illegal and compare this to the situation now. Go into detail in both examples so that the reader knows exactly what you mean.

Reading and Revising

Read your paragraph out loud, paying attention to your details in the explanation and examples. Be sure you have explained the cause-effect relationship at sufficient length for the reader to understand the consequences. Remove any unnecessary or repetitious details and add detail where an idea needs to be developed more. Talk out ideas while you are making revisions to speed up the process of rewriting. After checking your use of detail, carefully examine the organization, taking into consideration how it will affect the reader. Make sure you have included a topic sentence for your paragraph. Finally, write a second draft of the paragraph.

Critiquing in Collaboration

In groups of four or six, read your paragraphs out loud. Afterwards, pass a copy of your paragraph along with the Worksheet for Critiquing in Collaboration to your partners. When you note the strengths and weaknesses, give specific references. Be sure to include questions that the writers should answer within the paragraph.

Exercise

Polarization: Opinionnaire on Womanhood

This exercise analyzes opinions and exchanges points of view in order to develop more awareness of the different issues concerning women. By doing this you can gain insight into the various ways people interpret the statements listed below. Keep in mind that the purpose is to exchange opinions rather than argue about them.

Part I

In front of each statement, place one of the abbreviations from the list below to indicate the extent to which you agree or disagree with the statement.

SA—Strongly Agree

A—Agree

U—Uncertain

D—Disagree

SD—Strongly Disagree

_____ 1. Women should have the right to abortion on demand.

_____ 2. Free day care for children is a right all women should be able to demand.

_____ 3. Marriage is an institution that benefits males primarily.

_____ 4. Today's divorce laws are demeaning to women.

_____ 5. Employment practices in the United States discriminate against women.

_____ 6. The use of female sex appeal in advertising should be stopped.

_____ 7. Job vacancy notices should not mention sex.

_____ 8. Women should receive equal pay for equal work.

_____ 9. Women should receive preferential treatment right now as indemnity for past discrimination.

_____ 10. Women, because of their sensitivity, are superior to men in all work that does not rely primarily on brute strength.

_____ 11. Women should not be barred from careers because they are mothers.

_____ 12. The charge that women are overly emotional is a male "smokescreen."

_____ 13. Women are underrepresented in public office.

_____ 14. A woman should be able to have herself sterilized without her husband's permission.

_____ 15. Birth control information and devices should be available to any female over fourteen who requests them.

Part II

After you have filled out the questionnaire, get together in small groups to list those statements on which there was a great deal of agreement or disagreement. Then, go back to the statements that showed disagreement and examine all sides of the issue without arguing about them. Instead, group members should explain how they interpret each statement and what their attitude is about its meaning. Return to the statements that show agreement and express the reasons for these opinions to see how they compare.

 Writing Exercise
Opinionnaire on Womanhood

The purpose of this exercise is to write a paragraph that analyzes an opinion regarding women. Choose one of the statements you previously discussed and compose a paragraph using analysis as a major part of its development. Have at least one well-developed example or illustration to support your opinion. Consider the audience for your paragraph to be the readers of a women's magazine such as the now-defunct _Ms._ or _Working Woman_.

Prewriting

Think back to the exercise, and make notes on the ideas you and others brought up; write as many different statements as you can remember. Also, jot down any examples that were used to support this opinion, or think up examples that would be more effective.

Writing

Write your paragraph using the techniques of freewriting. Develop your explanation in as much detail as you can, and if you have difficulty composing part of it, try talking out your ideas by yourself or with others. Use a detailed example that will give the reader a clear idea of what you are saying in general about this subject. If possible, use more than one example to be more convincing.

Reading and Revising

Let some time elapse before you read your paragraph and then read it out loud. Be sure your explanation is written in enough detail so that your point cannot be misinterpreted. Check your examples to see that they, too, are developed completely. Rewrite any sentences that are awkward, repetitious, weak, or wordy. Then, check the sentence mechanics within your paragraph. As a final step, write a second draft of your paragraph.

Writing Exercise
Process

Think of a step-by-step procedure familiar to you and explain it in a fully developed paragraph. Be sure to choose a procedure or process that is not too complex to be fully explained, such as the art of taking a good photograph. Also, do not pick a subject that is too simple, such as addressing a letter. Consult the list of topics below for ideas or use a topic you find more interesting.

1. Tuning your car

2. Proper care of indoor plants

3. How to cook or bake ———

4. How to avoid injury while skiing

5. Safety precautions for ———

6. How to tell a lie

7. Talking your way out of a traffic ticket

8. Getting attention

9. How to cheat on an exam

10. Giving an excuse

11. Proper care of boots

12. Changing a tire

13. Building a good campfire

14. How Napoleon met his Waterloo

Prewriting

Choose one subject and list the steps involved. After you have finished the list, go back and make notes on each step, describing why it is important or any precautions or background that would be useful to the reader. Afterwards, check that all the steps are in order.

Writing

Following your list, write out this process so that all the steps are sequential. Explain and describe each step so that your readers know exactly what to do and why. Use visual detail to create a picture for them and make your instructions easier to interpret. After you have written out the entire process, check that you have included a topic sentence expressing an opinion.

Reading and Revising

Follow the usual procedure in reading and revising. Pay particular attention to the explanation of the steps. Make sure that it is easy for another person to understand and picture the process. Check that you have included any statements of caution and placed them properly. Write a second draft with the changes you feel are necessary.

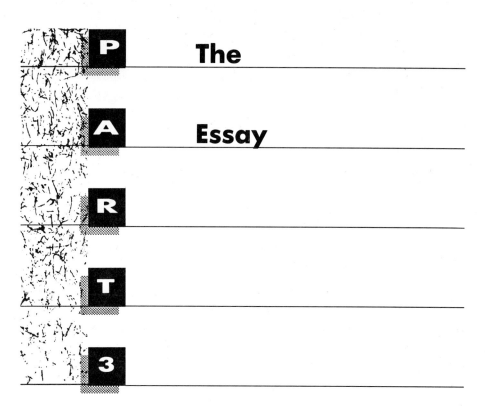

P A R T 3

The

Essay

8   The Essay

Much of the writing you do in college takes the form of essays, sometimes called themes or simply papers. We prefer the term "essay," coined in the sixteenth century by the French writer Montaigne, because it is perhaps the most common and because of its original meaning. *Essai* in French meant "attempt"; that is, the writer attempts to affect the readers' thinking by proving a point, demonstrating a truth, illustrating an opinion, and so on. Your purpose in writing essays, therefore, will be the same as in writing paragraphs—the main differences will be in scope and complexity. Your essays will almost always be longer than the single-paragraph or two-paragraph exercises you have attempted so far.

STRUCTURE OF THE ESSAY

The essay, like the paragraph you have been writing, can be divided into three parts: the introduction, the body, and the conclusion. The introduction presents the topic to be discussed, expresses the writer's attitude, and limits or defines the scope of the essay. The body of the composition consists of the paragraphs that support or develop the attitude expressed in the introduction. The conclusion ends the discussion, giving it a sense of completeness, and sometimes summarizes the main points made in the body of the essay.

The Body

The body is made up of paragraphs that develop the main ideas supporting the thesis statement. Like the paragraphs you have written for the previous chapters, each paragraph should be limited to one part of the main idea (one reason, way quality, cause, etc.) so that you can explain your reasoning in detail and give support. The types of paragraphs in the body of the essay—comparison, cause-effect, and so on—will depend on the topic and your purpose in writing. It is not necessary to use the same type of development in all the paragraphs; in a three-paragraph body, you might use three different methods of development.

Keep in mind that the body of the essay develops all of your supporting ideas. While the introduction may mention the primary supporting ideas and the conclusion may summarize them, the details, arguments, and explanations that prove or demonstrate these ideas must be presented in the body. Here you explain the reasoning involved, cite examples, give description or analyses—do whatever is necessary to convince the reader that your generalizations are valid and true.

Although each body paragraph develops a separate idea, there must be a clear relationship between each paragraph and the thesis and among the separate paragraphs. The same basic principles of *coherence* apply in essays as in paragraphs. To keep the ideas flowing smoothly and show the relationship between paragraphs, use the devices illustrated in the chapter on paragraphs: repeat key words and phrases and add appropriate transitional phrases.

Basic Organization

The easiest way to organize an essay is by order of time—chronological order. When you write about a sequence of events or describe a process, the ideas should be presented in the order in which they occur. An explanation of how you arrived at a certain attitude would probably be given in chronological order (When I was in junior high school, I used to believe . . .); the process of tuning an automobile engine would necessarily be presented in time sequence. Sometimes description can be given in chronological order. One of our students wrote an essay showing that the atmosphere in a hospital waiting room goes through many changes in the course of a single day. He described the room at several points in the day: early morning, noon, mid-afternoon, and late evening.

Another common method of organization is climactic order, in which the writer proceeds from the least important to the most important point. This can also be used in presenting causes and effects. With this method, the essay becomes more interesting as the reader continues to read; by presenting your most important point at the end, you place the greatest amount of emphasis on it. The decision as to which is the most significant point is a personal judgment by the writer that should be supported by the rest of the essay's content.

Introductions

There are two important purposes for the introduction: to attract the reader's interest and to explain the controlling idea or thesis statement of the essay. By beginning an essay with an introduction that attracts the reader's interest, you are more likely to keep a reader's attention throughout, and the reader will usually remember what you have said. An introduction that grabs the reader's attention also affects the person's attitude toward reading the essay. If an introduction is boring, it probably will make the reader expect to be bored by reading the remainder. If the introduction creates interest, the reader will perhaps have a positive attitude toward what you are saying, and be more receptive to your point of view or argument.

The reason for clearly stating the thesis statement in the introduction is to make the reader aware of the essay's purpose from the very beginning. If the introduction does not have this statement, the reader may have difficulty seeing the relationship among the various parts of the discussion; the thesis ties them together. The thesis is also important to you, the writer, because it helps keep your discussion unified; by constantly referring to your thesis, you can tell whether the ideas that occur to you relate closely enough to the main idea. For most of the essays you write in college, the introduction is generally limited to one paragraph; however, an introduction may occasionally be two or more paragraphs. For practical purposes, it is usually better to write the introduction after you have written the body of the paper. While writing the first and second drafts, you may come up with new ideas better than your original ones. If you wait until after you have completed the body of the essay, you will not have to make extensive revisions to your introduction.

The Thesis Statement

The main idea in an essay is expressed in the *thesis statement* that relates to the individual paragraphs as the topic sentence relates to the individual sentences in a paragraph. It states the controlling idea of the essay and tells the reader what to expect. The thesis statement is, thus, a generalization of the topic sentences in the body of the essay. It is an essential part of the introduction. In order to write your thesis statement, you must first determine the purpose of your essay.

Although the topic of an essay is a fairly large idea (compared with the paragraph), it still must be limited to a thesis that can be developed fully in the space allotted in a college essay or a newspaper editorial, or the like. You cannot fully discuss a subject like ecology in 500 to 600 words—you must deal with one part of it, for example, the harmful effects of a growing population on natural resources. And that is still pretty broad. A workable topic might be expressed in a thesis statement like this: *The beauty and purity of Lake Tahoe are being destroyed by the increasing amounts of waste materials being dumped into the lake.* This thesis might be developed with facts and statistics showing the different sources of waste materials, the increase in the amounts dumped, and the present and possible future effects on the lake.

Types of Introductions

There are many different ways to develop an introductory paragraph. The one you choose will depend on the topic, your attitude, and the effect you are trying to create. For instance, if you were writing about crime, you would probably want to begin by giving a shocking example. Here are a number of the most commonly used types of introduction.

Thesis-Analysis

This consists of a statement of the thesis preceded or followed by generalized statements that constitute the main supporting ideas developed in the body of the essay. Each idea becomes the topic of a paragraph. An advantage is that this introduction previews the organization and scope of the essay so that the reader knows exactly what the essay covers. The following are two examples of this kind of introduction.

> Effective listening is a technique that requires a great deal of self-control. This individual must be objective about what is being said; he must control his emotions about what is being said, and he must keep the subject that is being spoken of in the proper perspective.
>
> *Lisa Feldman, student*

> The main reason birth-order makes a difference in how one thinks about himself and reacts to others is that parents usually have a particular "emotional set" toward each child—a pattern of feeling and attitudes—depending on the child's place in the family succession. A second reason is that siblings tend to react with one another in ways directly related to their birth-order.
>
> *Peggy Hobbs, student*

Background-Thesis

In this introduction the writer explains background information so that the reader will understand the significance of the ideas the essay expresses. The introduction, thereby, informs the reader about a situation or problem in order to orient the reader to essential details. As a writer you do not want to take for granted that the reader already knows pertinent details, and this type of introduction makes sure that the reader is aware of essential information.

There are 435 members of the House of Representatives and 417 are white males. Ten of the others are women and nine are black. I belong to both of these minorities, which makes it add up right. That makes me a kind of sideshow attraction. I was the first American citizen to be elected to Congress in spite of the double drawbacks of being female and having skin darkened by melanin.

When you put it that way, it sounds like a foolish reason for fame. In a just and free society it would be foolish. That I am a national figure because I was the first person in 192 years to be at once a congressman, black, and a woman proves, I would think, that our society is not yet either just or free.

Shirley Chisholm, Introduction, Unbought and Unbossed, *Houghton-Mifflin, 1970*

An Unusual Angle

When you are writing about a very familiar topic, a good way to excite interest is to approach it from a new or uncommon perspective. The introduction for such an essay would summarize one or more familiar attitudes or approaches and contrast them with a new or unique way of looking at or understanding the topic.

The American public's ignorance of the urgent political issues of today is appalling. The public's attention has been channelled to inflation, recession, full employment, women's rights, and national defense by narrow-minded politicians seeking elective office by exploiting emotional issues. Each of these issues is important, but, with the exception of women's rights (an academic moral question), each is a small part of a complex international problem. Americans have long been conditioned to expect more, bigger, better, and faster. The economic well-being of this nation and the other developed countries of the world has depended on growth and expansion. Unfortunately, natural resources are not infinite in amount and are rapidly being exhausted by the mega-industrial nations.

Mike Miller, student

Contradiction

A similar way of introducing your topic is to contradict or disprove a commonly held idea. In presenting a new slant, you merely provide an additional way of looking at the subject without denying the truth of other points of view; however, the effectiveness of the contradiction approach depends on your ability to refute the other views concerning the subject. Consider the following example.

> The typical hyperactive child is a perpetual motion machine in human guise. He is a source of frustration to himself, his parents and teachers, and also to doctors. Time and again overactive youngsters have failed in school because they were considered to have brain damage or to be retarded. Through recent study it has been found that this is not true. There are many ways under study for reducing hyperactivity, or hyper-kinesis, which may help the hyperactive youngster to adjust to educational and social situations.
>
> *Kathy Solberg, student*

Example or Anecdote

In the section on paragraph development, we explained that examples were one of the most effective methods for supporting a statement. An example or examples can also be used to introduce an essay. With this technique, the writer uses one or more examples to begin with and follows with the thesis statement. The examples should, of course, be as interesting as possible to gain a reader's attention and propel the person to read further.

> When Evelyn Wagler was forced to douse herself with gasoline and then fatally burned by Boston ghetto teenagers last October, police officials were quick to point out that her death resembled a scene in "FUZZ," a movie on ABC, two nights before. In "FUZZ"—a police story filmed on location in Boston—teenagers were shown setting derelicts on fire for "kicks." Later in October this grisly scene was re-enacted in Miami, where a real derelict was the victim. Three boys, two 13 and one 12, were charged with first-degree murder.
>
> *Jean Davison, "TV Violence:*
> *The Triggered, the Obsessed and the Schemers"*

An anecdote is a short story, either real or hypothetical, used to dramatize the point you are about to make. In many cases this anecdote is a brief recounting of the writer's personal experience that led to a realization which became the subject of the essay. The story can also be about someone else's experience that the writer has either heard or read. A hypothetical anecdote tells what might happen under specified conditions, or what happens in general to a number of people.

> I awoke with a start! "My God, I haven't wet my bed in years," I muttered. The bed was soaked. As I turned to my wife, she sat up in bed with a shocked look on her face. "I think I broke my water," she

said. "What the Hell does that mean?" I asked. After all, I'd never had a pregnant wife before and was totally unprepared for the event. "Does that mean you are ready to go to the hospital?" I asked as I rushed to the bathroom for a towel. "I am not sure. I think I had better call Sharon again." Sharon is her cousin who, having had three small children of her own, gave my wife lots of advice throughout her pregnancy. I could have used some advice myself.

Patrick Skau, student

Quotations

A well-chosen quotation related to the topic often can express the writer's point of view in an extremely effective way. It may be a very concise summation about the subject; it may be a statement by an authority in the field; it may be a quotation that concisely expresses the attitude the writer intends to support or refute; it may be an expression that characterizes a particular individual; it may even be an invented statement, put into the mouth of an imaginary character to establish a point. Whatever the source of the quotation, it is effective partly because it gives the reader a sense of reality; one perceives it as authoritative, and is likely to approach the following discussion in a receptive frame of mind.

"It is a medical rule of thumb that among the patients a general practitioner sees on any day, half complain of symptoms directly stemming from anxiety. A majority of the rest have complaints that are at least partly caused by stress. The anti-anxiety drugs, tranquilizers such as Librium and Valium, are the number one prescriptions in America today, outdistancing antibiotics by far."

Many critics blame this excess of stress on our hectic paced lifestyle. But this, in itself, is not the sole reason. Instead, we are the victims of our reactions to its frantic pace.

Michael Miller, student

Question

When you begin your essay with a provocative question, or series of questions, you make your reader want to know the answer. Such a question is usually one with no easy answer, or the answer is one that you assume the reader is not aware of. It can also be a question most people have asked themselves but have not adequately answered. Consider the following examples.

What is news? It is the honest and unbiased and complete account of events of interest and concern to the public.

Duane Bradley, "What is News?" Reprinted from The Newspaper: Its Place in a Democracy, D. Van Nostrand Company, Inc.

Who is an alcoholic? The National Institute on Alcohol Abuse and Alcoholism puts the answer this way: An alcoholic is a person who is unable to choose whether he will drink or not, and if he does drink, is unable to choose whether he will stop or not. Although alcoholism usually follows ten years or so of problem drinking, there are people who apparently pass from abstinence to total alcoholism more rapidly. These instant alcoholics may have a biochemical imbalance or there may be some yet unknown heredity factor that predetermines alcoholism.

Linda Smith, student

Another example can be seen in the essay "Life After Life," where the author uses a single, short question as the entire first paragraph.

What is it like to die?

Conclusions

The conclusion of the essay is the writer's final opportunity to impress his or her point on the reader. And because it is the last thing the reader sees, it is the part most likely to be remembered so you should try to make it memorable. Rather than let the essay simply end, the conclusion should give an air of completeness to the discussion. To do this you not only need to restate the main ideas; you must draw a conclusion or make a judgment about the ideas and information you have presented and their significance. It is essential to emphasize the importance of the opinions you are stating so that the reader knows why your essay should be taken seriously. Be careful not to introduce any new ideas in the conclusion, ideas that need development or have not been mentioned in the body of the essay. There are many kinds of conclusions; some are described and illustrated below. Though they are shown individually, they are often used in combination.

Types of Conclusions

Restatement of Major Points

The most familiar type of conclusion has the writer simply restating the main ideas used to support the thesis statement. The key to maintaining interest in this kind of conclusion is to repeat the ideas, but not the actual sentences used previously; rather, rephrase the statements so that they appear fresh and are more emphatic. This conclusion is particularly effective in a long essay containing a number of important points, some of which the reader might otherwise forget. The simple restatement of the main ideas works as a memory device for the reader. The following conclusion, from an essay on the effects of television, includes both summary and interpretation.

> We have found that violence on prime-time network TV cultivates exaggerated assumptions about the threat of danger in the real world. Fear is a universal emotion, and easy to exploit. The exaggerated sense of risk and insecurity may lead to increasing demands for protection, and to increasing pressure for the use of force by established authority. Instead of threatening the social order, television may have become our chief instrument of social control.
>
> *George Gerbner and Larry Gross, "The Scary World of TV's Heavy Viewer,"* Psychology Today, *1976*

Quotation

As pointed out earlier, a quotation can lend an air of authority and reality to your essay. This is true in the conclusion as well as in the introduction. A well-chosen quotation allows you to end your discussion in a unique and memorable way. The quotation should compose only part of the conclusion; you must also add explanation to summarize the significance of the quoted passage and how it relates to the entire essay. The quotation that follows is the conclusion to a long discussion of the effects of having been near death.

> "When I was a little boy I used to dread dying. I used to wake up at night crying and having a fit. My mother and father would rush into the bedroom and ask what was wrong. I told them that I didn't want to die, but that I knew I had to and asked if they could stop it. My mother would talk to me and tell me, 'No, that's just the way it is and we all have to face it.' She said that we would do it all right. And years later after my mother died I would talk about death with my wife. I still feared it. I didn't want it to come.
>
> "But since this experience, I don't fear death. Those feelings vanished. I don't feel bad at funerals anymore. I kind of rejoice at them, because I know what the dead person has been through.
>
> "I believe that the Lord may have sent this experience to me because of the way I felt about death. Of course, my parents comforted me, but the Lord showed me, whereas they couldn't do that. Now, I don't talk about all this, but I know, and I am perfectly satisfied."
>
> *Dr. Raymond Moody, Jr., from* Life After Life, *Mockingbird Books, 1975*

Provocative Question

Questions can serve several purposes. If your question is thought-provoking, it should cause your readers to contemplate your subject for a considerable period of time, perhaps leading to other implications or further consequences. By asking a question you also allow readers to make up their minds, or at least you create that impression. Most people do not like to be told what to think, and here is one way to be more subtle when you are doing just that. The question may be expressed either directly or indirectly, as these two examples show. Also, the question may be rhetorical, one for which no answer is needed or for which the answer is obvious.

> No great optimism is justified . . . when it comes to cutting medical costs overall. Medicine cannot be made cheap, given the costs of its technology, and by its nature it cannot be anything but a seller's market. But U.S. health care bills do not have to shoot up as rapidly as they are doing now. The big question is whether doctors, hospital administrators, insurers and employers can devise ways to bring the public the benefits of technology at an affordable price, without a federal whip being held over them.
>
> *"Health Costs: What Limit?"* Time, *May 28, 1979*

> I have a clear conscience, because I have fulfilled my duties as a writer in all circumstances and because I will fulfill them even more successfully, more indisputably, when I am dead than I can while I am still alive. Nobody can bar the road to the truth. I am ready to accept death for the sake of the movement. But how many lessons do we need to teach us that the writer's pen should not be stopped while he still lives? Never once in our history have we been able to say this is so.
>
> *Aleksandr Solzhenitsyn, "Letter to the Fourth Congress of Soviet Writers,"* Survey, *No. 64 (July, 1967), Oxford University Press*

Prediction

In making a prediction you are requiring the reader to consider future consequences related to your subject that should emphasize the importance of your essay. Your prediction must be supported by the information in the body of your paper, and the logic of the relationship should be evident. If the relationship is not clear to the reader, your prediction will be confusing and will detract from the overall effect of your essay.

The White House and some elements in Congress seem to be lagging behind the rest of the country on the matter of reviving the CIA's capability. "The public mood is very supportive," says a top CIA official. "The question is how to mobilize that support." In the world as it is and not as it is sometimes fondly imagined, a major nation cannot function without a strong intelligence agency, and that is what is conspicuously missing in contemporary America. With the balance of power no longer as securely in America's favor as it once was, there may be little time left to get back into the intelligence business in a decisive way. Unless such a change is made, the damage that has been done by crippling the CIA may far outweigh the damage caused by the excesses of the agency when it was riding high and unchallenged.

"Strengthening the CIA," Time, *April 30, 1979*

(Note that the preceding example uses both prediction and quotation.)

Perhaps it is just as well that I conclude on this somberly precarious note. I hope I have made it clear that the potentialities for change and enrichment in the interpersonal world of the year 2000 most assuredly exist. There can be more of intimacy, less of loneliness, an infusion of emotional and intellectual learning in our relationships, better ways of resolving conflicts openly, man-woman relationships which are enriching, family relationships which are real, a sense of community which enables us to face the unknown. All of this is possible if as a people we choose to move into the new mode of living openly as a continually changing process.

Carl R. Rogers, "Interpersonal Relationships: U.S.A. 2000," Journal of Applied Behavioral Science, *4, no. 3, 1968: 265–280*

A decisive verdict in the case of "real" versus "reel" remains premature. Nevertheless, the evidence is encouraging for the proponents of videotaped trial materials: in no case has watching videotaped materials caused jurors to behave or decide any differently than they would at a live trial. In most instances, videotaping depositions or entire trials significantly cut the time needed to try each case. If research continues to produce similar results, television cameras, videotapes, and the other paraphernalia of modern electronics may become standard items in the courtroom. The research and practical results we have already have led such jurists as C. William O'Neill, the late chief justice of the Supreme Court of Ohio, to conclude, "The use of video trials on a major basis to eliminate delays has made national history. The success of this program established a landmark in jurisprudence in this country."

Gerald R. Miller and Norman E. Fontes, "Trial by Videotape,"
Psychology Today, *May, 1979*

(The preceding conclusion uses summary, quotation, and prediction.)

Recommendation

A technique similar to predicting what may happen is explaining what should happen. The purpose of many essays is not only to evaluate a situation, but also to confront the problems involved. In stating recommendations the writer is explaining the changes that should be implemented to make an improvement. The writer can also make an appeal for the reader to agree to a course of action that should be taken. Such appeals or recommendations often follow summaries. The first example below comes after a long discussion of metaphoric thought and the need to encourage such thinking in children.

> Educational efforts might be concentrated on developing metaphoric capacities that begin to evolve at an early age. For instance, parents of literally oriented schoolchildren might try more often to use figures of speech in situations that freshly illuminate topics of interest to the child—in describing, say, baseball players, rocket ships, or television programs. Or teachers, when working with children who find it difficult to produce expressive metaphors, might provide inviting linguistic frames: for instance, fill-in sentences such as, "The brightly colored dress seemed as noisy as '—'." As the clamor for basic skills continues to grow, it may be time for the fourth R—Rhetoric—to reenter the classroom.

*Howard Gardner and Ellen Winner, "The Child is Father to the Metaphor,"*Psychology Today, *May, 1979*

Plainly the citizen's plight is not subject to quickie remedy. Yet any solution would have to entail a shift in the relationship between the priests of knowledge and the lay public. The expert will have to play a more conscious role as citizen, just as the ordinary American will have to become ever more a student of technical lore. The learned elite will doubtless remain indispensable. Still, the fact that they are exalted over the public should not mean that they are excused from responsibility to it—not unless the Jeffersonian notion of popular self-rule is to be lost by default.

Frank Trippett, "A New Distrust of the Experts,"Time, May 14, 1979

In the next example, the author (speaker, actually) poses a rhetorical question that is really a call for action.

This nation is like a spring freshet; it overruns its banks and destroys all who are in its path. We cannot dwell side by side. Only seven years ago we made a treaty by which we were assured that the buffalo country should be left to us forever. Now they threaten to take that from us also. My brothers, shall we submit? or shall we say to them: "First kill me, before you take possession of my fatherland!"

Charles A. Eastman, trans., from "Sitting Bull Speaks"

Exercise
Limiting a Topic

Evaluate the following topics and determine which are too general or too limited to be developed in a 500-word essay. Indicate also those topics that could be developed adequately.

1. The power of positive thinking
2. Sex-role stereotyping in advertising
3. The ideal surfboard
4. Buying a used car
5. The impact of rock and roll on the United States
6. The best thing about McDonald's hamburgers
7. The Bermuda Triangle
8. How to choose a career
9. Interpreting your dreams
10. How to make espresso
11. The self-fulfilling prophecy

12. Taking care of indoor plants

13. How to succeed in college

14. Witchcraft

15. Fixing a flat tire

 Writing Exercise
Creating a Thesis Statement

In small groups choose five of the above topics and create a thesis statement for each that would be limited enough to be developed into a 500-word essay.

C h a p t e r

9 **Prewriting**

for the Essay

BRAINSTORMING IDEAS

Brainstorming was introduced in Chapter 1, and you have used it in several assignments. It can be applied to essays as well as paragraphs. This technique allows you to get a number of ideas about a subject on paper without evaluating their individual merits. You can use this method to think of different approaches, attitudes, opinions, advantages and disadvantages, causes and effects, qualities, reasons, and examples regarding your topic. You may also employ brainstorming to consider the purpose of an essay and the options open to you. Often after a class discussion brainstorming helps you to make notes on the major ideas expressed so that you remember them later when you begin to write.

Brainstorming ideas is not limited to sitting down at one time and thinking up ideas immediately. After choosing a topic for an essay, you may want to—or have to—wait several days before you find time to write. During this period you should come up with ideas at random that relate to your topic. Therefore, it is helpful to keep a sheet of paper or a notebook handy to write them down so that you don't forget them. You will then have some ideas available when you begin the rough outline or the first draft of your essay. When you have finished your list, you can evaluate it, crossing out those ideas that do not seem as important or interesting. Afterwards, you can group together similar ideas, opinions, and examples, so these can be turned into paragraphs when you make your outline.

OUTLINING IDEAS

Making an outline serves several important purposes. It allows you to see whether you have enough ideas and information to develop into an essay. It also gives you the opportunity to organize your ideas in a logical way, so the essay has a definite sense of direction. In addition, you can check the ideas in each paragraph to see that they relate directly to each other and that they all support the thesis statement. Furthermore, the process of writing the first draft can elicit new ideas you did not think of while brainstorming or outlining. As these ideas arise, you can write them down on the outline and consider substituting them if they seem more suitable or important.

Informal Outline

The first step in making a scratch outline is to write a topic sentence for each of the paragraphs that will make up the body of the essay and number them. You should refer to the groups of ideas in your brainstorming list. After you have written each topic sentence, you can make notes on the explanation you will use for each paragraph and the examples, facts, statistics, or description to support the main idea.

When you have finished outlining the body of your paper, you can compose a thesis statement for the entire essay, making sure it relates directly to each paragraph. Finally, make notes on the type of introduction and conclusion you will use.

Formal Outline

Many writers feel that a scratch outline is merely a list of subtopics and does not satisfactorily control the organization of an essay, especially one of more than 500 words. They prefer a more formal outline that clearly indicates the importance and relationship of the ideas. The great advantage of the formal outline is that it distinctly labels ideas according to their levels of importance and generality: the main-support ideas are indicated by Roman numerals (I, II, III, etc.) and often are paragraph topics; the more specific supporting ideas are designated by capital letters (A, B, C, etc.); such specific details as examples, important individuals, locations, etc., are marked by Arabic numerals (1, 2, 3, etc.), and so on through lowercase letters (a, b, c, etc.), which is usually as far as an outline goes. Remember that each level of an outline is a *division* of the one preceding it; thus, under II if you have A., you must have at least B. as well. Each item on a given level—say, capital letter—must be parallel (equal) in importance to the others on that level, must relate to the preceding level in the same way, and should be expressed in the same grammatical form.

Study the following examples of outlines for a 500-word essay. The first is a
topic outline, in which the items are units smaller than complete sentences. In
the second, a *sentence outline*, all the items are complete sentences. The outline
must be consistent—either all topics or all sentences—and the items similar in
structure.

The Unfriendly Skies

(Topic Outline)

Main Idea: Flying is becoming more dangerous.

  I. The aging fleet of planes.
    A. Problems with metal fatigue.
    B. Need to update maintenance procedures.
       March 8, 1989, United Airlines flight 811 cargo door detached, kill-
       ing nine passengers (*Time*, March 13, 1989).

  II. Counterfeit parts causing engine failures.
    A. Counterfeit or substandard parts substituted as new.
    B. Reconditioned parts sold as new.
       President of Execuair Corp. convicted of selling counterfeit actuators
       to the Air Force (*Fortune*, April 13, 1989).

  III. The continual threat of terrorism.
    A. Airlines targeted by terrorists.
    B. Hijackings.
    C. The use of time or remote control bombs.
       Pan Am flight 103 blown up over Scotland (*Time*, January 9, 1989).

Conclusion: The airline industry needs to take greater steps to ensure the
safety of the public.

The Unfriendly Skies

(Sentence Outline)

Main Idea: Flying is becoming more dangerous.

  I. The fleet of commercial planes is aging.
    A. Problems of metal fatigue have occurred due to the extended use of
       planes.
    B. Airlines need to update maintenance procedures in order to identify
       problems before they result in accidents.
       On March 8, 1989, United Airline's flight 811 cargo door detached
       in-flight, killing nine passengers (*Time*, March 13, 1989).

II. Counterfeit parts are causing engine failures.
   A. Counterfeit or substandard parts are substituted as new parts.
   B. Reconditioned parts are sold as new although they do not have the
      same life expectency.
      President of Execuair Corp. was convicted of selling counterfeit actu-
      ators to the Air Force (*Fortune,* April 13, 1989).

III. The continual threat of terrorism undermines the safety of flying.
   A. Airlines are targeted by terrorist groups.
   B. Despite the safety precautions, hijackings still persist.
   C. The use of time or remote control bombs has increased recently.
      Pan Am flight 103 was blown up over Scotland (Time, January 9,
      1989).

Conclusion: The airline industry needs to take greater steps to ensure the
safety of the public.

 Exercise
Outlining

Go back to the list of topics in the exercise titled Limiting a Topic at the end of
Chapter 8 and choose one idea for which you wrote a thesis statement. Develop
an outline for a 500-word, five-paragraph essay, following the example in this
chapter. Include as much relevant detail as you can and list specific examples,
facts, and so on that you could use for support.

WRITING THE FIRST DRAFT

As we have said before, in starting your essay you should begin with the
paragraphs that make up the body. You may use a number of approaches; all
the techniques mentioned in the first chapter apply to writing essays. You may
talk out ideas with others or use concentrated thinking or brainstorming. You
may wish to outline before you begin to write or, on the other hand, might want
to try freewriting to get started. Use the methods that work best for you, and be
aware of the alternatives that are available in case you have difficulty.

When you are involved in writing the first draft, write as automatically as
you can without stopping to make corrections or criticisms. In order to take
advantage of any ideas that emerge from the process of writing, write everything that comes to mind without evaluating it.

As a last step, you should write out the introduction and conclusion. They should be considered together and written after you have completed the body of the essay. As you know, the process of writing is a process of discovery. You many begin to write about a topic knowing full well what you want to say but while writing realize other ideas you had not considered. With these insights, you will change the content of the paragraphs in the body of the essay. By waiting until you have completed the body to write the introduction, you save having to rewrite it so that it matches the content of the essay. In considering the introduction and conclusion together, you can make sure that they are not too repetitious.

READING AND REVISING

Use the same techniques for reading and revising that you have been practicing. Focus your attention on the purpose of the essay and read each paragraph carefully, making notes on strengths and weaknesses, and writing out the explanation and/or details to overcome those weaknesses. As you are doing this, keep the needs of the reader in mind so that you will include the necessary detail. In addition, when you are reading and revising an essay, pay attention to the organization of your paragraphs and the unity of the essay overall. To maintain unity, you must check the content of each paragraph against the thesis of the essay. Review your introduction to see that you have included a thesis statement, that you have limited it, and that each paragraph relates directly to it. If you find that a paragraph's content does not relate to the thesis, you will need to revise it or replace it with one that has a more direct relationship to the thesis.

WRITING THE SECOND DRAFT

With your first draft and notes in front of you, write out the second draft, keeping in mind the purpose of the essay. Write out each of your paragraphs completely, including all the revisions you made. If you have difficulty, try composing sentences out loud or reading them to others in order to get ideas.

After you have completed the second draft, let it sit for awhile. Then read it carefully to see that you have explained your reasoning adaquately and developed each of your paragraphs in detail. At this point you should also proofread for punctuation, spelling, and grammar.

Exercise
I Was, I Am, I Will Be

This exercise evaluates what you have accomplished, how you have grown and changed, and how you expect to continue to develop as an individual. You are to draw three pictures of yourself. Each should be titled separately: (1) I was, (2) I am, and (3) I will be. For the first picture consider what you were like three to five years ago, the interests you had, the activities you were involved in, and your attitude toward yourself, others, and your situation. Draw a picture that best shows what you were like. Next, think about how much you have changed and draw a picture that shows in contrast what you are like now. Imagine what you will be like or what you would like to be like in five to seven years and draw a picture projecting this.

You can use many approaches in your drawings: one picture that represents a great deal about you, a collage showing a number of different things, a cartoon style, or abstract pictures. If you do not feel you draw very well, sketch out your pictures in pencil first and then color them in with crayons. Use as much detail as you can to make your pictures expressive and use color to add interest. Keep in mind that you are only representing your ideas in pictures—you will not be evaluated on the quality of your pictures.

Discussion

In either small groups or one large group, each student should display his or her pictures one at a time. The rest of the students should try to interpret what the picture represents by explaining the qualities and values each picture shows about the person who drew it, and interpreting what the picture expresses directly and indirectly. For instance, a picture might tell you directly that a person is going to college and indirectly that he or she is ambitious and resourceful. It may also indicate that the person is imaginative by the way the picture is composed. While the second and third pictures are shown, the students can, in addition, interpret the different ways in which the person has changed and grown.

Writing Exercise
I Was, I Am, I Will Be

In this exercise you are to write a five-paragraph essay including an introduction and conclusion. The body of your essay will contain three paragraphs: (1) I was, (2) I am, and (3) I will be. In each paragraph you should explain your reasoning and describe yourself, giving examples to illustrate what you are saying in general. As in the drawing exercise, concentrate on how much you have changed and expect to change. The main point is to contrast yourself with yourself. In addition, develop an attention-getting introduction and a comprehensive conclusion.

Prewriting

Refer to the three pictures you drew, and list the activities depicted in each. You need not feel restricted to those in your pictures—other ideas may have occurred since then that you feel are better; if so make note of them. Write down some of the interpretations that were made by students during the class. You might also make a list of qualities and values for each picture to use later when you are writing. Then make an outline of your essay.

Writing

Begin your essay by writing the paragraphs that will make up the body of your paper, saving the introduction and conclusion until last. Use the technique of freewriting to compose your paragraphs as quickly as you can. To write your "I Was" paragraph, look back at the drawing you made and revisualize yourself three to five years ago. Explain what you were like then, what were your attitudes about yourself and others, your interests and activities, and give examples or descriptions to illustrate what you are saying in general. In your "I Am" paragraph, concentrate on how much you have changed, explaining in detail what you are like now; if you feel you have not changed very much, describe how you have developed the qualities you had three to five years ago so the paragraph focuses on how you have grown. Again use examples or descriptions to develop your point. In the "I Will Be" paragraph, tell how you expect to continue to grow and change. Refer to your picture, and explain the changes you expect to make. In this paragraph, hypothetical or typical examples will support your opinion. As a final step, write an introduction and conclusion for your essay.

Reading and Revising

Wait until the next day to read and revise your essay. Keep in mind its purpose, and read it aloud to hear how it sounds, reviewing the paragraphs to see that they are unified and develop only one major idea. You will also want to check the main idea of each paragraph against the thesis statement to see that a direct relationship exists between them. Make sure that you have explained your reasoning in enough detail so that the reader can understand what you were like, how you have grown and how you expect to continue to grow and change. Then evaluate the examples and descriptions you have used to see that they include enough detail for the reader to get a clear picture of you. As you read each paragraph, make notes on the strengths and weaknesses, and write out revisions of the weaker sections in the margins or on a separate piece of paper. Be sure the introduction and conclusion are developed in enough detail. Afterwards, write out a second draft of your essay that includes all the changes you have noted.

10 Research

THE PROCESS OF RESEARCH

An essential part of developing an essay involves research to locate information about a topic. Your own experiences can illustrate your paragraphs, but the opinions, investigations, and studies of others can more convincingly establish the credibility of your opinions. Much of your research can be done at the library. However, you can conduct personal research, contacting individuals, companies, and institutions, or making your own investigations. The library, of course, is a primary source of published information—it offers books, professional journals, magazines, and newspapers.

To locate books, you can use three major sources. The card catalog lists the books available at the library and is organized alphabetically; you can look up books by subject, author, or title. Each card includes the author's name, the title of the book, the publisher, the publication date, the number of pages and illustrations, and the Library of Congress or Dewey Decimal system number. The Library of Congress or Dewey Decimal number is an identification number to help you find the book. Most college and university libraries have computer catalogs where you can look up books by subject, author, and title. Besides being easier to use, these computer catalogs are replacing the card catalog and contain a more complete listing of the books within the library. Many libraries have computer networks that are linked with other libraries or library systems, so if the book is not at your library, the computer will tell you what library has it. You can then order the book through interlibrary loan. Libraries that do not have this kind of computer network will still have access to an interlibrary loan service that enable you to obtain books. The third source of books is *Books in Print* and *Paperback Books in Print,* listings of books currently published in the United States. With them you can locate books by subject, author, and title.

You can use periodical indexes to find articles published in magazines, professional journals, and newspapers. These are bound volumes in which the articles are organized alphabetically by author and subject. Each listing gives the author's name, the title of the article, the date of publication, and the name of the periodical or an identification number. Some examples of these indexes are: *The Reader's Guide to Periodical Literature* (general magazines), *Applied Science and Technology Index* (professional journals), *Business Index* (professional journals), *ERIC* (articles in the field of education), *Humanities Index* (history, language and literature, literary and political criticism, performing arts, etc.), *Social Science Index* (anthropology, economics, environmental sciences, geography, law, political science, psychology, etc.), *Art Index*, *New York Times Index*, and *Los Angeles Times Index.* There are over a hundred indexes available, so you should consult the reference librarian about your topic before you begin to look through the indexes, or you might check the *Guide to Reference Books* by Sheely. In addition to the bound volumes, many libraries have indexes on compact discs for use in a computer. These can be helpful, for you can narrow the topic of your search and print out the information.

You may find additional information in abstracts. These books give summaries of professional reports and research in particular fields. Some examples are: *Psychological Abstracts, Women Studies Abstracts, Dissertation Abstracts International, Chemical Abstracts,* and *Education Abstracts.* These sources list the author and title of the work and summarize the information so that you can see whether it relates directly to your topic.

The library has still more sources of information that may be useful to you, so be sure to consult with the reference librarian.

You can gather additional information by contacting companies, institutes, government agencies, universities, and organizations. Many have reports, surveys, and documents that cannot be found in other sources. If you write a letter to one of these places, be sure to explain in detail the topic you are researching and the information you need—this saves time and avoids confusion. You may do further research by interviewing people who are knowledgeable about the subject or authorities in the field.

You can use a number of methods to make notes on the information you obtain from these sources. Most English handbooks suggest the use of index cards since they are a convenient way to collect and organize information. On each card you put the author, title, place and date of publication, and page numbers if necessary on one side. On the other side you write the information you will quote or paraphrase in your essay. You may also write this kind of information in a notebook on separate sheets of paper. Another common method is to photocopy the article or important pages from a book and underline or highlight the sections you wish to use.

CITING REFERENCES

As we mentioned before, there are two ways to use information from a source: you may quote directly or you may paraphrase (summarize and restate). In either case you must give credit to the source of the borrowed ideas or information through documentiation. This consists of notes on the pages where you use the borrowed material, as well as a bibliography (now usually titled "Works Cited") at the end of your paper in which you list all the publication data about each source to enable the reader to locate it in the library.

Again, two basic approaches apply: brief parenthetical documentation and the more traditional and formal footnote. For paragraphs and short essays like those you will be writing for this class, parenthetical documentation in the style preferred by the Modern Language Association will probably be enough. This requires only the author's last name and the number(s) of the page(s) from which you took the information, as in the following example.

> "Teachers appear to teach within a very limited repertoire of pedagogical alternatives emphasizing their own talk. . . . Few activities call for or even permit active student planning, follow through, and evaluation. . . . Commonly no space is available for small group work" (Goodlad 467).

Note that the closing parenthesis is placed before the period at the end of the sentence. The ellipses (. . .) indicate where one or more sentences have been left out. (An ellipsis consists of three spaced dots. The first dot in each of the preceding examples is the period at the end of a sentence.)

If you use the name of the author in your paragraph to introduce the quotation, you need only put the page number in parentheses, for example:

> When ideas are discussed in class, it is almost always in large groups in which Alvin Zander estimates "only 30 percent of those present do most of the commenting" (21).

Follow the same procedure when you paraphrase material from a specific page of a book or periodical. Many times, however, when you paraphrase, you are summarizing an idea that is developed over several pages in the source. In that case give the author's name and the inclusive pages, as in this example.

A composite portrait of the successful student would seem to show that he has a relatively high opinion of himself and is optimistic about his future performance (Ringness 21–35).

On a separate sheet at the end of your paper, give complete documentation of your sources in a list titled "Works Cited." Arrange the entries alphabetically, by the authors' last names, and supply the following information: author or authors, title of the work, publisher, place of publication, and date of publication. The entry for a book would be as follows.

Knowles, Malcom. *The Adult Learner: A Neglected Species.* Houston: Gulf Publishing Company, 1984. (Note the order of items and the punctuation.)

If there are two authors, list the first author's name last name first and the other's in regular order.

Schmuck, Richard A. and Patricia A. Schmuck. *Group Processes in the Classroom.* Dubuque, Iowa: Wm. C. Brown Company Publishers, 1983. (Note that the state where the book was published is included when the city may not be familiar.)

The entry for a magazine or journal article would be in this order.

Goodlad, John I. "A Study of Schooling: Some Implications for School Improvement." *Phi Beta Kappan* 64 (1983): 552–558. (In this case 64 refers to the volume number, 1983 is the year of publication, and 552–558 indicates the inclusive page numbers.)

For an unsigned article, the entry begins with the title of the article. Thus the example above, if there were no author, would begin "A Study of Schooling. . . ."

These few guidelines on documentation represent only the simplest acceptable approach; there are many situations that they do not cover. The most important things for you to remember about documentation are these:

Honesty and good scholarship demand that you give proper credit for all ideas not your own.

Documentation must include all the information your reader will need to locate the source for further research.

There is more than one style of documentation. What we have presented here should suffice for short papers. Be sure to ascertain the style preferred by your instructor and use it.

P A R T 4

Essays

and Exercises

he essays in the next four chapters provide examples of writing that illustrate different techniques and approaches. They are grouped together by topic so that you can compare their effectiveness. The accompanying questions offer a format by which you can evaluate essays, and the exercises give you the opportunity to discuss related topics that you will later develop into essays.

Chapter

11 Competition

and Cooperation

THE MYTHS OF COMPETITION

Alfie Kohn

In the first section of today's newspaper are stories about the indictment of a former government official, charged with using his influence to win lucrative contracts for his clients. There's another story about a prominent medical researcher who has admitted to fabricating his data. In the local news is the latest on that politician who was charged with accepting illegal campaign contributions. Move on to the business pages and read about bribery and insider trading in the stock market. And the sports section is filled as usual with reports of college recruiting scandals and the injuries from yesterday's game.

Because the articles are scattered throughout the paper, it is easy to overlook the common denominator in all this unhappy news. All of these incidents have taken place in the context of competition. Edging out rivals in the world of science, beating opponents for public office, staying ahead in the marketplace, scoring points on the field—all reflect our culture's obsession with winning. Competition is so pervasive, in fact, that many of us take it for granted, failing to notice its destructive consequences.

Competition can be defined as "mutually exclusive goal attainment": *my success requires your failure.* Put differently, two or more individuals are trying to achieve a goal that cannot be attained by all of them. The all-too-familiar pressure to be Number One grows out of this arrangement. We have become accustomed to living with it and quick to defend it. We have been trained, in other words, not only to compete but to believe there is value in doing so.

I have spent the last few years examining the arguments used to support competition and sorting through the evidence from various disciplines. My research has convinced me that these arguments ought more accurately to be called myths—that competition is neither necessary nor desirable. Here, then in the order of their popularity, are the four central myths of competition and what my research actually shows.

Myth 1: Competition Is Inevitable.

As with a range of other unsavory behaviors, we are fond of casually attributing competition to something called "human nature." Since this account is so popular, you might expect that there is considerable evidence to support it. In fact, it is difficult to find a single serious defense of the claim—let alone any hard data to back it up. It is not difficult at all, however, to come up with reasons to doubt that competition is inevitable.

Today, we in the U.S. especially tend to assume that our desperate quest to triumph over others must be universal. But half a century ago, anthropologist Margaret Mead and her colleagues found that competition was virtually unknown to the Zuni and Iroquois tribes and the Bathonga of southern Africa. Since then, cross-cultural observers have confirmed that the U.S. is more the exception than the rule. From the Inuit of Canada to the Tangu of Papua New Guinea, from Israeli kibbutzniks to farmers in Mexico cooperation is prized and competition generally avoided.

In their work with seven- to nine-year-olds, psychologists Spencer Kagan and Millard Madsen found that Mexican children quickly figured out how to cooperate on an experimental game, while those from the U.S. could not. In fact, 78 percent of the Anglo-American children "took the other child's toy away for no other reason than to prevent the other child from having it." Mexican children, whose socialization had been less competitive, did so only half as often.

Such findings strongly suggest that competitive behavior is a matter of social training and culture rather than a built-in feature of our nature. Further evidence comes from classroom experiments in which children have been successfully taught to cooperate. Gerald Sagotsky and his colleagues at Adelphi University, for example, trained 118 pairs of first- through third-grade students to work together instead of competing at a variety of tasks. Seven weeks later, a new experimenter introduced a new game to these children, and found that the lesson had stuck with them. Other researchers have shown that children taught to play cooperative games will continue to do so on their own time. And children and adults alike express a strong preference for the cooperative approach once they see first hand what it is like to learn or work or play in an environment that does not require winners and losers.

We might ask why we bother to train children from birth to compete—and to *want* to compete—if it really is part of our nature to do so. Far more plausible is the hypothesis that all of this socialization is not superfluous: competition is a learned behavior.

Myth 2: Competition Keeps Productivity High and Is Necessary for Excellence.

It is widely assumed that competition boosts achievement and brings out the best in us—and that without it life would be "a bland experience" and we would become "a waveless sea of nonachievers," as Spiro Agnew once put it. Many people who make such claims, however, have simply confused success with competition. This is easy to do in a society as wedded to winning as ours. But in fact the two concepts are quite different: I can succeed in knitting a scarf or writing a book without ever worrying whether it is better than yours. Or I can work *with* you—say, to write a report or build a house.

Which method is more productive—working against others (competition) or with others (cooperation)? The answer will take many by surprise, as it did psychologist Margaret Clifford. She assumed that a competitive game would help fifth-grade students learn a set of vocabulary words. In fact, it did nothing to improve their performance. One after another, researchers across the country have come to the same conclusion. David and Roger Johnson, educators at the University of Minnesota, recently analyzed 122 studies of classroom achievement conducted from 1924 to 1980. Sixty-five found that cooperation promotes higher achievement than competition, eight found the reverse, and 36 found no significant difference. Children simply do not learn better when education is transformed into a competitive struggle.

In the late 1970's, Robert Helmreich and his colleagues at the University of Texas decided to see whether this was also true in the "real world." They gave a personality test to 103 male scientists and found that those whose work was cited most often by their colleagues (a reasonable measure of achievement) were those who enjoyed challenging tasks but were not personally competitive. To be sure this surprising result wasn't a fluke, Helmreich conducted similar studies on businessmen, academic psychologists, undergraduates, pilots, and airline reservations agents. Each time he found exactly the same thing: a significant negative correlation between competitiveness and achievement.

On reflection, these results—and similar findings from scores of other studies in the workplace and the classroom—make perfect sense. First of all, trying to do well and trying to beat others really are two different things. Here sits a child in class, waving her arm wildly to attract the teacher's attention. When she is finally recognized, the student seems befuddled and finally asks, "Um, what was the question again?" Her mind is on edging out her classmates, not on the subject matter. These two goals often pull in opposite directions.

Second, competition is often highly stressful. The possibility of failure creates agitation if not outright anxiety, and this interferes with performance. Third, competition makes it difficult to share our skills, experiences, and resources as we can with cooperation. The latter does not assume that we will be selfless, but arranges things so that we sink or swim together and so have a powerful incentive to help each other.

Myth 3: Recreation Requires Competition.

It is remarkable, when you stop to think about it, that the only way many Americans can think of to have a good time is to play (or watch) highly structured games in which one individual or team must triumph over another. Grim, determined athletes who memorize plays and practice to the point of exhaustion in order to beat an opposing team—this is as close as our culture gets to a spirit of play.

Even children are pitted against one another as they conduct serious business on Little League fields. Sports psychologist Terry Orlick observed that such activities often leave their mark on young participants. "For many children," he wrote, "competitive sports operate as a failure factory which not only effectively eliminates the 'bad ones' but also turns off many of the good ones. . . . In North America it is not uncommon to lose from 80 to 90 percent of our registered organized sports participants by 15 years of age." Research in nonrecreational settings clearly shows that those who are not successful in initial competitions continue to perform poorly and drop out when given the chance.

Even the very youngest children get the message, as is obvious from the classic game of musical chairs. X players scramble for X − 1 chairs when the music stops. Each round eliminates one player and one chair until finally one triumphant winner emerges. Everyone else has lost and has been excluded from play for varying lengths of time. This is our idea of how children should have fun.

When Orlick reflected on the game, he asked what would happen if the players instead tried to squeeze onto fewer and fewer chairs until finally a group of giggling kids was crowded on a single chair. Thus is born a new game—one without winners and losers. The larger point is this: all games simply require achieving a goal despite the presence of an obstacle. Nowhere is it written that the obstacle must be other people; it can be a time limit or something intrinsic to the task itself—in which case no win/lose framework is required. We can even set up playful tasks so that everyone works together to achieve a goal—in which case opponents become partners.

It's also instructive to realize that the various benefits we attribute to our weekend contests actually do not require competition at all. Is exercise important to you? Competition is hardly necessary for that. Do you like teamwork? No need for a common enemy; in cooperative activities, such as making dinner together, *everyone* is on the same team. You say you value a sense of accomplishment? Aim at an objective standard—say, number of laps or weights—or try to exceed your previous record (which is typically known by the unfortunate misnomer "competing with oneself"). You want that joyous, almost mystical feeling of total immersion in an activity? Look into rock-climbing, jogging, dancing, or throwing pottery. The point, in short, is that recreation doesn't have to involve activities in which each player is trying to make the other fail.

Myth 4: Competition Builds Character.

Even if striving against others proves to be unproductive, some people may defend it as a way to become "stronger." Learning how to win and lose is supposed to toughen us and give us confidence. But this justification rings hollow because most of us intuitively sense that the consequences of struggling to be number one are generally unhealthy. As the anthropologist Jules Henry put it, "a competitive culture endures by tearing people down."

To a large extent, we compete to reassure ourselves that we are capable and basically good. The need to prove that we are better than others may be rooted in the fear that we are actually no good at all. Tragically, though, competing does nothing to strengthen the shaky self-esteem that gave rise to it.

On the contrary, trying to out-perform is damaging—first of all because most of us lose most of the time. The potential for humiliation, for being exposed as inadequate, is present in every competitive encounter. Even winning doesn't help because self-esteem is made to depend on the outcome of a contest, whereas psychological health implies an *unconditional* sense of trust in oneself. Moreover, victory is never permanent. King of the Mountain is more than a child's game; it is the prototype for all competition, since winning promptly establishes one as the target for one's rivals. In any case, the euphoria of victory fades quickly. Both winners and losers find they need more, not unlike someone who has developed a tolerance to a drug. It is a circular process: the more we compete, the more we need to compete.

The empirical evidence shows that competition is anything but constructive. Two sports psychologist, Bruce Ogilvie and Thomas Tutko, after studying some 15,000 athletes, could find no support for the belief that sport builds character. "Indeed, there is evidence that athletic competition limits growth in some areas," they concluded, after recording depression, extreme stress, and relatively shallow relationships among competitors. Many players "with immense character strengths" avoid competitive sports, they found. Other research has found that competition leads people to look outside themselves for evidence of their self-worth. On the other hand, cooperativeness is associated with emotional maturity and strong personal identity.

Even exploring these myths doesn't tell the whole story. Perhaps the most disturbing feature of competition is the way it can poison our personal relationships. Camaraderie and companionship, to say nothing of genuine friendship and love, scarcely have a chance to take root when we are defined as competitors.

In the workplace, you may try to remain friendly with your colleagues, but there is a guardedness, a part of the self held in reserve because you may be rivals tomorrow. Competition disrupts families, making the quest for approval a race and turning love into a kind of trophy. On the playing field, it is difficult to maintain positive feelings about someone who is trying to make you lose. And in our schools, students are taught to regard each other not as potential collaborators but as opponents, rivals, obstacles to their own success Small wonder that the hostility inherent in competition often erupts into outright aggression.

Ridding ourselves of the ill effects of rivalry is no easy task. It is not enough to get rid of "excessive" competition—cheating and win-at-all-costs fanaticism—because the trouble lies in the very heart of competition itself. All the problems mentioned here are due to the fundamental fact that one person can succeed only at the price of another's failure. If such an arrangement is to be altered, we must choose a radically new vision for our society, one grounded in cooperative work and play. Once the myths about competition are behind us, we can work to change the institutions that define us as opponents and devise healthier, more productive alternatives.

 Exercise

Questions

1. How is the essay organized?

2. What writing techniques does Kohn use to develop the essay? How effective are they?

3. State the thesis of the essay in one or two sentences.

4. Do you agree with Kohn that all four ideas about competition are myths?
   Do you agree with any of the ideas? If so, which? Why?

5. Kohn is especially concerned about the effects of competition on children. What in your own childhood experience suggests that competition does or does not build character or competence?

6. What are the ill effects of competition according to Kohn? To what extent do you agree with him?

7. According to the essay, how can we rid ourselves of the bad effects of rivalry? Do you agree or disagree? What other means are there to eliminate these effects?

COMPETITION AS A MIXED GOOD

Richard W. Eggerman

"Competition by its very nature is always unhealthy. Rivalry of any kind is both psychologically disastrous and philosophically unjustifiable." These claims made by Alfie Kohn in "Why competition?" (*The Humanist*, January/ February 1980) are too strong to be defensible. Although competition has certain negative features, there are positive aspects which should be noted. Competition is neither an unqualified evil, as Kohn would claim, nor an unqualified good, as a Vince Lombardi would have it. But it is on balance more likely to be a good than an evil.

The competitive persons is one who through his or her actions, indicates a keen concern for succeeding in situations that measure relative worth or excellence in an area. This usually involves attempting to beat another person, although it is possible to speak of persons competing against standards rather than persons. Furthermore, not every attempt at beating another persons counts as competition in the sense at issue here. We are interested in assessing the merits of rivalry when the rivalry is more for its own sake than for the sake of essential good, such as one's life or the lives of loved ones. When two soldiers fight to the death in hand-to-hand combat, there is clearly rivalry, but it would unnecessarily obscure issues to regard this as competition in the same sense that rivalry for its own sake is competition.

It may be unwise to assess in one category competition for children and competition for adults. It is reasonable to suppose that children may be peculiarly liable to dangers of comparison of relative worth in a way that adults are not, just as it is reasonable to suppose that children should not be exposed to pornography, violence and so forth. One cannot presume that, if competition is a healthy activity on balance for the normal adult, it will also be a healthy activity for the child. In order to avoid blurring what may be significantly different categories, I shall restrict the assessment of competition to only adults.

Some claims against competition are valid. It can lead to cheating, whether by tempting one to fabricate sources in the course of a debate or to improve one's lie on the golf course. This does not, of course, show that it must or even usually does not lead to cheating, nor does it show that cheating, in the context of sport makes a person more apt to cheat in noncompetitive areas, as filing an income tax return. Nonetheless, cheating, even when done only occasionally and in the context of a sport, is still morally wrong. If competitive pressure tends to incite people to commit such a wrong, then this is a mark against competition.

A particularly insidious aspect of cheating is the tendency of competition to obscure the very wrongness of certain actions as long as everyone is doing them. For instance, dishonest practices in college athletic recruiting have gone on for so long as the result of pressures to win that the ability of the persons involved to recognize the difference between right and wrong seems largely to have withered. It is now perceived by some schools as a part of the game to entice would-be players with cars, female companionship, no-work jobs and even altered high school transcripts. Cheating when one is aware of the wrongness of it is bad enough, but cheating to such an extent that one's moral sensibilities become anesthetized is surely worse.

Some suggest that competition leads one to regard opponents with suspicion and contempt. This happens often enough to be noteworthy. The tactic of "psyching up" by developing an artificial contempt or hatred has been publicized in some notable cases; Muhammad Ali in his earlier years, the "Mad Hungarian" relief pitcher, Al Hrabosky, and tennis stars John MacEnroe and Ilie Nastase come immediately to mind. The situation is surely out of hand when the contempt becomes contagious and causes fans also to treat rivals with contempt, leading to incidents of violence. Competition sometimes leads persons to such behavior; whether such attitudes in fact make victory more likely is debatable.

Another questionable aspect of competition is its tendency to lead persons to perform under conditions which threaten long-term impairment to their health. "Playing while injured" is seen as meritorious rather than silly. It is an indictment of competition that it could tempt persons to risk permanent disability for the sake of the big game.

Closely allied is the phenomenon of using drugs to improve one's performance artificially whether it be by blocking pain, increasing endurance beyond nature's limits, or increasing aggressiveness. Such chemical stimulation risks long-term injuries, but the pressures of competition cause persons to disregard this.

Other claims made against competition are without serious merit. Kohn, for example, suggests that competition is anti-humanistic because in it one person's success depends upon another person's failure. But it not always true that A's succeeding must involve B's failing. And, even when this is the case, it does not follow that the situation is anti-humanistic (if one assumes this word to mean something like "at odds with the development of one's desireable human potential").

In competition, losing should not necessarily be seen as failing. If a runner finishes behind Bill Rogers in the marathon but runs the race twenty minutes faster than he has ever before, one cannot say that he has failed. If a person enters a city tennis tournament and is eliminated in the third round, he cannot be said to have failed if neither he nor anyone else expected him to survive the first round. The point is simple: failure in competition is not to be identified with losing *per se* but rather with performing below reasonable expectations. Only when one could reasonably have expected to win does losing mean failing. In most competition someone wins and someone or many lose, but this does not mean that many (or even *any*) have performed below reasonable expectations and have, therefore, failed.

Even when two persons of equal ability, both with strong expectations of winning, are competing in an important contest, it does not follow that the situation is anti-humanistic. In some cases, loss (when seen as failure) may lead to a deterioration of the personality in some important way, but it is flagrantly wrong to imply that it must do so. Psychological studies indicate that competitive persons are apt to be self-assertive, tough-minded, self-sufficient, forthright, emotionally detached, and cheerfully optimistic with an absence of severe mood swing. Failures simply do not lead in a consistent way to deleterious effects upon the psyche of the competitor, for he or she realizes that competition (perhaps unlike real life) will provide him or her with another day and a second chance. Failure will cause short-term disappointment, but only a hedonist of a very simplistic sort would equate short-term disappointment with anti-humanism.

Kohn suggests that the competitor is caught on a treadmill, never able to enjoy real satisfaction because there are always others who are, or soon will be, better than he or she. But this also ignores the matter of reasonable expectations. The awareness that others are better is not *per se* a source of dissatisfaction unless the competitor can reasonably expect to be the very best; the awareness that others may become better is surely not a source of dissatisfaction, since no one can reasonably expect to remain the best forever. Such a claim would come closer to being defensible if it were to suggest that competitors seldom enjoy real satisfaction because they seldom are realistic in their expectation. But even this is quite dubious, for competitors, in spite of brief periods of heady and unreasonable expectation, usually do entertain fairly realistic impressions of what they are capable and usually realize that even if they are "the best" they are not going to win all the time.

The "agony of defeat" approach to sport may give the opposite impression, but it probably has more to do with television's attempt to hype than with a genuine feature of competition. This is not to suggest that there are no keen disappointments involved in competition but rather that the view of the competitor as *perpetually* insecure or unsatisfied is generally quite fictional.

What are the virtues of competition? Frequently persons attempt to defend it by pointing to various good results that allegedly follow from it, such as character building, cooperation, and catharsis of anti-social tendencies. Most psychological studies, however, indicate that these consequentialist approaches to defending competition are doubtful if not simply false.

The virtue of competition is more likely to be intrinsic in character. Competition is enjoyable to most persons who participate in it. This is confirmed by the increasing numbers of persons who participate in city softball, tennis, and golf leagues. Such hedonistic reasons should not be considered alone but should be considered.

More importantly, competition offers an opportunity for deep pride to those who move beyond the level of casual involvement. The serious competitor who has worked to master his or her sport feels real accomplishment at what he or she can do. Competitors find that it is the competitive situation which routinely leads them to new levels of performance, often feats they did not know they were capable of. Runners frequently discover that a tough race leads them to performances they never dreamed possible, performances far superior to anything they can push themselves to in training. In such situations, one feels completely invigorated, very much in contrast to much of the humdrum routine of daily life. Perhaps under harsher conditions persons would not feel the pride which is generated from excelling at artificial challenges presented by competition, for the necessities of survival would provide sufficient feelings of accomplishment. But for many persons today the task of providing shelter and food has become too easy to provide feelings of real accomplishment. In the absence of such natural sources of pride, persons seek substitutes, and competition fits the bill excellently.

This is not, of course, to suggest that competition is the only way in which one can obtain a sense of pride in accomplishment today, nor that everyone who so competes will receive such benefits. But it is a plausible source, and this recommends it highly. Nor am I claiming that the virtues of competition in this regard should take priority over other activities which have more fundamental claims upon the person. It would be wrong for a person to neglect his children while "fulfilling" himself continuously on the golf course. Competitive rewards are basically self-centered, a fact which places them behind most moral *obligations* in any reasonable ranking of priorities. But they are still valuable, personal rewards—a fact too often overlooked by critics of competition.

Do competition's liabilities outweigh its assets, or vice versa? I am inclined to claim that *most* persons who engage in competition benefit from the experience and, further, that, if a minimal amount of consideration were given to the true nature of competitive activity, almost everyone who tried it would benefit. Let us imagine the case of enlightened competitors—persons who take a bit of time to assess what they want from competition and how best to achieve it.

Enlightened competitors have reasonable expectations about their performances. They are not frustrated at the mere perception that others are better, as long as they can see themselves as making reasonable improvement. They are not terribly upset by an occasional lapse in performance, for they know that it is unreasonable to expect to play one's best game every time out. They will upon reflection see that cheating is antithetical to their goals of deep pride, rather than a means to it, for cheating vitiates their reward. It destroys the possibility of pride at performing well and thwarts the goal of drawing out maximal levels of performance. With a bit more reflection, they see that playing while injured or drugged is at odds with the most effective pursuit of their goals of maximal long-term development, for victories purchased today at the expense of risking permanent damage are too much of a risk. And, finally, they regard worthy rivals with gratitude and respect, rather than contempt, for they realize that it is only through their pushing themselves to the limit that they discover what those limits are.

The enlightened competitor may seem a rather utopian character, especially against the backdrop of competition as usually witnessed in professional or major college sports. This fact has more to do with the corruption of genuine competition at such levels of sport than with intrinsic problems of competition. When persons perform for a paycheck or scholarship rather than for intrinsic pride and achievement, cheating, intimidation, risk of debilitating injury, and the like may make sense—but only then. The enlightened competitor seems less utopian when one looks at the level of city league play, local tennis and running clubs, and so forth. Persons approaching the enlightened competitor exist in large numbers at this level, where personal monetary gain is not a factor. Their competition is to them a source of pride, without the slightest desire to cheat or hold opponents in contempt.

Competition is a mixed good; it does have risks. Competition makes some persons anything but enlightened competitors. But critics such as Kohn have painted a far too bleak picture of it. The suspicious, contemptuous, deceitful, and insecure competitor—too often portrayed as typical—is far more the exception than the rule at the level of sport where persons still rival simply for the sake of the rivalry.

Exercise
Questions

1. What is the purpose of this essay?

2. Who is the intended audience?

3. How is it organized?

4. What writing techniques does Eggerman use within the essay?
    How effective are they?

5. Eggerman states that "enlightened" competitors "regard worthy rivals
    with gratitude and respect, rather than contempt." Do your own ob-
    servations of people competing bear out this belief?

6. Do you believe that people in competitive situations "are not frustrated
    at the mere perception that others are better, as long as they can see
    themselves as making reasonable improvement"? How often do you
    think people entertain the "perception that others are better?"

7. Do young competitors fit the definition of the "enlightened competi-
    tor"? Do they use drugs to enhance performance, play when injured,
    cheat in order to win, or intimidate their rivals, leading to violence?

8. How does Eggerman's essay compare with Kohn's? Which is the more
    convincing? Explain why.

WINNING—AN ANCIENT TRADITION

James G. Thompson

*However some moderns romanticize the Olympic Games, winning was not a by-
product but integral to ancient athletics. The Greeks called it arete—excellence—
and victory was the way to get it.*

Educators have sometimes criticized coaches' desire to win, yet the longing
to win is natural regardless of interest. Like so many areas of human en-
deavor, the roots of our athletic heritage are etched in ancient Greek history. The nearly 1200 year reign of the ancient Olympic Games is
testimony to the continuity of the Greeks' athletic involvement. In addition
to the Olympics, other national festivals—the Pythian, Isthmian, and Nem-
ean Games—prompted scholars to claim that the Greeks' national athletic
system was a unique aspect of their culture (Wilken, 1967; Hamilton, 1930;

Young, 1984). Apart from these four national festivals, there were hundreds of local athletic festivals held annually. The attention the Greeks devoted to athletics and the emphasis they placed on winning may be relevant to modern-day coaches.

The Greeks' teaching specialists within their educational system collectively were called didaskaloi (teachers); among them was the *gymnastes* (coach) (Forbes, 1971). The responsibilities of coaches and physical education teachers in Greek antiquity were similar to our present-day system, yet quite different in their approach and intent to subject matter. The Greeks placed an enormous importance on winning in athletics—so much so that no recognition was given to second place at the national athletic festival competitions. The preoccupation with winning is not necessarily an outgrowth of our modern-day athletic beliefs.

Arete

The Greeks had many lofty ideals. Two, *arete* and *kaloskagathos*, were closely linked with athletics. *Arete*, defined as excellence, clearly fits what some scholars have called the insatiable desire for the ancient Greeks to compete. The spirit of adventure and competition seemed to be inherent in the Greek character (Gardiner, 1930, DeRomilly, 1963). Their competitive nature, which was designed to achieve human *arete*, permeated all levels of their culture; therefore, athletics ranked high in their value system. The joy they derived from competition was testing physical skills against those of an opponent. This motive was equally strong in individuals skilled in rhetoric, music, and drama. It was not considered out of place for athletic festivals to have oratory, musical, and drama as well as athletic contests. In all, the object was to win. The incentive to win at Olympia, for example, went far beyond the desire to be crowned with an olive wreath, the symbol of victory at the Games. Solid evidence shows that in the case of Athenian athletes, the winners were awarded generous prizes. As early as the 6th century B.C., and perhaps even earlier, Athenian victors were paid money equal in amount to what it would have taken an average wage earner nearly eight years to accumulate (Plutarch; Young, 1984).

Kaloskagathos

While *arete* dealt with excellence, *kaloskagathos*, not as easily defined but linked with athletics, can be thought of as representing the desirable external and internal qualities developed through athletic participation. Athletic training helped produce the body symmetry sought after then as well as today. As symbols of aesthetic consciousness, Greek art and sculpture underscore the Greeks' desire to achieve external beauty. The discipline, sacrifice, and training athletes endure to achieve success is well known. The same commitments were made by athletes in ancient Greece. The *gymnastes* would coach their athletes with the same intensity as present-day coaches to achieve the same outcome—victory. In fact, ancient Olympic law mandated an eleven-month training period for all athletes prior to the Games. Moreover, the training and coaching of Greek athletes was highly organized and scientific (Harris, 1967). The Greeks believed that the training, sacrifices, and commitments made by those who properly prepared for competition would help mold them into productive citizens of their respective city-states.

Victory

Victory was so important in antiquity that the Greeks were victims of the same pitfalls that plague modern-day athletes. The inability of some athletes to keep the quest for victory in proper balance led to violation of Olympic rules. These violations were usually of two kinds: bribing an opponent to lose a contest, and misrepresenting a city-state (claiming to be a Spartan, but actually being a citizen of Athens). While these infractions were few in number throughout the long history of the Olympics, they did exist. The Greeks dealt severely with these violations. Guilty athletes were banished from any future Olympic festivals and they were required to erect bronze, life-size statues of Zeus in whose honor the Games were held. These *Zanes* lined the entrance way to the Olympic stadium and were engraved with the name of the guilty athlete as well as the city-state he represented (Swaddling, 1980). Since there was only one entrance and exit to the Olympic stadium, the names of the violators were in full view of the thousands of spectators who attended the Games every four years.

Demanding the Best

The desire to excel is an admirable trait. Whether in art, music, drama, or athletics the quest for excellence is necessary to success. In our present-day educational/athletic system, winning is as it should be, important. Should one prepare for an examination to do poorly? Likewise, should one practice and prepare for a contest to lose? Of course not. The competitive process demands the best—excellence—from participants. Perhaps Charles B. "Bud" Wilkinson, former head football coach at the University of Oklahoma said it best.

The competitive process, without any question, is what has made America. As long as we preserve this attitude, I feel that we will maintain our position as the world's greatest nation. Very frankly, we coaches are guardians of a prime example of the competitive process. We are the one group that say simply, line it up and let's see who can win. Fair start, same course, and let's see who can win and to the victor belongs the glory. You simply cannot take the competitive element out of the competition, as some people would like to do. If you are involved in a competitive game, the idea is to play the best you can, to make the sacrifices and give the dedication and devotion to insure your best possible performance. Anybody who wants to erode this factor is destroying the priceless contribution that we in competitive athletics can make to our society. (In Fuoss & Trappman, 1979)

It seems that the ancient Greeks and our present society have in common the inherent trait of being a highly competitive people. To be taught to win is no sin; in fact, to do otherwise may be sinful to the opposite extreme. If athletes are coached to perform to their maximum abilities then they achieve victory regardless of the outcome.

References

DeRomilly, J. (1963). *Thucydides and the Athenian imperialism* (Philip Thody, Trans.) (p. 77). New York: Cornell University Press.

Forbes, C. A. (1971). *Greek physical education* (pp. 136, 68). New York: The Century Company.

Fuoss, D., & Troppman, R. (1979). *Creative management techniques in interscholastic athletes* (p. 52). New York: John Wiley.

Gardiner, E. N. (1930). *Athletics of the ancient world* (p. 2). London: Oxford at the Clarendon Press.

Hamilton, E. (1930). *The Greek way* (pp. 19–31) New York: W. W. Norton & Co.

Harris, H. (1967). *Greek athletes and athletics* (p. 173). London: Indiana University Press.

Plutarch. *Solon* (I. Scott-Kilvert, Trans.) (23.3). Baltimore: Penguin Books Ltd.

Swaddling, J. (1980). *The ancient olympic games* (p. 41). London: British Museum Publications Ltd.

Wilcken, U. (1967). *Alexander the great* (G. C. Richards, Trans.) (p. 299). New York: W. W. Norton & Co.

Young, D. C. (1984). *The olympic myth of Greek amateur athletics* (pp. viii, 122–133). Chicago: Ares Publishers, Inc.

Exercise

Questions

1. What is the thesis of the essay? Is it stated in a single sentence?

2. Identify the topic sentence in Paragraph two. What is the effect of its placement?

3. How is the essay organized? Is the organization effective? Explain.

4. In discussing the "pitfalls" attendant on the Greeks' emphasis on victory, Thompson states that the infractions such as bribery were "few in number." In the same paragraph he reports that the guilty athletes were required to erect life-size statues of Zeus, and these statues "lined the entrance way to the Olympic stadium." Is that a contradiction? If so, does it diminish the effectiveness of the essay?

5. "If athletes are coached to perform to their maximum abilities, then they achieve victory regardless of the outcome." Can you reconcile this closing statement with the arguments and attitude that prevail in the essay?

6. Can excellence be equated with winning? Does Thompson suggest such an equation?

FOOTBALL BREAKS MORE THAN BONES

Ellen Goodman

LIVING: *If compassion is an innate human trait, why don't men seem to have any?*

It was an average week. A separated shoulder or two, a few broken bones, ligament damage to a couple of knees. The football coverage sounded like grand rounds on the orthopedic ward.

Then Jeff Fuller barreled his 49er helmet into an opponent on the 29-yard-line. It was what commentators call "a possible career-ending injury." It was also a possible walk-ending injury, a possible move-his-body-ending injury, but nobody put it that way. Was his neck broken? The game went on. Round up the usual casualties.

I am no football fan. I do not share the allure of this alleged sport. Thousands of pounds of human flesh and armor pound more thousands across the turf, Astro and real, Saturdays, Sundays, Monday nights. But watching Fuller being carefully carted off the field, I know why I am hooked on the dynamics of the thing.

Somewhere in the middle of every game, the same thing happens. A man is knocked down and writhes in pain. The team plays on. A man is carted off in a stretcher and replaced. The game goes on. As I watch, I have come to wonder: Is this what men mean when they talk about team players?

All my life, I have heard about the disadvantage women have in business because most don't play team sports. It is said that we don't know what it is like to be turf buddies, to get muddied together, to win together. Togetherness.

The ultimate model is, I am told, this all-American, only-American sport called football. It is true that on this turf men work together for victory. But on this same turf, they are trained to block a teammate's injury out of their minds. Also trained to be hauled out of the way.

This is the image of a team we take from football: a group of people strong and close enough to go for it together, but not intimate enough to stop and take care of each other.

Not long ago, I talked with Harvard's Carol Gilligan, who has studied moral development in children. She has observed the different ways grade-school boys and girls generally deal with sports. When a boy is injured, he is taken off the field while the others continue. When a girl is injured, the game stops while they gather around the one who was hurt.

When does that break occur? Most children, even the littlest boys and girls, express compassion when another of their kind is hurt. Is it taught out of boys on the playing fields? Is it how they are prepared for war or business or just manhood?

When do people learn that to be a "pro" in many worlds you have to equip yourself with blinders against the weak and the injured? Do they have to learn first to ignore their own feelings?

I don't think that every game should halt while a splinter is removed or that every business deal should be sidetracked by injured feelings. Indeed, there are times when people, especially women, get paralyzed by the opposite problem: their fear of causing pain or even making others angry.

But it occurs to me that this image of teamwork may be all too successful a training for business in an era of takeovers and lean, mean strategies. Today, competitiveness is the key word. Those who would be winners often learn not to care when colleagues are cut from the "team." The bottom line may indeed reward those who aren't distracted by bodies on the field.

What would happen in America if just once the pros stopped playing ball until they found out if a teammate had indeed broken his neck? The producers, the coaches, the advertisers would scream.

But they just might send abroad a startling new image of a team player: not an interchangeable digit on a shirt. Somewhere down in the

Pop Warner Leagues and in the living room there would be a small flash of understanding: "Pros" also take care of each other. In time, we might learn to play the serious games with much less pain.

 Exercise

Questions

1. How would you describe Goodman's tone, or attitude, in this essay? How did you arrive at that description? What effect does it have on your reaction to the essay?

2. What is the thesis of this essay?

3. What techniques of development does Goodman use? How effective are they?
    Give some examples.

4. What main points does Goodman make against competition? How well are they developed?

5. Is Goodman's comparison of how girls and boys deal with sports accurate?

6. How does this essay compare with Alfie Kohn's? Eggerman's?

7. How much of Goodman's objection is to violence, rather than to competition? Are the two necessarily interrelated? Explain. How does this affect the overall impact of the essay?

 Exercise

Collaborative Learning

Considering the experiences you have had in this class discussing, writing, and critiquing in collaboration, answer the following questions:

1. What were the advantages for each? Explain them and give examples.

2. What were the disadvantages? Describe them and give examples.

3. Consider the other classes you are taking. How many use cooperative learning techniques? In what ways? What are the advantages and disadvantages of the teaching approach used?

4. How can you use collaborative techniques in other classes, on the job, and within your family?

 Writing Exercise

Collaboration and Competition

The purpose of this essay is to develop your own ideas about collaboration and competition. Using one of the topics from the essays or exercises, write a five- to six-paragraph essay. Some ideas you may consider are the advantages or disadvantages of competition or cooperation, ways to alter competition so that it is more humanistic, and any of the other subtopics that arose during the discussions. Write this essay as though you were going to enter it in an essay contest for a local service organization such as the Rotary Club.

Prewriting

Brainstorm a list of possible topics, and choose one most interesting to you; then, brainstorm several opinions related to the topic to see the different approaches you may use in your essay. Pick one opinion and outline the paragraphs that will make up the body of the essay, limiting each paragraph to a reason, way, or cause-effect so that you can develop it in detail.

Writing

Use the techniques that you have learned for writing and emphasize the explanation of your reasoning. Use detailed examples to illustrate what you are saying in general so that the reader can fully understand your concepts. When you have finished writing the body of the essay, compose the introduction, including a limited thesis statement and the conclusion.

Reading and Revising

Use the standard methods of reading and revising, and, in addition, concentrate on the primary and secondary support of your paragraphs. Check the paragraphs in the essay body; are they closely related to the thesis? Finally, write a second draft of the essay, incorporating your notes on revisions.

Chapter

12 Pivotal Experiences

SHAME

Dick Gregory

I never learned hate at home or shame. I had to go to school for that. I was about seven years old when I got my first big lesson. I was in love with a little girl named Helene Tucker, a light-complected little girl with pigtails and nice manners. She was always clean and she was smart in school. I think I went to school then mostly to look at her. I brushed my hair and even got me a little old handkerchief. It was a lady's handkerchief, but I didn't want Helene to see me wipe my nose on my hand. The pipes were frozen again, there was no water in the house, but I washed my socks and shirt every night. I'd get a pot, and go over to Mr. Ben's grocery store, and stick my pot down into his soda machine. Scoop out some chopped ice. By evening the ice melted to water for washing. I got sick a lot that winter because the fire would go out at night before the clothes were dry. In the morning I'd put them on, wet or dry, because they were the only clothes I had.

Everybody's got a Helene Tucker, a symbol of everything you want. I loved her for her goodness, her cleanliness, her popularity. She'd walk down my street and my brothers and sisters would yell, "Here comes Helene," and I'd rub my tennis sneakers on the back of my pants and wish my hair wasn't so nappy and the white folks shirt fit me better. I'd run out on the street. If I knew my place and didn't try come too close, she'd wink at me and say hello. That was a good feeling. Sometimes I'd follow her all the way home, and shovel the snow off her walk and try to make friends with her momma and her aunts. I'd drop money on her stoop late at night on my way back from shining shoes in the taverns. And she had a daddy, and he had a good job. He was a paper hanger.

I guess I would have gotten over Helene by summertime, but something happened in that classroom that made her face hang in front of me for the next twenty-two years. When I played the drums in high school it was for Helene and when I broke track records in college it was for Helene and when I started standing behind microphones and heard applause I wished Helene could hear it, too. It wasn't until I was twenty-nine years old and married and making money that I finally got her out of my system. Helene was sitting in that classroom when I learned to be ashamed of myself.

It was on a Thursday. I was sitting in the back of the room, in a seat with a chalk circle drawn around it. The idiot's seat, the troublemaker's seat.

The teacher thought I was stupid. Couldn't spell, couldn't read, couldn't do arithmetic. Just stupid. Teachers were never interested in finding out that you couldn't concentrate because you were so hungry, because you hadn't had any breakfast. All you could think about was noontime, would it ever come? Maybe you could sneak into the cloakroom and steal a bite of some kid's lunch out of a coat pocket. A bite of something. Paste. You can't really make a meal out of paste, or put it on bread for a sandwich, but sometimes I'd scoop a few spoonfuls out of the paste jar in the back of the room. Pregnant people get strange tastes. I was pregnant with poverty. Pregnant with dirt and pregnant with smells that made people turn away, pregnant with cold and pregnant with shoes that were never bought for me, pregnant with five other people in my bed and no daddy in the next room, and pregnant with hunger. Paste doesn't taste too bad when you're hungry.

The teacher thought I was a troublemaker. All she saw from the front of the room was a little black boy who squirmed in his idiot's seat and made noises and poked the kids around him. I guess she couldn't see a kid who made noises because he wanted someone to know he was there.

It was on a Thursday, the day before the Negro payday. The eagle always flew on Friday. The teacher was asking each student how much his father would give to the community chest. On Friday night, each kid would get the money from his father, and on Monday he would bring it to the school. I decided I was going to buy me a daddy right then. I had money in my pocket from shining shoes and selling papers, and whatever Helene Tucker pledged for her daddy I was going to top it. And I'd hand

the money right in. I wasn't going to wait until Monday to buy me a
daddy.

I was shaking, scared to death. The teacher opened her book and started calling out names alphabetically.

"Helene Tucker?"

"My daddy said he'd give two dollars and fifty cents."

"That's very nice, Helene. Very, very nice indeed."

That made me feel pretty good. It wouldn't take too much to top that.
I had almost three dollars in dimes and quarters in my pocket. I stuck my
hand in my pocket and held onto the money, waiting for her to call my
name. But the teacher closed her book after she called everybody else in
the class.

I stood up and raised my hand.

"What is it now?"

"You forgot me."

She turned toward the blackboard. "I don't have time to be playing
with you, Richard."

"My Daddy said he'd . . . "

"Sit down. Richard, you're disturbing the class."

"My daddy said he'd give . . . fifteen dollars."

She turned around and looked mad. "We are collecting this money for
you and your kind, Richard Gregory. If your Daddy can give fifteen dollars
you have no business being on relief."

"I got it right now, I got it right now. My Daddy gave it to me to turn
in today. My Daddy said . . . "

"And furthermore." she said, looking right at me, her nostrils getting
big and her lips getting thin and her eyes opening wide, "we know you
don't have a Daddy."

Helene Tucker turned around, her eyes full of tears. She felt sorry for
me. Then I couldn't see her too well because I was crying, too.

"Sit down, Richard."

And I always thought the teacher kind of liked me. She always picked
me to wash the blackboard on Friday, after school. That was a big thrill, it
made me feel important. If I didn't wash it, come Monday the school
might not function right.

I walked out of school that day, and for a long time I didn't go back
very often. There was shame there.

Now there was shame everywhere. It seemed like the whole world had
been inside that classroom, everyone had heard what the teacher had said,
everyone had turned around and felt sorry for me. There was shame to the
Worthy Boys Annual Christmas Dinner for you and your kind, because everyone knew what a worthy boy was. Why couldn't they just call it the
Boy's Annual Dinner, why'd we have to give it a name? There was shame

in wearing the brown and orange and white plaid mackinaw the welfare gave to 3,000 boys. Why's it have to be the same for everybody so when you walked down the street the people could see you were on relief? It was a nice warm mackinaw and it had a hood. And my Momma beat me and called me a little rat when she found out I stuffed it in the bottom of a pail full of garbage way over on Cottage Street. There was shame in running out to meet the relief truck. I hated that truck, full of food for you and your kind, I ran into the house and hid when it came. And I started to sneak through alleys, to take the long way home so the people going into White's Eat Shop wouldn't see me. Yeah, the whole world heard the teacher that day, we all know you don't have a Daddy.

 Exercise

Questions

1. What is the theme of this essay?

2. How has the author organized his material?

3. What overall effect did this experience have on the author? Do such experiences usually have this kind of effect?

4. Would the essay have been as effective without the use of dialogue? Why? What does this tell you about the use of quotations?

5. Why did Dick Gregory say that his daddy would give fifteen dollars?

6. How well is Mr. Gregory's teacher characterized? What is she like? How well does the author develop her character?

7. What did Helene represent to the author?

8. What did your first boyfriend or girlfriend mean to you, and how did you act around him or her?

MARGARET

Maya Angelou

Recently a white woman from Texas, who would quickly describe herself as a liberal, asked me about my hometown. When I told her that in Stamps my grandmother had owned the only Negro general merchandise store since the turn of the century, she exclaimed, "Why, you were a debutante." Ridiculous and even ludicrous. But Negro girls in small Southern

towns, whether poverty-stricken or just munching along on a few of life's
necessities, were given as extensive and irrelevant preparations for adult-
hood as rich white girls shown in magazines. Admittedly the training was
not the same. While white girls learned to waltz and sit gracefully with a
tea cup balanced on their knees, we were lagging behind, learning the
mid-Victorian values with very little money to indulge them. (Come and
see Edna Lomax spending the money she made picking cotton on five
balls of ecrutatting thread. Her fingers are bound to snag the work and
she'll have to repeat the stitches time and time again. But she knows that
when she buys the thread.)

We were required to embroider and I had trunkfuls of colorful dish-
towels, pillowcases, runners and handkerchiefs to my credit. I mastered
the art of crocheting and tatting, and there was a lifetime's supply of
dainty doilies that would never be used in sacheted dresser drawers. It
went without saying that all girls could iron and wash, but the finer
touches around the home, like seeing a table with real silver, baking roasts
and cooking vegetables without meat, had to be learned elsewhere. Usually at the source of those habits. During my tenth year, a white woman's
kitchen became my finishing school.

Mrs. Viola Cullinan was a plump woman who lived in a three-bed-
room house somewhere behind the post office. She was singularly unat-
tractive until she smiled, and then the lines around her eyes and mouth
which make her look perpetually dirty disappeared, and her face looked
like the mask of an impish elf. She usually rested her smile until late afternoon when her women friends dropped in and Miss Glory, the cook,
served them cold drinks on the closed-in porch.

The exactness of her house was inhuman. This glass went here and
only here. That cup had its place and it was an act of impudent rebellion
to place it anywhere else. At twelve o'clock the table was set. At 12:15
Mrs. Cullinan sat down to dinner (whether her husband had arrived or
not). At 12:16 Miss Glory brought out the food.

It took me a week to learn the difference between a salad plate, a
bread plate and a dessert plate.

Mrs. Cullinan kept up the tradition of her wealthy parents. She was
from Virginia. Miss Glory, who was a descendant of slaves that had
worked for the Cullinans, told me her history. She had married beneath
her (according to Miss Glory). Her husband's family hadn't had their
money very long and what they had "didn't mount to much."

As ugly as she was, I thought privately, she was lucky to get a husband above or beneath her station. But Miss Glory wouldn't let me say a
thing against her mistress. She was very patient with me, however, over
the housework. She explained the dishware, silverware and servants' bells.
The large round bowl in which soup was served wasn't a soup bowl, it

was a tureen. There were goblets, sherbet glasses, ice-cream glasses, wine glasses, green glass coffee cups with matching saucers, and water glasses. I had a glass to drink from, and it sat with Miss Glory's on a separate shelf from the others. Soup spoons, gravy boat, butter knives, salad forks and carving platter were additions to my vocabulary and in fact almost represented a new language. I was fascinated with the novelty, with the fluttering Mrs. Cullinan and her Alice-in Wonderland house.

Her husband remains, in my memory, undefined. I lumped him with all the other white men that I had ever seen and tried not to see.

On our way home one evening, Miss Glory told me that Mrs. Cullinan couldn't have children. She said that she was too delicate-boned. It was hard to imagine bones at all under those layers of fat. Miss Glory went on to say that the doctor had taken out all her lady organs. I reasoned that a pig's organs include the lungs, heart and liver, so if Mrs. Cullinan was walking around without those essentials, it explained why she drank alcohol out of unmarked bottles. She was keeping herself embalmed.

When I spoke to Bailey about it, he agreed that I was right, but he also informed me that Mr. Cullinan had two daughters by a colored lady and that I knew them very well. He added that the girls were the spitting image of their father. I was unable to remember what he looked like, although I had just left him a few hours before, but I thought of the Coleman girls. They were very light-skinned and certainly didn't look very much like their mother (no one ever mentioned Mr. Coleman).

My pity for Mrs. Cullinan preceded me the next morning like the Cheshire cat's smile. Those girls, who could have been her daughters, were beautiful. They didn't have to straighten their hair. Even when they were caught in the rain, their braids still hung down straight like tamed snakes. Their mouths were pouty little cupid's bows. Mrs. Cullinan didn't know what she missed. Or maybe she did. Poor Mrs. Cullinan.

For weeks after, I arrived early, left late and tried very hard to make up for her barrenness. If she had had her own children, she wouldn't have had to ask me to run a thousand errands from her back door to the back door of her friends. Poor old Mrs. Cullinan.

Then one evening Miss Glory told me to serve the ladies on the porch. After I set the tray down and turned toward the kitchen, one of the women asked, "What's your name, girl?" It was the speckled-faced one. Mrs. Cullinan said, "She doesn't talk much. Her name's Margaret."

"Is she dumb?"

"No. As I understand it, she can talk when she wants to but she's usually quiet as a little mouse. Aren't you, Margaret?"

I smiled at her. Poor thing. No organs and couldn't even pronounce my name correctly.

"She's a sweet little thing, though."

"Well, that may be, but the name's too long. I'd never bother myself. I'd call her Mary if I was you."

I fumed into the kitchen. That horrible woman would never have the chance to call me Mary because if I was starving I'd never work for her. I decided I wouldn't pee on her if her heart was on fire. Giggles drifted in off the porch and into Miss Glory's pots. I wondered what they could be laughing about.

Whitefolks were so strange. Could they be talking about me? Everybody knew that they stuck together better than the negroes did. It was possible that Mrs. Cullinan had friends in St. Louis who heard about a girl from Stamps being in court and wrote to tell her. Maybe she knew about Mr. Freeman.

My lunch was in my mouth a second time and I went outside and relieved myself on the bed of four-o'clocks. Miss Glory thought I might be coming down with something and told me to go on home, that Momma would give me some herb tea, and she'd explain to her mistress.

I realized how foolish I was being before I reached the pond. Of course Mrs. Cullinan didn't know. Otherwise she wouldn't have given me the two nice dresses that Momma cut down, and she certainly wouldn't have called me a "sweet little thing." My stomach felt fine, and I didn't mention anything to Momma.

That evening I decided to write a poem on being white, fat, old and without children. It was going to be a tragic ballad. I would have to watch her carefully to capture the essence of her loneliness and pain.

The very next day, she called me by the wrong name. Miss Glory and I were washing up the lunch dishes when Mrs. Cullinan came to the doorway. "Mary?"

Miss Glory asked, "Who?"

Mrs. Cullinan, sagging a little, knew and I knew. "I want Mary to go down to Mrs. Randall's and take her some soup. She's not been feeling well for a few days."

Miss Glory's face was a wonder to see. "You mean Margaret, ma'am. Her name's Margaret."

"That's too long. She's Mary from now on. Heat that soup from last night and put it in the china tureen and Mary, I want you to carry it carefully."

Every person I know had a hellish horror of being "called out of his name." It was a dangerous practice to call a Negro anything that could be loosely constructed as insulting because of the centuries of their having been called niggers, jigs, dinges, blackbirds, crows, boots and spooks.

Miss Glory had a fleeting second of feeling sorry for me. Then as she handed me the hot tureen she said, "Don't mind, don't pay that no mind.

Sticks and stones may break your bones, but words. . . . You know, I been working for her for twenty years."

She held the back door open for me. "Twenty years. I wasn't much older than you. My name used to be Hallelujah. That's what Ma named me, but my mistress give me 'Glory,' and it stuck. I likes it better too."

I was in the little path that ran behind the houses when Miss Glory shouted, "It's shorter too."

For a few seconds it was a tossup over whether I would laugh (imagine being named Hallelujah) or cry (imagine letting some white woman re-name you for her convenience). My anger saved me from either outburst. I had to quit the job, but the problem was going to be how to do it. Momma wouldn't allow me to quit for just any reason.

"She's a peach. That woman is a real peach." Mrs. Randall's maid was talking as she took the soup from me, and I wondered what her name used to be and what she answered to now.

For a week I looked into Mrs. Cullinan's face as she called me Mary. She ignored my coming late and leaving early. Miss Glory was a little an-noyed because I had begun to leave egg yolk on the dishes and wasn't putting much heart in polishing the silver. I hoped that she would com-plain to our boss, but she didn't.

Then Bailey solved my dilemma. He had me describe the contents of the cupboard and the particular plates she liked best. Her favorite piece was a casserole shaped like a fish and the green glass coffee cups. I kept his instructions in mind, so on the next day when Miss. Glory was hang-ing out clothes and I had again been told to serve the old biddies on the porch, I dropped the empty serving tray. When I heard Mrs. Cullinan scream, "Mary!" I picked up the casserole and two of the green glass cups in readiness. As she rounded the kitchen door I let them fall on the tiled floor.

I could never absolutely describe to Bailey what happened next, be-cause each time I got to the part where she fell on the floor and screwed up her ugly face to cry, we burst out laughing. She actually wobbled around on the floor and picked up shards of the cups and cried, "Oh, Momma. Oh, Momma, I sorry."

Miss Glory came running in from the yard and the women from the porch crowded around. Miss Glory was almost as broken up as her mis-tress. "You mean to say she broke our Virginia dishes? What we gone do?"

Mrs. Cullinan cried louder, "That clumsy nigger. Clumsy little black nigger."

Old speckled-face leaned down and asked, "Who did it, Viola? Was it Mary? Who did it?"

Everything was happening so fast I can't remember whether her action preceded her words, but I know that Mrs. Cullinan said, "Her name's Margaret, goddamn it, her name's Margaret." And she threw a wedge of the broken plate at me. It could have been the hysteria which put her aim off, but the flying crockery caught Miss Glory right over her ear and she started screaming.

I left the front door wide open so all the neighbors could hear.

Mrs. Cullinan was right about one thing. My name wasn't Mary.

 Exercise

Questions

1. What is the purpose of the essay?

2. How is it organized?

3. How is Mrs. Cullinan described? How much does the author tell the reader about her character?

4. What is the significance of Mrs. Cullinan's changing Margaret's name?

5. What does Miss Glory represent?

6. In what way was this experience like a finishing school? What did the author learn?

THE PHYSICAL MISEDUCATION OF A FORMER FAT BOY

Louie Crew

When I was six, a next-door neighbor gave me my first candy bar, and I fattened immediately in a home where food was love. It is hardly surprising that when I first entered physical education courses in the eighth grade my coaches were markedly unimpressed or that thereafter I compensated by working harder at books, where I was more successful. Although I did learn to take jokes about my size and experienced the "bigness" of being able to laugh at myself (the standard fat man's reward), at thirty-five I am furious to recall how readily and completely my instructors defaulted in their responsibilities to me. Some remedies I have learned in my thirties persuade me that it is not inevitable that the system would continue to fail other fat boys.

My personal remedies for physical ineptitude have a firm base in ideas. Four years ago I weighed 265 pounds. Only my analyst needs to know how much I consequently hated myself. In six months I took off 105 pounds and initiated a regular jogging and exercising schedule that has gradually, very gradually, led to increase self-confidence. Yet my physical education teachers in secondary school and college never showed the least interest in my physical problems, never sat down and initiated the simplest diagnosis of my physical needs, never tempted me into the personal discoveries that I had to wait more than a decade to make for myself.

Instead, my physical educators offered two alternatives. Either I could enter the fierce competitive sports that predominate in our culture and therein make and accept the highest mark I could achieve; or I could opt for the less-competitive intramurals, modeled after the big boys' games, and accept my role as a physically incompetent human being, sitting on the sidelines to cheer for a chosen team of professionals. These limited alternatives were repeatedly justified as teaching me how it is out in the "real world," in "the game of life," allegedly divided between the participators and the watchers.

Now, as I jog in midwinter dawn, all muffled with socks over my hands, making tracks with the rabbits in Carolina dew, I am not competing with anyone, unless I whimsically imagine Father Time having to add another leaf to my book. I am celebrating me, this morning, this pair of worn-out tennis shoes, the tingle in my cheeks, the space being cleared in my stomach for my simple breakfast when I get back. . . . I was very articulate at fourteen—fat—but articulate and I believe that a sympathetic, interested coach could have shared this type of insight, this type of reality, with me, and perhaps thereby he could have teased me into the discoveries I had to make many years later. But the coach would have had to love kids like me more than he loved winning if he had hoped to participate in my physical education. I had no such coach.

Perhaps an athletic friend could have shared insights into my physical needs and suggested alternative fulfillments. I certainly had many athletic friends, because I sought avidly to compensate for my physical failures by liking and being liked by athletes. Unfortunately, these friends were all schooled in the competitive rules of keeping trade secrets and of enjoying and hoarding compliments. Human sharing had not been a part of their education.

I recall how at thirty-two I tentatively jogged around a block for the first time, how the fierce hurt in my gut was less bothersome than the fear that I would not make it. I had to learn to love myself for making it, and for making it again the next day, rather than to participate in my hecklers' mockery of the sweating fat man. I remember jogging no faster at sixteen and being laughed at by the coach, who kept me that much longer a prisoner in my role as the jovial class clown.

I became a water boy and trainer, winning the school's award for

"most unselfish service." Is not the role familiar? I even served two sum-
mers as a camp counselor. I could not walk to first base without puffing. I
had been taught well.

My physical educators were signally unimaginative. We played only
the few sports that had always been played in our area. Further, they
maintained a rigid separation between "sports" and "play." Football, baseball, basketball, and track were "sports." Fishing, hiking, boating, and jogging were "play." Golf was "play" until you had a team that won five
trophies; then you developed the cool rhetoric of "sport."

I remember going on a boy-scout trip in the Talledega National Forest
in Alabama for a week. My anticipation was immense. I liked the woods. I
liked walking. I liked the sky, trees, rocks, ferns. . . . We were to walk
only about five or ten miles a day through a wilderness, camping out
around an authentic chuck wagon that would move in advance during the
day. The trip itself, however, was a nightmare for me. The coach/scoutmas-
ter led at a frantic pace, because he wanted to get each lap done with and,
as he said he wanted "to make men" out of us. The major activity was to
race ahead so as to enjoy "breathers" while waiting to heckle us slower
folk when we caught up. When we came to a clearing overlooking the vast
chasms of blue-green shimmer, the biggest breach of the unwritten code
would have been to stop to look for ten minutes. The trip was to get
somewhere (nobody quite knew why or where), not to be somewhere.

For a long time I treasured illusions that my experiences with physical
miseducation resulted merely from my provincial isolation, that real professionals elsewhere had surely identified and rectified these ills. But as I
have moved from south to west to east, even to England, I have found
very few real physical educators. Almost no one is interested in educating
individuals to discover their own physical resources and to integrate them
with all other personal experiences. Almost everyone is interested in developing ever-better professionals to provide vicarious entertainment for a
physically inept society.

Most of the professional literature describes the training of professional
sportsmen and evaluates the machinery developed to serve this training.
My favorite example of this perverse pedantry is my friend's M.A. thesis
studying the effects of various calisthenics on sweat samples. One is scared
to imagine what secretions he will measure for his doctoral dissertation.
Yet it is fashionable to mock medieval scholars for disputing how many angels could stand on the head of a pin!

Once while working out in gymnasium at the University of Alabama, I
jestingly asked some professionals how many pounds I would have to be
able to lift to be a man. To my surprise, I received specific answers: one
said 280 pounds (he could lift 285); another said, "one's own weight"; another. . . . But I was born a man! It is surely perverse for a man to trap
himself by confusing *being* with *becoming*.

Exercise

Questions

1. State the thesis of the essay in one sentence.

2. How is this essay organized?

3. How did the author's instructors default in their responsibilities?

4. What difference could a sympathetic coach have made in the author's life?

5. What overall effect has this experience had on the author?

Exercise

Your Helene Tucker

Part I

As Dick Gregory says, "Everybody's got a Helene Tucker, a symbol of everything you want." For Dick Gregory, she was an incentive to excel, a reason to accomplish what others made him feel he was incapable of achieving. Though everyone has a Helene Tucker, yours may not have been a girlfriend. She or he may have been a friend, a relative, a teacher, or other person who gave you the desire to attempt goals that you would not otherwise have tried.

Think of someone who had this effect on you and visualize the person and the situation. Use your imagination like a motion picture to review the sequence of events. Then, write a short essay about this incident. Describe the situation and this person in detail, and relate what happened during this time. Be sure to tell why the individual had this effect on you, and what you were able to achieve because of it. You may conclude by looking back on that experience now.

Part II

In small groups, read your essays aloud, in order to share these experiences; then answer the following questions.

1. What different kinds of people have inspired the members of your group? In what different ways did they do this?

2. What did these people show you about yourselves?

3. How did this experience affect your life at the time? How does it continue to affect you?

Writing Exercise

This exercise explores the topics and issues presented in the three previous essays and relates them to your own experience. Using one of the topics, write a five- to six-paragraph essay. Some of the ideas you may consider are: shame and how it affects people, a personal experience that made a significant change in your life, and any of the other subtopics that came up during the discussions. You may also revise the essay you wrote for "Your Helene Tucker." (If you select that essay, you need not read the instructions on prewriting and writing.)

Prewriting

Brainstorm a list of possible topics, and choose the one that is the most interesting to you; then brainstorm some related opinions. Pick one and outline the paragraphs that will make up the body of the essay, limiting each paragraph to a reason, way, quality, or cause-effect so that you can develop it in detail. If you are writing about a personal experience that made a change in your life, make notes on the events or situation that preceded the experience, the sequence of events involved, the roles other people played in it, and finally the change that resulted from the experience.

Writing

Use the technique of freewriting and write out your first draft as automatically as you can. Try to visualize the experience so that you can recall details. When you have finished writing the body of the essay, compose the introduction, including a limited thesis statement, and the conclusion.

Reading and Revising

Use the methods of reading and revising that you have been practicing, and check that you have included primary and secondary support in your paragraphs. Also, review the paragraphs in the body of the essay to see that they are closely related to the thesis. Finally, write a second draft of the essay, using the notes you have made on revisions.

Critiquing in Collaboration

In small groups, pass a copy of your essay and the Worksheet for Critiquing in Collaboration to your partners. Follow the usual procedure in critiquing, pointing out the strengths and weaknesses and any questions that the writer should answer. Each essay should be read by at least two people.

Intercultural Communication

FEAR AND REALITY IN THE LOS ANGELES MELTING POT

Joel Kotkin

On a warm afternoon in Long Beach, at Pei Lin, a Cambodian restaurant on Anaheim Street, Indochinese teen-agers, dressed like Valley girls, clutch their schoolbooks and cluster around the big-screen Mitsubishi in the corner, lip-syncing along with MTV. Across the room, middle-aged refugees stare blankly as they drink their tea.

Marc Wilder, an urban planner and a former Long Beach City Council member, sits at one of the tables, eating a fish and rice lunch and considering the impact of immigration on Southern California.

"Anything will be possible here in the future," he says. "These people who are coming here can succeed or they can fail. They can be our hope or our downfall."

Immigration has become *the* irresistible force in the life of Southern California. In 1970, only 11% of the Los Angeles area population was foreign-born; a decade later, 22% was foreign-born, and predictions by the Southern California Assn. of Governments puts the figure at close to a third by the turn of the century. Last year, the Immigration and Naturalization service issued 122,268 new green cards in the seven-county Southern California region. The immigrants came from Mexico and El Salvador and China and Vietnam and Ireland, some 30 countries in all, with a majority fitting under the headings Latino and Asian. Next year, 40% of Southern

California's population, by birth or ancestry, will be either Latino or Asian. In another 20 years, according to projections from SCAG, those groups will make up an absolute majority in the region.

Already, in the Mid-Wilshire district, in Monterey Park, in Orange County's Westminster or along Anaheim Street in Long Beach, a stranger to Southern California would think the region's predominant language was Korean, Chinese, Vietnamese or Cambodian. And in the Los Angeles Basin, in a huge arc stretching from San Fernando to Santa Ana, Latinos, a majority of them immigrants, form the second-largest concentration of Spanish speakers in North America (the first is Mexico City).

For Marc Wilder, this is a geography of hope—a unique opportunity to build a bracing, multiracial, multicultural urban civilization. "We are going to be different than anywhere," he says, "and we are going to do things differently because a Cambodian, a Hispanic and a Jew share the same space. . . . We will see new kinds of institutions made by new kinds of people."

Wilder's hopeful vision of a future built on immigration is evidently not shared by most Southern Californians. A Los Angeles Times Poll conducted in January found that 57% of the residents polled agreed that there are "too many immigrants here." The result echoed a 1986 poll in Los Angeles and Orange counties that found 55% agreement with the statement "immigration is a change for the worse." And throughout the region, there are widespread concerns that massive immigration is threatening our economic future, our social cohesion and our quality of life.

The anti-immigration mood shows up in blatant ways. Last year, for instance, then-Monterey Park Mayor Barry Hatch dispatched a letter—on city stationery—to the leading presidential candidates calling the immigrants "a horde of invaders," linking undocumented foreigners with "drug runners, terrorists and criminals" and suggesting a five-year ban on all immigration.

This year, in Westminster, the commercial hub for Orange County's estimated 85,000 Vietnamese, vandals have attacked at least eight signs that direct motorist to the "Little Saigon" shopping district. In April, the City Council there rejected a request for a parade of Vietnamese veterans groups honoring those who died fighting along-side American soldiers in the Vietnam War.

"It's my opinion that you're all Americans and you'd better be Americans. If you want to be Vietnamese, go back to South Vietnam," City Councilman Frank Fry told the organizers of the South Vietnam Armed Forces Day. "That may be unfair," he added, "but that's my opinion, and I'm sure that it is the opinion of a lot of people around here."

The Federation for American Immigration Reform, an anti-immigration lobby, links newcomers to such issues as crowded freeways, soaring housing costs and overcrowded schools. "The immigrants are resented strongly because of their impact on livability," says Los Angeles City Councilman Ernani Bernardi, a member of FAIR's national board of advisers. "We just can't accommodate the population. They can't *all* come here."

Among many of the region's blacks and some native Latinos, there is fear that the new immigrants will usurp both their homes and jobs, leaving their communities even poorer and less empowered. And even among the liberal and academic elites of the Westside, long the self-styled supporters of minority rights, there is mounting concern. "One leading liberal told me the other day that immigrants were eating up the resources and that they are not like their parents or grandparents," relates Antonia Hernandez, executive director of the Mexican American Legal Defense and Educational Fund.

The anti-immigration mood can be summarized in three basic fears: the fear that natives will be displaced from jobs and neighborhoods, the fear that immigrants will be caught in a growing underclass and the fear that this extraordinary wave of newcomers will not or cannot fit in—and become Americans. These fears can be attributed to simple racism or nativism; they can be explained by tightening economic realities; they can be traced to the demonstrable changes that add up to a lost Southern California "paradise."

They can also be challenged. There is evidence—in the *barrios*, along Anaheim Street, in Westwood's "Little Tehran," in Monterey Park, in Koreatown and throughout the new Los Angeles—that the pessimism is unfounded, that the future can be cast in positive terms, that immigration can help revive dying communities, strengthen the changing economy and, with an interplay of cultures and values, become a source of innovation in the region.

"Maybe," says Marc Wilder as he finishes his tea in the Pei Lin restaurant, "we are already evolving into something new and exciting. And, maybe we don't even know it."

Debunking the Displacement Theory

Some Southern Californians would have it that if high-paying jobs are scarce, traffic is a nightmare and property values in their neighborhoods have escalated beyond reach, the new immigrants are to blame. For instance, nearly 60% of all blacks in Southern California and almost half of the whites, according to a 1983 Urban Institute poll, were convinced that immigrants are taking jobs from native-born Americans. And that feeling often broadens to sweeping generalizations. "The jobs that used to go to blacks are now going to Latinos," complains Fritizer Hopkins, a community leader with the Southern California Organizing Committee, which represents 83,000 families in the south Los Angeles area.

In fact, the jobs that immigrants take are new jobs: low-wage, low-benefit positions in the burgeoning manufacturing and service industries responsible for the rapid expansion—at nearly three times the national rate—of the Southern California economy. To a large extent, these additional jobs helped the region recover from the loss of thousands of unionized blue-collar positions, which disappeared when employers such as GM and Firestone closed down their Southern California operations during the 1970s and early 1980s. The jobs are part of a new economy—and they are jobs that natives do not want.

"Young blacks don't want to start at the bottom," says George Givens, chief organizer for the Southern California Organizing Committee, as we drove through the industrial districts in the grim eastern reaches of South-Central Los Angeles, where the vast majority of workers appear to be Latinos. "If a job doesn't pay $15 an hour, you don't want to do it."

Such anecdotal evidence against the displacement theory is also supported by the bulk of economic research. A 1988 report issued by the highly respected National Bureau of Economic Research in Cambridge, Mass., concluded that immigrants do not cause unemployment among native-born Americans. The bureau and other researchers found that cities with large-scale immigration, such as Los Angeles or Miami, actually created more high-paying jobs for natives, including blacks, than areas with fewer newcomers. According to a report from UCLA, from 1979 to 1987, Los Angeles experienced an increase of 11.3% in high-paying jobs, compared with 8.5% nationwide.

That's partly because having a large pool of low-wage immigrant workers allows small subcontractor firms to cut the price of parts and components they sell to larger companies. Those lower prices help keep production costs in bigger American companies close to those in overseas factories, maintains Wayne Cornelius, director of the Center for U.S.-Mexico Studies at UC San Diego, and thousands of high-paying industrial jobs are preserved for native-born Americans. Without the contributions of the immigrants, Cornelius and other economists suggest, these better-paying jobs would have long ago migrated "offshore."

Another major charge against immigrants is that they depress wage rates for native-born workers. But recent studies by both the Urban Institute and NBER have concluded that the influx of low-cost Hispanic labor has had no appreciable negative effect on wage rates for native-born workers. "There's absolutely no evidence that immigration hurts wage rates," sums up NBER's Richard Freeman, who is also a professor of economics at Harvard University. "The average American benefits from immigration—and there's not a major economist who disagrees with that. (Immigrants) produce more than they consume—everybody benefits."

There is a softer side to the displacement theory, a sense among long-time residents that the successes of immigrants somehow threaten the quality of life for natives. Some have seen their communities transformed as revitalization sparked by immigrants has been accompanied by congestion, increased inconvenience and the possibility of displacement. "A way of life is disappearing, and it's brought out the worst in people," says Antinio Bitonti, an 80-year-old retired deputy L.A. County assessor who lives in Westminster. "Many of these people have been here 20 or 30 years and haven't caught up with the changes in Southern California." Immigrants are an easy target for their resentments.

Seventeen years ago, when Bitonti first moved to Westminster from Long Beach, it was a sleepy, almost-bucolic place. "Right around the street here I picked tomatoes," Bitonti recalls. "I picked strawberries down at the corner of Magnolia and Bolsa."

Today, the strawberry fields are gone, replaced by bustling dim-sum restaurants, noodle houses and ginseng parlors, all part of a $100-million thriving commercial center with more than 700 businesses owned by Southeast Asians. Los Angeles leads the nation in both Latino- and Asian-owned business, including more than 7,000 enterprises run by Koreans alone. And Orange County, according to a recent U.S. Department of Commerce study, has the country's third-largest number of Asian-owned businesses, after Los Angeles and Honolulu.

For Bitonti and his neighbors at the Mission Del Amo trailer park, the immigrants' success has brought distress. As Vietnamese-driven development has lifted commercial property values along Bolsa Avenue from $7 to $70 a square foot since the early 1980s, the pressure on owners of trailer parks to sell has mounted. Caught between capitalist economics and the demographic tidal wave, the retirees in the mobile home parks feel threatened, and hostility toward the Vietnamese has mounted.

"At least 50% are prejudiced, even members of my own family," Bitonti says. "People call them gooks. It's wrong, but there's a lot of prejudice here."

Sally Ringbloom, one of Bitonti's neighbors, says she thinks of the Vietnamese every time she turns left onto Bolsa. "The traffic has become terrible. It takes forever to make that turn, and they (the Vietnamese) are the worst drivers in the world."

Ringbloom says she once hoped "to die here" but now plans to move. So does her daughter, who lives with her family on the other side of the 405 Freeway in Huntington Beach. "My grandkids don't like it anymore. There's too much traffic, too many immigrants. They've made life difficult for Americans."

As unpleasant as Ringbloom's assertions might be, they do reflect an undeniable fact that immigration increases population pressures. For Ringbloom or for the average commuter fuming in morning traffic on the

San Bernardino or Ventura freeways, immigrants became the focal point for the ever-growing complaints about getting there from here.

But in reality, notes David Diaz, a city planner from the heavily Latino El Sereno district of Los Angeles, immigrants generally are not the ones spending hours clogging the roadways. Most cluster closer to downtown and the industrial areas of the city, and they are likely to commute by RTD or drive only a short distance.

"If people are so concerned about smog and traffic, maybe they should look at the people who are coming from the Northeast or Midwest," suggest Diaz, sitting on the porch of his closed-in home. "Those are the guys who are commuting from out in the suburbs, not the *Mexicanos* who are riding the bus from East L. A. The *real* problem is our political infrastructure won't move. It won't get the job done to blame the powerless first."

Beyond the Underclass

If Southern Californians feel threatened by the successes of newcomers, they're equally disturbed by the specter of the immigrants' failure. One vision of many who fear immigration is that Southern California's newest residents and the generations that follow will be trapped at the bottom of society and never find an upward path. They see these groups as likely prisoners of a welfare-dependent, crime-ridden underclass unable to find jobs and soon not even trying.

These fears were bolstered earlier this year by a report from UCLA's Graduate School of Architecture and Urban Planning. "The Widening Divide" analyzed income inequality and poverty in Los Angeles, and its findings concerning Latinos and some Asian groups, many of whom are recent immigrants, were most troublesome. The report showed a growing gap between the haves and the havenot groups and predicted that the latter were potentially destined to remain struck at the bottom of an emerging "two-tier" society. In short, according to the report, many immigrants may never acquire the skills or be offered the opportunities necessary for upward mobility.

The key word is *may*. The UCLA study only indicated a trend, not a current reality. The report repeatedly stresses that government and industry can intervene and provide better educational occupational opportunities in order to avert such a two-tier society.

The effect of such opportunities is demonstrable. At Windline/Amanet, a small manufacturing company typical of the industries that are fueling L.A.'s booming economy, one positive scenario for the future is unfolding.

Mario Toledo came to Los Angeles illegally from Guatemala in 1981, when he was 16. He spoke no English, had no industrial or trade skills and had only a 10th-grade education. Toledo worked at a series of menial jobs, then found work on the assembly line at Windline, putting together marine-safety products for close to the minimum wage.

After three years on the job, he has applied for citizenship in the amnesty process and moved up the ladder at the company. He is making close to $7 an hour building prototypes for new equipment. His wife, Rosa, 19, a Mexican immigrant whom he met at Windline, also started there at about the minimum wage and also has advanced quickly. She now makes $6.50 an hour inspecting aerospace components. Together, their earnings, boosted by overtime, add up to nearly $30,000 a year. The Toledos are bonafide American dreamers.

For Rosa and Mario, life in Los Angeles has been tough, but not the Dickensian hell portrayed in the UCLA study. They live with two other immigrant couples in a $650-a-month apartment in Culver City near Rosa's mother, who occasionally cares for the Toledos' 18-month-old son, Mario Jr. And encouraged by Windline's president, Robert Barbour, both are learning English. About a quarter of the company's 40 employees, like the Toledos, are new immigrants, and the company pairs non-English-speaking employees with natives to teach them the language on the job. Windline also offers Spanish-language job training and videos, and those who learn English are eligible for promotions and training for higher-paying jobs. Rosa takes classes at night to finish her high school education and plans someday to attend college.

"It was hard to be here at first, but now we feel we're going up in the world," she says, during a break at the Marina del Rey factory. "You know, when we started, we had nothing in a positive direction."

Significant research underlines that "positive direction." In 1982, University of Illinois researcher Barry Chiswick found that the longer immigrants stay in the United States, the less likely they are to be in poverty.

And a key study completed in 1985 by the RAND Corp. also challenged the notion that immigrants are doomed to poverty. The study focused on Mexican immigrants (the largest segment of Latino newcomers), and it assessed the achievements of members of three generations. The report's author, demographer Kevin McCarthy, summarized the results as consistent with the traditional American immigrant pattern: "The process is . . . three-generational . . . with poorly educated immigrants coming in and filling the lowest-level jobs, their children getting more education and then moving into skilled blue-collar jobs, and then the next generation, if they get the additional education, moving into the white-collar jobs."

But at the end of the report, McCarthy injected a warning: Shrinking numbers of mid-level, steppingstone jobs, along with other economic factors, might halt the traditional pattern of upward mobility. And although McCarthy found evidence that educational levels had improved over the generations, he stressed that that process must continue if immigrants were to make it in America.

The UCLA study, four years later, found that the situation in Los Angeles came closer to McCarthy's warnings than to his positive assessment of the progress so far. The study showed that in areas such as income level, occupational attainment, education and households in poverty, the overall situation for Latino immigrants, in particular, had worsened over a 20-year period. More full-time workers lived in poverty; more jobs paid low wages, and more Latinos held them than any other group; more native-born and immigrant Latinos were dropping out of school (at rates of almost 70% for the foreign-born, 40% for native-born). Latino immigrants might still be improving their lot from generation to generation, but they were falling further and further behind Anglo society.

"There was good opportunity in the past," says Paul M. Ong, the study director. "You could end up in a middle-income job with just a ninth-grade education. There were enough blue-collar jobs around to propel you. But the economy is not producing the jobs it used to; the opportunities aren't as plentiful. And if you are a minority, studies show you will end up in a school district that performs badly."

There is some information, however, that recent studies did not consider. For example, the education data used by UCLA come from public-school sources and do not include the thousands of Latino students who attend Catholic schools. In the Catholic School System of the Archdiocese of Los Angeles, which includes schools in Los Angeles, Ventura and Santa Barbara, 44,135 Latino children—46% of the Catholic school system's enrollment—attend classes. According to recent surveys, they possess reading skills equal to those of their Anglo peers in the parochial system and superior to those of whites attending public schools. And the dropout rate is similar to the Anglo dropout rate for Catholic schools: less than 1%.

But even Latinos who fail to finish school should not be cast too quickly into the underclass mold of crime, hopelessness, broken families and disenfranchisement from the working world. Latino immigrants in Southern California are for the most part actively and notably involved in the job market. The UCLA report emphasized this: Latino immigrants constitute the vast majority of Los Angeles' *working* poor. And perceptions bear out its statistics: "You just don't have the sort of long-term unemployment (among Latinos) that you have in South-Central," says El Sereno planner Diaz. "These people are making ends meet. You simply don't have the sort of urban defeatism you associate with some of the big cities back East."

Despite polls showing that some believe Latinos are welfare-dependent and violent, the RAND study indicates that Latinos are half as likely as the average Californian to be on welfare. And prison records and arrest rates show that Latinos commit crimes at rates slightly lower than those for the Anglo and black populations.

Latino immigrants' family structure, too, defies the underclass stereotype. Somewhat more than 60% of all Latino households, for instance, are headed by married couples, a figure that is likely to be much higher in immigrant families. That number is significantly higher than the rates for either whites or blacks. Only the households of Asians, as a group, are close to this percentage. Family cohesion may explain how Latino and Asian immigrants succeed despite a lack of education and employment in low-wage jobs.

 Exercise

Questions

1. What is the purpose of the essay?

2. What method of organization does the author use?

3. How does the lack of a formal introduction and conclusion affect you as a reader?

4. What is the function of quotations in the essay? Explain.

5. What are the mounting concerns about the increase of various cultures in southern California?

6. What is the displacement theory? How well is it explained? How well does the author "debunk" it? What sources does he use and how effective are they?

7. What are the fears associated with employment? How well does the author dispel them? Explain.

PREJUDICE IN INTERCULTURAL COMMUNICATION

Richard W. Brislin

The Functions of Prejudice

When people react negatively to others on an emotional basis, with an absence of direct contact or factual material about the others, the people are said to behave according to prejudice. The concept of prejudice has been subjected to first-rate research investigations by psychologists and sociologists. One of the conclusions of this research is that "prejudice" is a far more complex concept than would be judged from the way the word is

used in ordinary, everyday usage. This complexity has to be understood if
the problems of prejudice are to be addressed effectively.

An understanding of prejudice can begin if its functions are analyzed.
Katz[1] has written the clearest presentation of the functions of various attitudes which people hold, and these can be applied to the more specific
case of prejudicial attitudes. In addition, the functions can be applied to
the sorts of intercultural contact under scrutiny at this conference. In the
past, the majority of research has dealt with interpersonal contact within
countries, especially Black-White relations. The four functions that attitudes
serve for people are:

1. *The utilitarian or adjustment function.* People hold certain prejudices
because such attitudes lead to rewards, and lead to the avoidance of pun-
ishment, in their culture. For instance, people want to be well liked by
others in their culture. If such esteem is dependent upon rejecting members of a certain group, then it is likely that the people will indeed reject
members of the outgroup. Or, if jobs are scarce and if people from a
certain group want those jobs, it is adjustive to believe that members of
a certain group have no responsibility in work settings. Thus there will be
less competition for the desired employment.

2. *The ego-defensive function.* People hold certain prejudices because they
do not want to admit certain things about themselves. Holding the prejudice protects the people from a harsh reality. For instance, if a person is
unsuccessful in the business world, (s)he may believe that members of a
certain successful group are a scheming bunch of cheaters. This belief protects the individual from the self-admission that (s)he has inadequacies.
Another example involves experiences that most people have during childhood, no matter what their culture. People believe, as part of their basic
feelings of self-esteem, that they have grown up in a society where proper
behavior is practiced. These people may look down upon members of
other cultures (or social classes within a culture) who do not behave "correctly." This prejudicial attitude, then, serves the function of protecting
people's self-esteem.

3. *The value-expressive function.* People hold certain prejudices because
they want to express the aspects of life which they highly prize. Such aspects include basic values of people concerning religion, government, society, aesthetics, and so forth. Katz[2] emphasizes that this function is related
to an individual's "notion of the sort of person he sees himself to be." For
example, people who discriminate against members of a certain religious
group may do so because they see themselves as standing up for the one
true God (as defined by their own religion). As a more intense example,
people have engaged in atrocities toward outgroup members so as to retain
the supposed values of a pure racial stock (again their own).

4. *The knowledge function.* People hold certain prejudices because such

attitudes allow individuals to organize and structure their world in a way that makes sense to them. People have a need to know about various aspects of their culture so that they can interact effectively in it. But the various aspects are so numerous that various discrete stimuli must be categorized together for efficient organization. People then behave according to the category they have organized, not according to the discrete stimuli.[3] Often these categories are stereotypes that do not allow for variation within a category. For instance, if people believe that members of a certain cultural group are childlike and cannot be given any responsibility, they may employ that stereotype upon meeting a member of that group. Given a set of stereotypes, people do not have to think about each individual they meet. They can then spend time on the many other matters that compete for their attention during an average day. The prejudicial stereotypes thus provide knowledge about the world. The problem, of course, is that the stereotypes are sometimes wrong and always overdrawn.[4]

Certain prejudices can serve several functions, particularly so when an individual's entire life span is considered. Young children develop a prejudice to please their parents (adjustment), continue to hold it because of what they learn in school (knowledge), and behave according to the prejudice since they wish to express their view of themselves (value). Programs to change prejudice often fail because the most important function, or functions, are not recognized. Most change-oriented programs are concerned with presenting well-established facts about the targets of prejudice. But such a program will only change people's attitudes which serve the knowledge function. Much more work has to be done on finding ways to change prejudices that serve the other thee functions. This is a research area that should yield very important payoffs to careful investigators.

The Forms of Prejudice

In addition to an understanding of the functions of prejudice, it is also important to consider various forms that prejudice takes in its expression. The range of such expression is large.

1. *Red-neck racism.* Certain people believe that members of a given cultural group are inferior according to some imagined standard and that the group members are not worthy of decent treatment. The term "red-neck" comes from the Southern United States where world attention was focused on the White majority's treatment of Blacks during political demonstrations prior to the Civil Rights Act of 1964. The type of prejudice summarized by the term "red-neck" however, is found all over the world. This extreme form of prejudice has most often been assessed by asking people to agree or disagree with statements like this:[5] "The many faults, and the general

inability to get along, of (*insert name of group*) who have recently flooded our community, prove that we ought to send them back where they came from as soon as conditions permit." "(*insert name of group*) can never advance to the standard of living and civilization of our country due mainly to their innate dirtiness, laziness, and general backwardness." All of us cringe at the thought of such tasteless, abhorrent sentiments. But we all know that such prejudices exist, and all of us can give many examples from the countries in which we have lived. Formal education has had a tremendous influence on lowering the incidences of red-neck racism. Research has shown that as the number of years of formal education increases, the incidence of racism decreases. However, I do feel that we need accurate figures on the current levels of such prejudice, and only large scale surveys can give us this information. It is possible that attendees at a conference such as this one underestimate the current levels of red-neck racism since they do not normally interact with people who hold such views.

   2. *Symbolic racism.* Certain people have negative feelings about a given group because they feel that the group is interfering with aspects of their culture with which they have become familiar. The people do not dislike the group per se, and they do not hold sentiments that are indicative of red-neck racism. Symbolic racism[6] is expressed in terms of threats to people's basic values and to the status quo. When directly questioned, people will assert that members of a certain group are "moving too fast" and are making illegitimate demands in their quest for a place in society. Symbolic racism is expressed by responses to questions like these (the answer indicative of symbolic racism is noted in parentheses):

> "Over the past few years, (*insert name of group*) have gotten more economically than they deserve." (agree)
> "People in this country should support ————————————— in their struggle against discrimination and segregation." (disagree)
> "————————————— are getting too demanding in their push for equal rights." (agree)

   Sentiments like these are probably more widespread than red-neck feelings among members of the affluent middle class in various countries. Again, however, exact figures are unavailable, and this lack hampers intelligent planning for programs to deal with this form of prejudice. It is important to understand the differences between red-neck and symbolic racism. People who hold symbolic sentiments do not view themselves as red-necks, and so programs aimed at changing extreme racist views (such programs are presently most common) are doomed to failure. McConahay and Hough[7] are accurate when they state that current change programs seem incomprehensible to holders of symbolic views "and they do not understand what all the fuss is about. This enables racism to be considered somebody else's problem while holders of symbolic views concentrate upon their own private lives."

3. *Tokenism.* Certain people harbor negative feelings about a given group but do not want to admit this fact to themselves. Such people definitely do not view themselves as prejudiced and they do not perceive themselves as discriminatory in their behavior. One way that they reinforce this view of themselves is to engage in unimportant, but positive, intergroup behaviors. By engaging in such unimportant behaviors people can persuade themselves that they are unprejudiced and thus they can refuse to perform more important intergroup behaviors. For instance, Dutton[8] found that if people gave a small amount of money to an outgroup, they were less willing to later donate a large amount of their time to a "Brotherhood Week" campaign emphasizing intergroup relations and goodwill. Other people in the Dutton study donated time to the Brotherhood Week if they had previously not been asked to give the small sum of money. The small amount of money, then, was a token that allowed some people to persuade themselves that they are unprejudiced and so don't have to prove themselves again by engaging in the more important, time-consuming behavior.

4. *Arms-length prejudice.* Certain people engage in friendly, positive behavior toward outgroup members in certain situations but hold those same outgroup members at an "arm's length" in other situations. The difference across situations seems to be along a dimension of perceived intimacy of behaviors.[9] For semi-formal behaviors such as (1) casual friendships at a place of employment, (2) interactions between speaker and audience at a lecture, or (3) interactions at a catered dinner party, people who harbor an arm's-length prejudice will act in a friendly, positive manner. But for more intimate behaviors such as (1) dating, (2) interactions during an informal dinner held at someone's home or (3) relations between neighbors, people will act in a tense, sometimes hostile manner. Frankly, I have observed this sort of arm's-length prejudice at places where such behavior would ideally not be expected, as at the East-West Center. I have observed a Caucasian social psychologist (who has long lectured on prejudice), during a visit to my home, become non-communicative and ultimately rude when my Chinese-American neighbor unexpectedly dropped in for a visit. This form of prejudice is hard to detect since people who engage in it seem so tolerant of outgroup members much of the time.

5. *Real likes and dislikes.* Certain people harbor negative feelings about a given group because members of the group engage in behaviors that people dislike. This fifth category is derived from more common sense than scholarly literature, and it represents an expression of my feelings that not all prejudice should be looked upon as an indication of some sickness or flaw. People *do* have real likes and dislikes. No one person is so saintly as to be tolerant and forgiving toward all who engage in behaviors (s)he dislikes. For instance, littering really bothers me, and there are certain groups more likely to leave their trash on the ground after a picnic. Sometimes they are from cultures where servants or laborers are expected to do such cleanup. But my realization of the group's background does not lessen my dislike of litter. Seeing members of a certain group engage in such disliked behaviors, I am less likely to interact pleasantly with other members of the group in the future. My recommendation is to give more attention to this common, but heretofore neglected, type of everyday prejudice.

6. *The familiar and unfamiliar.* People who are socialized into one culture are likely to become familiar and thus comfortable with various aspects of that culture. These people, when interacting with members of another culture, are likely to experience behaviors or ideas that are unfamiliar and hence they are likely to feel uncomfortable. Consequently, the people are likely to prefer to interact with members of their own cultural group. What might seem like prejudice and discrimination to an onlooker, then, may be simply a reflection of people's preference for what is comfortable and non-stressful. In a study of interaction among members of nine ethnic groups on Guam,[10] I found that informants were able to verbalize this reason for people's choices of friends. An informant from the Marshall Islands wrote:

> Culture makes these groups stick together. Somebody might not get along with one from another country. He likes to find some friends who have the same beliefs he has, and he could only find these characteristics with the people from his own country.

And a resident of Truk wrote about the type of strained conversation that can arise when members of different groups interact:

> A Trukese who has never experienced the cold winter of the U.S. could not comprehend and intelligently appreciate a Statesider telling him the terrible winter they had in Albany anymore than a person from Albuquerque who has never seen an atoll could visualize the smallness of the islets that make up such an atoll. (Truk, of course, is an atoll.)

I believe that this sort of mild prejudice based on what is familiar and unfamiliar is the sort of phenomenon recently referred to by the United States Ambassador to the United Nations, Andrew Young.[11] In mid-1977 Young labeled a number of people as "racists,"[12] but in explaining his use of the term he clearly was referring to a lack of understanding and an insensitivity regarding other cultural groups. When questioned by the press,

Young had to admit that the insensitivity and misunderstanding stem from unfamiliarity. As with the type of prejudice described under "real likes and dislikes," this everyday type of behavior deserves more attention from behavioral scientists and educators than it has heretofore received.

Notes

1. D. Katz, "The functional approach to the study of attitudes," *Public Opinion Quarterly*, 1960, 24, pp. 164–204.

2. Katz, 1960, p. 173.

3. H. Triandis, "Culture training, cognitive complexity and interpersonal attitudes." In R. Brislin, S. Bochner, and W. Lonner (eds.). *Cross-Cultural Perspectives on Learning* (New York: Wiley/Halsted Division, 1976) pp. 39–77.

4. The fact that I use the term "prejudicial stereotypes" does not mean that stereotypes and prejudice are isomorphic. *Some* stereotypes stem from prejudicial attitudes, and only these are discussed in this paragraph. More generally, stereotypes refer to any categorization of individual elements that mask differences among those elements. Stereotypes are absolutely necessary for thinking and communicating since people cannot respond individually to the millions of isolated elements they perceive every day. They must group elements together into categories, and then respond to the categories. Stereotypes are a form of generalization that involve names of some group of people and statements about that group. Thus when we speak of "conservatives" or "academics" or "educators," we are using stereotypical categories that mask individual differences within those categories. Stereotypes will always be a factor in any sort of communication, a fact that must be realized in any analysis of communication between individuals from different backgrounds. I mention this because, recently, I have found difficulty in encouraging multicultural groups to discuss stereotypes since the link between prejudice and stereotypes has become so strong. Stereotypes have acquired a distasteful status. Refusal to deal with them, however, means a refusal to deal with one of the most basic aspects of thinking and communication.

5. These statements are adapted from the analysis of such questionnaire items by R. Ashmore, "The problem of intergroup prejudice," in B. Collins, *Social Psychology* (Reading, Mass: Addison-Wesley, 1970) pp. 245–296.

6. J. McConahay and J. Hough, "Symbolic racism," *Journal of Social Issues*, 1976, 32(2), pp. 23–45.

7. McConahay and Hough, 1976, p. 44.

8. D. Dutton, "Tokenism, reverse discrimination, and egalitarianism in interracial behavior," *Journal of Social Issues*, 1976, 32(2), pp. 93–107.

9. H. Triandis and E. Davis, "Race and belief as determinants of behavioral intentions," *Journal of Personality and Social Psychology*, 1965, 2, pp. 715–725.

10. R. Brislin, "Interaction among members of nine ethnic groups and the belief-similarity hypotheses," *Journal of Social Psychology*, 1971, 85, pp. 171–179.

11. Playboy, July, 1977; also analyzed in *Newsweek*, June 20, 1977, p. 34.

12. An "unfortunate" use of the term, Ambassador Young eventually admitted.

 Exercise

Questions

1. What are the four functions of prejudice? Summarize each of them.

2. What are the different forms of prejudice? Summarize them. How do they serve to perpetuate prejudice?

3. State the thesis of the essay in one sentence.

4. How is this essay organized?

5. What methods of development has the author used. How effective are they?

6. Can understanding the functions and forms of prejudice help a person to overcome prejudice? How?

7. How else can people overcome their prejudices?

COMMUNICATION IN A GLOBAL VILLAGE

Dean C. Barnlund

Nearing Autumn's close.
My neighbor—
How does he live, I wonder?
                Basho

These lines, written by one of the most cherished of *haiku* poets, express a timeless and universal curiosity in one's fellow man. When they were written nearly three hundred years ago, the word "neighbor" referred to people very much like one's self—similar in dress, in diet, in custom, in lan-guage—who happened to live next door. Today relatively few people are surrounded by neighbors who are cultural replicas of themselves. Tomor-row we can expect to spend most of our lives in the company of neighbors who will speak in a different tongue, seek different values, move at a dif-ferent pace, and interact according to a different script. Within no longer than a decade or two the probability of spending part of one's life in a for-eign culture will exceed the probability a hundred years ago of ever leaving the town in which one was born. As our world is transformed our neigh-bors increasingly will be people whose life styles contrast sharply with our own.

The technological feasibility of such a global village is no longer in doubt. Only the precise date of its attainment is uncertain. The means al-ready exist: in telecommunication systems linking the world by satellite, in aircraft capable of moving people faster than the speed of sound, in com-puters which can disgorge facts more rapidly than men can formulate their questions. The methods for bringing people closer physically and electron-ically are clearly at hand. What is in doubt is whether the erosion of cul-tural boundaries through technology will bring the realization of a dream or a nightmare. Will a global village be a mere collection or a true commu-nity of men? Will its residents be neighbors capable of respecting and uti-lizing their differences, or clusters of strangers living in ghettos and united only in their antipathies for others?

Can we generate the new cultural attitudes required by our technologi-cal virtuosity? History is not very reassuring here. It has taken centuries to learn how to live harmoniously in the family, the tribe, the city state, and the nation. Each new stretching of human sensitivity and loyalty has taken generations to become firmly assimilated in the human psyche. And now we are forced into a quantum leap from the mutual suspicion and hostility that have marked the past relations between peoples into a world in which mutual respect and comprehension are requisite.

Even events of recent decades provide little basis for optimism. Increas-ing physical proximity has brought no millennium in human relations. If anything, it has appeared to intensify the divisions among people rather than to create a broader intimacy: Every new reduction in physical distance has made us more painfully aware of the psychic distance that divides people and has increased alarm over real or imagined differences. If today people occasionally choke on what seem to be indigestible differences be-tween rich and poor, male and female, specialist and nonspecialist within cultures, what will happen tomorrow when people must assimilate and cope with still greater contrasts in life styles? Wider access to more people will be a doubtful victory if human beings find they have nothing to say to one another or cannot stand to listen to each other.

Time and space have long cushioned intercultural encounters, confining them to touristic exchanges. But this insulation is rapidly wearing thin. In the world of tomorrow we can expect to live—not merely vacation—in societies which seek different values and bide by different codes. There we will be surrounded by foreigners for long periods of time, working with others in the closest possible relationships. If people currently show little tolerance or talent for encounters with alien cultures, how can they learn to deal with constant and inescapable coexistence?

Anyone who has truly struggled to comprehend another person—even those closest and most like himself—will appreciate the immensity of the challenge of intercultural communication. A greater exchange of people between nations, needed as that may be, carries with it no guarantee of increased cultural empathy; experience in other lands often does little but aggravate existing prejudices. Studying guidebooks or memorizing polite phrases similarly fails to explain differences in cultural perspectives. Programs of cultural enrichment, while they contribute to curiosity about other ways of life, do not cultivate the skills to function effectively in the cultures studied. Even concentrated exposure to a foreign language, valuable as it is, provides access to only one of the many codes that regulate daily affairs: human understanding is by no means guaranteed because conversants share the same dictionary. (Within the United States, where people inhabit a common territory and possess a common language, mutuality of meaning among Mexican-Americans, White-Americans, Black-Americans, Indian-Americans—to say nothing of old and young, poor and rich, pro-establishment and anti-establishment cultures—is a sporadic and unreliable occurrence.) Useful as all these measures are for enlarging appreciation of diverse cultures, they fall short of what is needed for a global village to survive.

What seems most critical is to find ways of gaining entrance into the assumptive world of another culture, to identify the norms that govern face-to-face relations, and to equip people to function within a social system that is foreign but no longer incomprehensible. Without this kind of insight people are condemned to remain outsiders no matter how long they live in another country. Its institutions and its customs will be interpreted inevitably from the premises and through the medium of their own culture. Whether they notice something or overlook it, respect or ridicule it, express or conceal their reactions will be dictated by the logic of their own rather than the alien culture.

Every culture expresses its purposes and conducts its affairs through the medium of communication. Cultures exist primarily to create and preserve common systems of symbols by which their members can assign and exchange meanings. Unhappily, the distinctive rules that govern these symbol systems are far from obvious. About some of these codes, such as language, we have extensive knowledge. About others, such as gestures and facial codes, we have only rudimentary knowledge. On many others—

rules governing topical appropriateness, customs regulating physical contact, time and space codes, strategies for the management of conflict—we have almost no systematic knowledge. To crash another culture with only the vaguest notion of its underlying dynamics reflects not only a provincial naivete but a dangerous form of cultural arrogance.

It is differences in meaning, far more than mere differences in vocabulary, that isolate cultures, and that cause them to regard each other as strange or even barbaric. It is not too surprising that many cultures refer to themselves as "The People," relegating all other human beings to a subhuman form of life. To the person who drinks blood, the eating of meat is repulsive. Someone who conveys respect by standing is upset by someone who conveys it by sitting down; both may regard kneeling as absurd. Burying the dead may prompt tears in one society, smiles in another, and dancing in a third. If spitting on the street makes sense to some, it will appear bizarre that others carry their spit in their pocket; neither may quite appreciate someone who spits to express gratitude. The bullfight that constitutes an almost religious ritual for some seems a cruel and inhumane way of destroying a defenseless animal to others. Although staring is acceptable social behavior in some cultures, in others it is a thoughtless invasion of privacy. Privacy, itself, is without universal meaning.

Note that none of these acts involves an insurmountable linguistic challenge. The words that describe these acts—eating, spitting, showing respect, fighting, burying, and staring—are quite translatable into most languages. The issue is more conceptual than linguistic; each society places events in its own cultural frame and it is these frames that bestow the unique meaning and differentiated response they produce.

As we move or are driven toward a global village and increasingly frequent cultural contact, we need more than simply greater factual knowledge of each other. We need, more specifically, to identify what might be called the "rulebooks of meaning" that distinguish one culture from another. For to grasp the way in which other cultures perceive the world, and the assumptions and values that are the foundation of these perceptions, is to gain access to the experience of other human beings. Access to the world view and the communicative style of other cultures may not only enlarge our own way of experiencing the world but enable us to maintain constructive relationships with societies that operate according to a different logic than our own.

Sources of Meaning

To survive, psychologically as well as physically, human beings must inhabit a world that is relatively free of ambiguity and reasonably predictable. Some sort of structure must be placed upon the endless profusion of incoming signals. The infant, born into a world of flashing, hissing, moving images, soon learns to adapt by resolving this chaos into toys and tables, dogs and parents. Even adults who have had their vision or hearing restored through surgery describe the world as a frightening and sometimes unbearable experience; only after days of effort are they able to transform blurs and noises into meaningful and therefore manageable experiences. It is commonplace to talk as if the world "has" meaning to ask what "is" the meaning of a phrase, a gesture, a painting, a contract. Yet when thought about, it is clear that events are devoid of meaning until someone assigns it to them. There is no appropriate response to a bow or a handshake, a shout or a whisper, until it is interpreted. A drop of water and the color red have no meaning, they simply exist. The aim of human perception is to make the world intelligible so that it can be managed successfully; the attribution of meaning is a prerequisite to and preparation for action.

People are never passive receivers, merely absorbing events of obvious significance, but are active in assigning meaning to sensation. What any event acquires in the way of meaning appears to reflect a transaction between what is there to be seen or heard, and what the interpreter brings to it in the way of past experience and prevailing motive. Thus the attribution of meanings is always a creative process by which the raw data of sensation are transformed to fit the aims of the observer.

The diversity of reactions that can be triggered by a single experience— meeting a stranger, negotiating a contract, attending a textile conference—is immense. Each observer is forced to see it through his own eyes, interpret it in the light of his own values, fit it to the requirements of his own circumstances. As a consequence, every object and message is seen by every observer from a somewhat different perspective. Each person will note some features and neglect others. Each will accept some relations among the facts and deny others. Each will arrive at some conclusion, tentative or certain as the sounds and forms resolve into a "temple" or "barn," a "compliment" or "insult."

Provide a group of people with a set of photographs, even quite simple and ordinary photographs, and note how diverse are the meanings they provoke. Afterward they will recall and forget different pictures, they will also assign quite distinctive meanings to those they do remember. Some will recall the mood of a picture, others the actions; some the appearance and others the attitudes of persons portrayed. Often the observers cannot agree upon even the most "objective" details—the number of people, the precise location and identity of simple objects. A difference in frame of mind—fatigue, hunger, excitement, anger—will change dramatically what they report they have "seen."

It should not be surprising that people raised in different families, exposed to different events, praised and punished for different reasons, should come to view the world so differently. As George Kelly has noted, people see the world through templates which force them to construe events in unique ways. These patterns or grids which we fit over the realities of the world are cut from our own experience and values, and they predispose us to certain interpretations. Industrialists and farmer do not see the "same" land; husband and wife do not plan for the "same" child; doctor and patient do not discuss the "same" disease; borrower and creditor do not negotiate the "same" mortgage; daughter and daughter-in-law do not react to the "same" mother.

The world each person creates for himself is a distinctive world, not the same world others occupy. Each fashions from every incident whatever meanings fit his own private biases. These biases, taken together, constitute what has been called the "assumptive world of the individual." The world each person gets inside his head is the only world he knows. And it is this symbolic world, not the real world, that he talks about, argues about, laughs about, fights about.

Intercultural Encounters

Every culture attempts to create a "universe of discourse" for its members, a way in which people can interpret their experience and convey it to one another. Without a common system of codifying sensations, life would be absurd and all efforts to share meanings doomed to failure. This universe of discourse—one of the most precious of all cultural legacies—is transmitted to each generation in part consciously and in part unconsciously. Parents and teachers give explicit instruction in it by praising or criticizing certain ways of dressing, of thinking, of gesturing, of responding to the acts of others. But the most significant aspects of any cultural code may be conveyed implicitly, not by rule or lesson but through modelling behavior. The child is surrounded by others who, through the mere consistency of their actions as males and females, mothers and fathers, salesclerks and policemen, display what is appropriate behavior. Thus the grammar of any culture is sent and received largely unconsciously, making one's own cultural assumptions and biases difficult to recognize. They seem so obviously right that they require no explanation.

In *The Open and Closed Mind*, Milton Rokeach poses the problem of cultural understanding in its simplest form, but one that can readily demonstrate the complications of communication between cultures. It is called the "Denny Doodlebug Problem." Readers are given all the rules that govern his culture: Denny is an animal that always faces North, and can move only by jumping; he can jump large distances or small distances, but can change direction only after jumping four times in any direction: he can jump North, South, East or West, but not diagonally. Upon concluding a jump his master places some food three feet directly West of him. Survey-ing the situation, Denny concludes he must jump four times to reach the food. No more or less. And he is right. All the reader has to do is explain the circumstances that make his conclusion correct.

The large majority of people who attempt this problem fail to solve it, despite the fact that they are given all the rules that control behavior in this culture. If there is difficulty in getting inside the simplistic world of Denny Doodlebug—where the cultural code has already been broken and handed to us—imagine the complexity of comprehending behavior in soci-eties where codes have not yet been deciphered. And where even those who obey these codes are only vaguely aware and can rarely describe the underlying sources of their own actions.

If two people, both of whom spring from a single culture, must often shout to be heard across the void that separates their private worlds, one can begin to appreciate the distance to be overcome when people of differ-ent cultural identities attempt to talk. Even with the most patient dedica-tion to seeking a common terminology, it is surprising that people of alien cultures are able to hear each other at all. And the peoples of Japan and the United States would appear to constitute a particularly dramatic test of the ability to cross an intercultural divide. Consider the disparity between them.

Here is Japan, a tiny island nation with a minimum of resources, buf-feted by periodic disasters, overcrowded with people, isolated by physical fact and cultural choice, nurtured in Shinto and Buddhist religions, perme-ated by a deep respect for nature, nonmaterialist in philosophy, intuitive in thought, hierarchical in social structure. Eschewing the explicit, the monu-mental, the bold and boisterous, it expresses its sensuality in the form of impeccable gardens, simple rural temples, asymmetrical flower arrange-ments, a theatre unparalleled for containment of feeling, an art and litera-ture remarkable for their delicacy, and crafts noted for their honest and earthy character. Its people, among the most homogeneous of men, are modest and apologetic in manner, communicate in an ambiguous and evocative language, are engrossed in interpersonal rituals and prefer inner serenity to influencing others. They occupy unpretentious buildings of wood and paper and live in cities laid out as casually as farm villages. Suddenly from these rice paddies emerges an industrial giant, surpassing rival nations with decades of industrial experience, greater resources, and a larger reserve of technicians. Its labor, working longer, harder and more frantically than any in the world, builds the earth's largest city, constructs some of its ugliest buildings, promotes the most garish and insistent ad-vertising anywhere, and pollutes its air and water beyond the imagination.

And here is the United States, an immense country; sparsely settled, richly endowed, tied through waves of immigrants to the heritage of Europe, yet forced to subdue nature and find fresh solutions to the problems of survival. Steeped in the Judeo-Christian tradition, schooled in European abstract and analytic thought, it is materialist and experimental in outlook, philosophically pragmatic, politically equalitarian, economically competitive, its raw individualism sometimes tempered by a humanitarian concern for others. Its cities are studies in geometry along whose avenues rise shafts of steel and glass subdivided into separate cubicles for separate activities and separate people. Its popular arts are characterized by the hugeness of Cinemascope, the spontaneity of jazz, the earthy loudness of rock; in its fine arts the experimental, striking, and monumental often stifle the more subtle revelation. The people, a smorgasbord of races, religions, dialects, and nationalities, are turned expressively outward, impatient with rituals and rules, casual and flippant, gifted in logic and argument, approachable and direct yet given to flamboyant and exaggerated assertion. They are curious about one another, open and helpful, yet display a missionary zeal for changing one another. Suddenly this nation whose power and confidence have placed it in a dominant position in the world intellectually and politically, whose style of life has permeated the planet, finds itself uncertain of its direction, doubts its own premises and values, questions its motives and materialism, and engages in an orgy of self criticism.

It is when people nurtured in such different psychological worlds meet that differences in cultural perspectives and communicative codes may sabotage efforts to understand one another. Repeated collisions between a foreigner and the members of a contrasting culture often produce what is called "culture shock." It is a feeling of helplessness, even of terror or anger, that accompanies working in an alien society. One feels trapped in an absurd and indecipherable nightmare.

It is as if some hostile leprechaun had gotten into the works and as a cosmic caper rewired the connections that hold society together. Not only do the actions of others no longer make sense, but it is impossible even to express one's own intentions clearly. "Yes" comes out meaning "No." A wave of the hand means "come," or it may mean "go." Formality may be regarded as childish, or as a devious form of flattery. Statements of fact may be heard as statements of conceit. Arriving early, or arriving late, embarrasses or impresses. "Suggestions" may be treated as "ultimatums," or precisely the opposite. Failure to stand at the proper moment, or failure to sit may be insulting. The compliment intended to express gratitude instead conveys a sense of distance. A smile signifies disappointment rather than pleasure.

If the crises that follow such intercultural encounters are sufficiently dramatic or the communicants unusually sensitive, they may recognize the source of their trouble. If there is patience and constructive intention the confusion can sometimes be clarified. But more often the foreigner, without knowing it leaves behind him a trail of frustration, mistrust, and even hatred of *which he is totally unaware.* Neither he nor his associates recognize that their difficulty springs from sources deep within the rhetoric of their own societies. Each sees himself as acting in ways that are thoroughly sensible, honest and considerate. And—given the rules governing his own universe of discourse—each is. Unfortunately, there are few cultural universals, and the degree of overlap in communicative codes is always less than perfect. Experience can be transmitted with fidelity only when the unique properties of each code are recognized and respected, or where the motivation and means exist to bring them into some sort of alignment.

When people within a culture face an insurmountable problem they turn to friends, neighbors, associates, for help. To them they explain their predicament, often in distinctive personal ways. Through talking it out, however, there often emerge new ways of looking at the problem, fresh incentive to attack it, and alternative solutions to it. This sort of interpersonal exploration is often successful within a culture for people share at least the same communicative style even if they do not agree completely in their perceptions or beliefs.

When people communicate between cultures, where communicative rules as well as the substance of experience differs, the problems multiply. But so, too, do the number of interpretations and alternatives. If it is true that the more people differ the harder it is for them to understand each other, it is equally true that the more they differ the more they have to teach and learn from each other. To do so, of course, there must be mutual respect and sufficient curiosity to overcome the frustrations that occur as they flounder from one misunderstanding to another. Yet the task of coming to grips with differences in communicative styles—between or within cultures—is prerequisite to all other types of mutuality.

 Exercise

Questions

1. What is the purpose of the essay? Who is its intended audience? How does this affect the way the essay is written?

2. How is the essay organized?

3. What methods of development has the author used? How effectively has he used them?

4. Why is it difficult for people to adopt new cultural attitudes? How well does the author explain this?

5. How does the difference in meanings of actions or gestures of people affect intercultural communication?

6. Why is it important that people "inhabit a world that is relatively free of ambiguity and reasonably predictable"? (first paragraph from Sources of Meaning)

7. How do intercultural encounters affect communication? Explain. Can these effects be changed?

 Exercise

Intercultural Communication

In small groups, consider what you know about other cultures and what you have learned from your experiences with people of other cultures; then answer the following questions.

1. What positive effects have different cultures made on the world and on your own culture?

2. What have you learned personally from people of different cultures?

3. What difficulties, conflicts, or misunderstandings have you experienced with people of other cultures?

4. What can you learn from these problems and how can you overcome them?

 Exercise

Your Own Culture

In small groups, brainstorm the personal qualities, social values, and individual and overall accomplishments associated with your culture. Consider the attitudes expressed about religion, marriage and the family, personal conduct, and how your culture encourages people to behave and give examples for each as illustrations. In addition, describe any other things people should know about your culture in order to fully understand it. Also, write down any common misunderstandings about your culture, how they came about, and why they are inaccurate.

Exercise
Intercultural Communication

In small groups, consider specific methods that you can use to develop intercultural communication. Take into consideration these particular situations:

1. In your personal life

2. At your school

3. In your community

4. In your country

 Writing Exercise

Use one of the topics from the essays or exercises and write a six-paragraph essay. Some ideas you may consider are the fears associated with other cultures, the causes or effects of prejudice, ways to improve intercultural communication, perceptions that block intercultural communication, and any of the other subtopics that came up during the discussions. Follow the usual procedure for prewriting, writing, and reading and revising to compose your essay.

14   Death and Life

After Death

LIFE SUPPORT VS. DEATH

Marlene Sparling

Our society is undergoing many changes in attitudes. One of these changes is our ideas about dying. This is because, for the first time in history, we have the ability to keep people alive artificially almost indefinitely. Decisions are now having to be made that past generations did not even have to imagine, and it has caused many of us to take a hard look at the value of life.

At no time in history have we been able to control life and death to the extent we do today. Along with this ability comes the question, do we have the right?

This ability carries with it the necessity for society to define just what is death. Traditionally, the definition of death has been the absence of breathing and heartbeat. However, with the invention of life-support machines, we need a new definition.

Last August, a judge in Boston stated for the first time ever that death was cessation of brain activity; however, the man standing trial for the murder has appealed on the grounds that there is really no legal definition of death. Although the victim's brain activity ceased two days after the assault, he was breathing and his heart was beating until the life-support machines were disconnected five days later. The defense claims that it was

207

the withdrawal of life-support machines that caused the man's death, and not the defendant's actions.

There is a great deal of confusion in both the medical and legal worlds about the definition of death. Perhaps brain death should be legal death because, while blood can be pumped through the body and air forced into lungs by a machine, no machine exists that can keep a brain functioning after it has died.

Some doctors may say they are preserving life, but are they really? It depends on how one defines life. Life is more than functioning organs and a beating heart. Life is more than just physically being alive. It's experiencing life. The machines cannot accomplish that for us.

We live in a highly contradictory society. Without making a judgment one way or the other, the fact is that abortions are performed every day for convenience sake. Yet we keep hooking up people to life-support machines when their organs have stopped functioning and they are, for all intents and purposes, dead. It matters not if their brain is beyond repair and they are only technically alive. The are reduced to an artificially breathing organism. Some feel that this is the final degradation. Living and dying should both be done with dignity. Each person should be able to define for himself what that dignity is.

We should allow each person to decide for himself whether or not he wants to be kept alive artificially, and we should respect his wishes.

However, there is one good reason for keeping a dead person's organs functioning. It should be acceptable when organs need to be kept viable for transplant purposes. But this should be done as quickly as possible, and a person should know of this possibility when he chooses to donate his organs.

Life-support systems are used not only on people who have died, but on the terminally ill also. It should be remembered that the patient does have certain rights. He has the right to know important details of his illness. He has the right to refuse treatment and to die in his own way. These rights should not be denied him. A problem arises when the patient, because of coma or mental incompetence, cannot exercise these rights. Because of these problems, there exists a document called The Living Will that can be signed while a person is able to make a rational decision. However, California is the only state to legally recognize The Living Will. It should be remembered that The Living Will does not authorize euthanasia. It will only stop a doctor from prolonging a person's life artificially when he is terminally ill. It allows a person to choose to die naturally.

We should be aware of the fact that for some, extreme agony or loss of independence may be more horrible than death. It is hypocritical to say we would not want artificial life-support for ourselves and then turn around and allow it to be done to others. Forcing others to stay alive when they are terminal and want to die is cruel.

It seems man is trying to conquer death with his sophisticated medical equipment. He may be able to delay it, but he cannot abolish it. Death is something we all have in common since we will all have to face it one way or another. We all want to deny the possibility, but denying will not make it disappear.

Most of us have a certain amount of fear about death. It seems only the very young and the very old do not fear death. They don't fear death because they haven't picked up on our fears yet. The old don't seem to fear death as much as the rest of us because they may understand it very well and sometimes even welcome it. Maybe they see no need to hold onto past fears. Some seem to be more ready than others. I remember when my grandfather died last year. He knew he was dying, and he waited for all of his children to come to his bedside. As soon as he had seen each one, he died. It seemed as if, to him, it was a long awaited trip. He told me once how he was looking forward to seeing his wife again. That was what death was to him, seeing my grandmother again.

He was at peace. I hope for that kind of death. I also hope it doesn't come too soon.

 Exercise

Questions

1. How is this essay organized?

2. What major points does the author make about the subject of euthanasia?

3. What techniques of development does she use? How well do they work? Could she have used more?

4. Is man trying to conquer death with his sophisticated machinery?

5. Why do people try to keep relatives alive when there is no hope for recovery?

6. Should you be able to choose when you want to die? Should you be able to terminate an incurable illness?

7. What is our attitude toward people who commit suicide or attempt suicide? Should you have the right to terminate your life whenever you want?

LEARNING ABOUT DEATH

Jeffery Schrank

They think they're so smart giving the kids garbage like Johnny Tremain *and* Giants of the Earth *and* Macbeth, *but do you know, I don't think there's a single kid in the whole joint who would know what to do if somebody dropped dead.*

Paul Zindel, *The Pigman*

Every day 5,000 Americans do it. Die, that is. If the death is a "natural" one (usually meaning slow, smelly, and painful), there is a two-by-two-inch obituary written by a frustrated novelist often working, appropriately enough, on the graveyard shift. If the death is "unnatural" (usually meaning caused by a machine of some sort), the victim often receives a larger notice. If the corpse once owned an unusually large amount of money, his write-up is even larger.

His friends light candles, sing songs, shed tears, sprinkle water on the corpse and themselves, pay the undertaker, and go back to their daily routine of avoiding the same fate. They huddle together in crowds; they perform rituals, have babies, build monuments, madly scribble their own version of "Kilroy was here," pay life-insurance installments, and during breakfast read every gory detail of the latest mass murder. As Kurt Vonnegut would say, "So it goes."

If all the people who ever lived on the face of the planet earth would return from the dead, we the survivors would be outnumbered thirty to one. If each of our thirty ghosts came to America, they would notice in those still alive an almost obsessive fear of the experience called death. They would notice a repression of thoughts, of scientific study, and of feelings about the one event that is inevitable for man.

Much of our culture is a response, however inadequate, to the fear of death. This fear is an active motivation force among all people, including those young enough to be studying in high school and those old enough to be teaching. Perhaps we instinctively realize what it took Dr. Nathan Schock ten years of research to discover: namely that almost all bodily functions start declining around age eighteen to twenty. At thirty they begin deteriorating at a faster rate, which remains constant until death. In plain language, we go over the hill at twenty, and the downgrade steepens after thirty. Much of what we do in the name of teaching, art, creativity, and work is a secret but desperate attempt to avoid the inevitable decline.

"Death is the most important question of our time," according to psychohistorian Robert Jay Lifton. It might be at the root of more of our problems than we suspect. At one of the first New York radical bombings the explanatory letter claimed that "In death-directed America, there is only one way to a life of love and freedom: to attack and destroy the forces of death." And the founding document of the now all but defunct SDS, the Port Huron Statement, was forged under the stark realization that "we may be the last generation in the experiment of living."

In spite of death's universality and power, science has rarely challenged the belief that death is not a phenomenon which can be subjected to scientific study. The doubling of the bibliography relating to death in the past few years is proof that scientists are just now beginning to realize the value of death study.

A Theory

I have a pet theory that goes something like this: what a particular culture considers obscene reveals its most threatening fear. Obscenity is a social way of enforcing a taboo, of keeping a subject away from the dinner table. Death is becoming the new obscenity.

Our attitude toward death is to deny and brand as taboo rather than confront. Dr. Rollo May, writing in *Love and Will*, says, "The ways we repress death and its symbolism are amazingly like the ways the Victorians repressed sex. . . . Death is not talked of in front of the children, not talked about at all if we can help it."

In the Middle Ages, when Church history *was* history, the most obscene comment one could make was antireligious in character. Many of these religious obscenities or profanities still exist today, but are not as shocking or blasphemous as they were in the religion-saturated Middle Ages. Expressions such as damn and hell can even appear in popular education magazines today without raising the proverbial eyebrow. An innocent expression such as *holy mackerel* is little heard today and would cause no shock if used in public. However, in Medieval France it was an accusation of being God's whore. *Bloody* as used by the English in "a bloody good show" dates back to a contraction of the expression *By Our Lady*, referring to the Virgin Mary. *Hocus Pocus* is another term now harmless which was once a sacrilegious blasphemy. The phrase is a corruption of the Latin word of concentration used in a Catholic Mass. *Gee* and *gads* were once vulgar references to God and Christ but are now common interjections.

Once religion began to lose its hold, hell, damnation, and blessed virginity became less frightening or awe-inspiring and have today all but lost their shock value.

Today almost anyone, when asked to think of a list of three "dirty" words, 99.9 percent of the time will choose words relating to sex and the body. We have met the enemy and they are we; our greatest fear is our body and its enjoyment.

But from Esalen to *Oh! Calcutta!* we are rediscovering the body. Concomitant with this rediscovery of the body, four-letter sex and body words are finding their ways into higher levels of respectability. Eventually these words might assume the mild taboos we today attach to the religious profanities of the Middle Ages.

As values change, a new obscenity will become socially unacceptable. The new obscenity will be death.

Already we see signs of certain death words surrounded with an aura of bluntness or impropriety. *Cemeteries* have turned into gardens; graves have given way to *plots* or *resting places; corpses* (perish the word) are not *buried* but *laid to rest*. And people *pass away* instead of just plain *dying*. Try talking about death at the dinner table some time and decide if a bit of the taboo hasn't already descended.

Having overcome our fear of the wrath of God, having at least begun to learn to enjoy our bodies, we are still afraid of the unknown we call death.

Exercise
Questions

1. How does the author say people react to death when they are confronted by it?

2. Why do people like to read about gory murders?

3. Is much of what we do in the name of teaching, art, creativity, and work a secret but desperate attempt to avoid our inevitable decline?

4. How might death be at the root of more of our problems than we suspect?

5. What things have been considered obscene? Why does Schrank use so many examples of terms that used to be considered obscene?

6. With reference to "A Theory," do people still consider sex obscene? What does this tell you about them?

7. Are four-letter words becoming more respectable? Are there any that are still shocking? Why?

8. Why don't people talk about death? Is death obscene? Does it help to talk about it?

9. Why does the author use the quotation at the beginning of his essay? How effective is it?

10. Does death make life more meaningful or meaningless?

LIFE AFTER LIFE

Raymond A Moody, Jr., M.D.

What is it like to die?

That is a question which humanity has been asking itself ever since there have been humans. Over the past few years, I have had the opportunity to raise the question before a sizable number of audiences. These groups have ranged from classes in psychology, philosophy, and sociology through church organizations, television audiences, and civic clubs to professional societies of medicine. On the basis of this exposure, I can safely say that this topic excites the most powerful of feelings from people of many emotional types and walks of life.

Yet, despite all this interest it remains true that it is very difficult for most of us to talk about death. There are at least two reasons for this. One of them is primarily psychological and cultural: The subject of death is taboo. We feel, perhaps only subconsciously, that to be in contact with death in any way, even indirectly, somehow confronts us with the prospect of our own deaths, draws our own deaths closer and makes them more real and thinkable. For example, most medical students, myself included, have found that even the remote encounter with death which occurs upon one's first visit to the anatomical laboratories when entering medical school can evoke strong feelings of uneasiness. In my own case, the reason for this response now seems quite obvious. It has occurred to me in retrospect that it wasn't entirely concern for the person whose remains I saw there, although that feeling certainly figured, too. What I was seeing on that table was a symbol of my own mortality. In some way, if only pre-consciously, the thought must have been in my mind, "That will happen to me, too."

Likewise, talking about death can be seen on the psychological level as another way of approaching it indirectly. No doubt many people have the feeling that to talk about death at all is in effect to conjure it up mentally, to bring it closer in such a way that one has to face up to the inevitability of one's own eventual demise. So, to spare ourselves this psychological trauma, we decide just to try to avoid the topic as much as possible.

The second reason it is difficult to discuss death is more complicated, as it is rooted in the very nature of language itself. For the most part, the words of human language allude to things of which we have experience through our own physical senses. Death, though, is something which lies beyond the conscious experience of most of us because most of us have never been through it.

If we are to talk about death at all, then we must avoid both social taboos and the deep-seated linguistic dilemmas which derive from our own inexperience. What we often end up doing is talking in euphemistic analogies. We compare death or dying with more pleasant things in our experience, things with which we are familiar.

Perhaps the most common analogy of this type is the comparison between death and sleep. Dying, we tell ourselves, is like going to sleep. This figure of speech occurs very commonly in everyday thought and language as well as in the literature of many cultures and many ages. It was apparently quite common even in the time of the ancient Greeks. In The Iliad, for example, Homer calls sleep "death's sister," and Plato, in his dialogue The Apology, puts the following words into the mouth of his teacher, Socrates, who has just been sentenced to death by an Athenian jury.

> [Now, if death is only a dreamless sleep,] it must be a marvelous
> gain. . . .

This same analogy is embedded in our own contemporary language. Consider the phrase "to put to sleep." If you present your dog to a veterinarian with the instruction to put him to sleep, you would normally mean something very different than you would upon taking your wife or husband to an anesthesiologist with the same words. Others prefer a different, but related analogy. Dying, they say is like forgetting. When one dies, one forgets all one's woes; all one's painful and troubling memories are obliterated.

As old and as widespread as they may be, however, both the "sleeping" and the "forgetting" analogies are ultimately inadequate in so far as comforting us is concerned. Each is a different way of making the same assertion. Even though they tell us so in a somewhat more palatable way, both say, in effect, that death is simply the annihilation of conscious experience, forever. If this is so, then death really doesn't have any of the desirable features of sleeping and forgetting. Sleeping is a positive, desirable experience in life because waking follows it. A restful night's sleep makes the waking hours following it more pleasant and productive. If waking did not follow it, the benefits of sleep would not be possible. Similarly, annihilation of all conscious experience implies not only the obliteration of all painful memories, but of all pleasant ones, too. So upon analysis, neither analogy is close enough to give us real comfort facing death.

There is another view, however, which disavows the notion that death is annihilation of consciousness. According to this other, perhaps more ancient tradition, some aspect of the human being survives even after the physical body ceases to function and is ultimately destroyed. This persistent aspect has been called by many names, among them psyche, soul, mind, spirit, self, being, and consciousness. By whatever name it is called, the notion that one passes into another realm of existence upon physical death is among the most venerable of human beliefs. There is a graveyard in Turkey which was used by Neanderthal men approximately 100,000 years ago. There, fossilized imprints have enabled archaeologists to discover that these ancient men buried their dead in biers of flowers, indicating that they perhaps saw death as an occasion of celebration—as a transition of the dead from this world to the next. Indeed, graves from very early sites all over the earth give evidence to the belief in human survival of bodily death. In short, we are faced with two contrasting answers to our original question about the nature of death, both of ancient derivation, yet both widely held even today. Some say that death is annihilation of consciousness; others say with equal confidence that death is the passage of the soul or mind into another dimension of reality. In what follows I do not wish in any way to dismiss either answer. I simply wish to give a report on a search which I have personally undertaken.

As I became more widely known for this interest, doctors began to refer to me persons whom they had resuscitated and who reported unusual experiences. Still others have written to me with reports after newspaper articles about my studies appeared.

At the present time, I know of approximately 150 cases of this phenomenon. The experiences which I have studied fall into three distinct categories:

(1) The experiences of persons who were resuscitated after having been thought, adjudged, or pronounced clinically dead by their doctors.

(2) The experiences of persons who, in the course of accidents or severe injury or illness, came very close to physical death.

(3) The experiences of persons who, as they died, told them to other people who were present. Later, these other people reported the content of the death experience to me.

Despite the wide variation in the circumstances surrounding close calls with death and in the types of persons undergoing them, it remains true that there is a striking similarity among the accounts of the experiences themselves. In fact, the similarities among various reports are so great that one can easily pick out about fifteen separate elements which recur again and again in the mass of narratives that I have collected. On the basis of these points of likeness, let me now construct a brief, theoretically "ideal" or "complete" experience which embodies all of the common elements, in the order in which it is typical for them to occur.

Hearing the News

Numerous people have told of hearing their doctors or other spectators in effect pronounce them dead. One woman related to me that,

> I was in the hospital, but they didn't know what was wrong with me. So Dr. James, my doctor, sent me downstairs to the radiologist for a liver scan so they could find out. First, they tested this drug they were going to use on my arm, since I had a lot of drug allergies. But there was no reaction, so they went ahead. When they used it this time, I arrested on them. I heard the radiologist who was working on me go over to the telephone, and I heard very clearly as he dialed it. I heard him say, "Dr. James, I've killed your patient, Mrs. Martin." And I knew I wasn't dead. I tried to move or to let them know, but I couldn't. When they were trying to resuscitate me, I could hear them telling how many c.c.'s of something to give me, but I didn't feel the needles going in. I felt nothing at all when they touched me.

Feelings of Peace and Quiet

Many people describe extremely pleasant feelings and sensations during the early stages of their experiences. After a severe head injury, one man's vital signs were undetectable. As he says,

> At that point of injury there was a momentary flash of pain, but then all the pain vanished. I had the feeling of floating in a dark space. The day was bitterly cold, yet while I was in the blackness all I felt was warmth and the most extreme comfort I have ever experienced . . . I remember thinking, "I must be dead."

A woman who was resuscitated after a heart attack remarks,

> I began to experience the most wonderful feelings. I couldn't feel a thing in the world except peace, comfort, ease—just quietness. I felt that all my troubles were gone, and I thought to myself, "Well how quiet and peaceful, and I don't hurt at all."

The Noise

In many cases, various unusual auditory sensations are reported to occur at or near death. Sometimes these are extremely unpleasant. A man who "died" for twenty minutes during an abdominal operation describes "a really bad buzzing noise coming from inside my head. It made me very uncomfortable . . . I'll never forget that noise." Another woman tells how as she lost consciousness she heard a loud ringing. It could be described as a buzzing. "And I was in a sort of whirling state." I have also heard this annoying sensation described as a loud click, a roaring, a ganging, and as a "whistling sound, like the wind."

The Dark Tunnel

Often concurrently with the occurrence of the noise, people have the sensation of being pulled very rapidly through a dark space of some kind. Many different words are used to describe this space. I have heard this space described as a cave, a well, a trough, an enclosure, a tunnel, a funnel, a vacuum, a void, a sewer, a valley, and a cylinder. Although people use different terminology here, it is clear that they are all trying to express some one idea. Let us look at one account in which the "tunnel" figures prominently.

> This happened to me when I was a little boy—nine years old. That was twenty-seven years ago, but it was so striking that I have never forgotten it. One afternoon I became very sick, and they rushed me to the nearest hospital. When I arrived they decided they were going to have to put me to sleep, but why I don't know, because I was too young. Back in those days they used ether. They gave it to me by putting a cloth over my nose, and when they did, I was told afterwards, my heart stopped beating. I didn't know at that time that that was exactly what happened to me, but anyway when this happened, I had an experience. Well, the first thing that happened—now I am going to describe it just the way I felt—was that I had this ringing noise brrrrrrrnnnnnnnnng-brrrrrrrrrnnnnnng-brrrrrrrrn-nnnnnng, very rhythmic. Then I was moving through this—you're going to think this is weird—through this long dark place. It seemed like a sewer or something. I just can't describe it to you. I was moving, beating all the time with this noise, this ringing noise.

Out of the Body

Prior to their experiences, the persons I have interviewed were not, as a group, any different from the average person with respect to this attitude (to exist without a physical body). That is why, after his rapid passage through the dark tunnel, a dying person often has such an overwhelming surprise. For, at this point he may find himself looking upon his own physical body from a point outside of it, as though he were "a spectator" or "a third person in the room" or watching figures and events "on stage

in a play" or "in a movie." Let us look now at portions of some accounts
in which the uncanny out-of-body episodes are described.

A woman recalls,

> About a year ago, I was admitted to the hospital with heart trouble, and
> the next morning, lying in the hospital bed, I began to have a very severe
> pain in my chest. I pushed the button beside the bed to call for the
> nurses, and they came in and started working on me. I was quite uncom-
> fortable lying on my back so I turned over, and as I did I quit breathing
> and my heart stopped beating. Just then, I heard the nurses shout, "Code
> pink! Code pink!" As they were saying this, I could feel myself moving
> out of my body and sliding down between the mattress and the rail on the
> side of the bed—actually it seemed as if I went through the rail—on down
> to the floor. Then, I started rising upward, slowly. On my way up, I saw
> more nurses come running into the room—there must have been a dozen
> of them. My doctor happened to be making his rounds in the hospital so
> they called him and I saw him come in, too. I thought, "I wonder what
> he's doing here." I drifted on up past the light fixture—I saw it from the
> side and very distinctly—and then I stopped, floating right below the ceil-
> ing, looking down. I felt almost as though I were a piece of paper that
> someone had blown up to the ceiling.
>
> I watched them reviving me from up there. My body was lying down
> there stretched out on the bed, in plain view, and they were all standing
> around it. I heard one nurse say, "Oh, my God! She's gone!," while an-
> other one leaned down to give me mouth-to-mouth resuscitation. I was
> looking at the back of her head while she did this. I'll never forget the way
> her hair looked; it was cut kind of short. Just then, I saw them roll this
> machine in there, and they put the shocks on my chest. When they did, I
> saw my whole body just jump right up off the bed, and I heard every
> bone in my body crack and pop. It was the most awful thing!
>
> As I saw them below beating on my chest and rubbing my arms and
> legs, I thought, "Why are they going to so much trouble? I'm just fine
> now."

Several persons have told me of having feelings of unfamiliarity toward
their bodies, as in this rather striking passage.

> Boy, I sure didn't realize that I looked like that! You know, I'm only used
> to seeing myself in pictures or from the front in a mirror, and both of
> those look flat. But all of a sudden there I—or my body—was and I could
> see it. I could definitely see it, full view, from about five feet away. It took
> me a few moments to recognize myself.

In one account, this feeling of unfamiliarity took a rather extreme and
humorous form. One man, a physician, tells how during his clinical
"death" he was beside the bed looking at his own cadaver, which by then
had turned the ash gray color assumed by bodies after death. Desperate

and confused, he was trying to decide what to do. He tentatively decided just to go away, as he was feeling very uneasy. As a youngster he had been told ghost stories by his grandfather and paradoxically, he "didn't like being around this thing that looked like a dead body—even if it was me."

A young woman gave a very impressive account of such feelings when she told me that,

> I thought I was dead, and I wasn't sorry that I was dead, but I just couldn't figure out where I was supposed to go. My thought and my con- sciousness were just like they are in life, but I just couldn't figure all this out. I kept thinking, "Where am I going to go? What am I going to do?" and "My God, I'm dead! I can't believe it!" Because you never really be- lieve, I don't think, fully that you're going to die. It's always something that's going to happen to the other person, and although you know it you really never believe it deep down. . . . And so I decided I was just going to wait until all the excitement died down and they carried my body away, and try to see if I could figure out where to go from there.

Another person reported,

> (When I came out of the physical body) it was like I did come out of my body and go into something else. I didn't think I was just nothing. It was another body . . . but not another regular human body. It's a little bit dif- ferent. It was not exactly like a human body, but it wasn't any big glob of matter, either. It had form to it, but no colors. And I know I still had something you could call hands.
>
> I can't describe it. I was more fascinated with everything around me— seeing my own body there, and all—so I didn't think about the type of body I was in. And all this seemed to go so quickly. Time wasn't really an element—and yet it was. Things seem to go faster after you get out of your body.

Meeting Others

Quite a few have told me that at some point while they were dying— sometimes early in the experience, sometimes only after other events had taken place—they became aware of the presence of other spiritual beings in their vicinity, beings who apparently were there to ease them through their transition into death, or, in two cases, to tell them that their time to die had not yet come and that they must return to their physical bodies.

> I had this experience when I was giving birth to a child. The delivery was very difficult, and I lost a lot of blood. The doctor gave me up, and told my relatives that I was dying. However, I was quite alert through the

whole thing, and even as I heard him saying this I felt myself coming to. As I did, I realized that all these people were there, almost in multitudes it seems, hovering around the ceiling of the room. They were all people I had known in my past life, but who had passed on before. I recognized my grandmother and a girl I had known when I was in school, and many other relatives and friends. It seems that I mainly saw their faces and felt their presence. They all seemed pleased. It was almost as if I were coming home, and they were there to greet or to welcome me. All this time, I had the feeling of everything light and beautiful. It was a beautiful and glorious moment.

The Being of Light

What is perhaps the most incredible common element in the accounts I have studied, and is certainly the element which has the most profound effect upon the individual, is the encounter with a very bright light. Typically, at its first appearance this light is dim, but it rapidly gets brighter until it reaches an earthly brilliance. Yet, even though this light (usually said to be white or "clear") is of an indescribable brilliance, many make the specific point that it does not in any way hurt their eyes, or dazzle them, or keep them from seeing other things around them (perhaps because at this point they don't have physical "eyes" to be dazzled).

Despite the light's unusual manifestation, however, not one person has expressed any doubt whatsoever that it was a being, a being of light. Not only that, it is a personal being. It has a very definite personality. The love and warmth which emanate from this being to the dying person are utterly beyond words, and he feels completely at ease and accepted in the presence of this being. He senses an irresistible magnetic attraction to this light. He is ineluctably drawn to it.

I knew I was dying and that there was nothing I could do about it, because no one could hear me . . . I was out of my body, there's no doubt about it, because I could see my own body there on the operating room table. My soul was out! All this made me feel very bad at first, but then, this really bright light came. It did seem that it was a little dim at first, but then it was this huge beam. It was just a tremendous amount of light, nothing like a big bright flashlight, it was just too much light. And it gave off heat to me; I felt a warm sensation.

It was a bright yellowish white—more white. It was tremendously bright; I just can't describe it. It seemed that it covered everything, yet it didn't prevent me from seeing everything around me—the operating room, the doctors and nurses, everything. I could see clearly, and it wasn't blinding.

At first, when the light came, I wasn't sure what was happening, but then, it asked, it kind of asked me if I was ready to die. It was like talking to a person, but a person wasn't there. The light's what was talking to me, but in a voice.

Now I think that the voice that was talking to me actually realized that I wasn't ready to die. You know, it was just kind of testing me more than anything else. Yet, from the moment the light spoke to me, I felt really good—secure and loved. The love which came from it is just unimaginable, indescribable. It was a fun person to be with! And it had a sense of humor, too—definitely!

The Review

The initial appearance of the being of light and his probing, non-verbal questions are the prelude to a moment of startling intensity during which the being presents to the person a panoramic review of his life. It is often obvious that the being can see the individual's whole life displayed and that he doesn't himself need information. His only intention is to provoke reflection.

This review can only be described in terms of memory, since that is the closest familiar phenomenon to it, but it has characteristics which set it apart from any normal type of remembering. First of all, it is extraordinarily rapid. The memories, when they are described in temporal terms, are said to follow one another swiftly, in chronological order. Others recall no awareness of temporal order at all. The remembrance was instantaneous; everything appeared at once, and they could take it all in with one mental glance. However it is expressed, all seem in agreement that the experience was over in an instant of earthly time.

> After all this banging and going through this long, dark place, all of my childhood thoughts, my whole entire life was there at the end of this tunnel, just flashing in front of me. It was not exactly in terms of pictures, more in the form of thought, I guess. I can't exactly describe it to you, but it was just all there. It was just all there at once, I mean, not one thing at a time, blinking off and on, but it was everything, everything at one time. I thought about my mother, about things that I had done wrong. After I could see the mean little things I did as a child, and thought about my mother and father, I wished that I hadn't done these things, and I wished I could go back and undo them.

The Border or Limit

In a few instances, persons have described to me how during their near-death experience they seemed to be approaching what might be called a border or a limit of some kind. This has taken the form, in various accounts, of a body of water, a gray mist, a door, a fence across a field, or simply a line. Though this is highly speculative, one could raise the question of whether there might not be some one basic experience or idea at the root of all of them. If this is true, then the different versions would merely represent varying individual ways of interpreting, wording or remembering the root experience. Let us look at an account in which the idea of a border or limit plays a prominent role.

> I died from a cardiac arrest, and, as I did, suddenly found myself in a rolling field. It was beautiful, and everything was an intense green—a color unlike anything on earth. There was light—beautiful, uplifting light—all around me. I looked ahead of me, across the field, and I saw a fence. I started moving towards the fence, and I saw a man on the other side of it, moving towards it as if to meet me. I wanted to reach him, but I felt myself being drawn back, irresistibly. As I did, I saw him, too, turn around and go back in the other direction, away from the fence.

Coming Back

Obviously, all the persons with whom I have talked had to "come back" at some point in their experience. Usually, though, an interesting change in their attitude had taken place by this time. Remember that the most common feelings reported in the first few moments following death are a desperate desire to get back into the body and an intense regret over one's demise. However, once the dying person reaches a certain depth in his experience, he does not want to come back, and he may even resist the return to the body. This is especially the case for those who have gotten so far as to encounter the being of light. As one man put it, most emphatically, "I never wanted to leave the presence of this being."

> (1) After I came back, I cried off and on for about a week because I had to live in this world after seeing that one. I didn't want to come back.

> (2) When I came back, I brought with me some of the wonderful feelings I had over there. They lasted for several days. Even now I feel them sometimes.

In a few instances, persons have expressed the feeling that the love or prayers of others have in effect pulled them back from death regardless of their own wishes.

> I was with my elderly aunt during her last illness, which was very drawn out. I helped take care of her, and all that time everyone in the family was praying for her to regain her health. She stopped breathing several times, but they brought her back. Finally, one day she looked at me and said,

"Joan, I have been over there, over to the beyond and it is beautiful over there. I want to stay, but I can't as long as you keep praying for me to stay with you. Your prayers are holding me over here. Please don't pray any more." We did all stop, and shortly after that she died.

Effects on Lives

The effects which their experiences have had on their lives seem to have taken a subtler, quieter form. Many have told me that they felt that their lives were broadened and deepened by their experience, that because of it they became more reflective and more concerned with ultimate philosophical issues.

> I try to do things that have more meaning, and that makes my mind and soul feel better. And I try not to be biased, and not to judge people. I want to do things because they are good, not because they are good to me. And it seems that the understanding I have of things now is so much better. I feel like this is because of what happened to me, because of the places I went and the things I saw in this experience.

There is a remarkable agreement in the "lessons," as it were, which have been brought back from these close encounters with death. Almost everyone has stressed the importance in this life of trying to cultivate love for others, a love of a unique and profound kind. One man who met the being of light felt totally loved and accepted, even while his whole life was displayed in a panorama for the being to see. He felt that the "question" that the being was asking him was whether he was able to love others in the same way. He now feels that it is his commission while on earth to try to learn to be able to do so.

In addition, many others have emphasized the importance of seeking knowledge. During their experiences, it was intimated to them that the acquisition of knowledge continues even in the after-life. One woman, for example, has taken advantage of every educational opportunity she has had since her "death" experience.

Another man offers the advice, "No matter how old you are, don't stop learning. For this is a process, I gather, that goes on for eternity."

New Views of Death

As one might reasonably expect, this experience has a profound effect upon one's attitude towards physical death, especially for those who had not previously expected that anything took place after death. In some form or another, almost every person has expressed to me the thought that he is no longer afraid of death. This requires clarification, though. In the first place, certain modes of death are obviously undesirable, and secondly, none of these persons are actively seeking death. They all feel that they have tasks to do as long as they are physically alive and would agree with the words of a man who told me, "I've got quite a lot of changing to do before I leave here." Likewise, all would disavow suicide as a means by which to return to the realms they glimpsed during their experiences. It is just that now the state of death itself is no longer forbidding to them. Let us look at some passages in which such attitudes are explained.

> When I was a little boy I used to dread dying. I used to wake up at night crying and having a fit. My mother and father would rush into the bedroom and ask what was wrong. I told them that I didn't want to die, but that I knew I had to, and asked if they could stop it. My mother would talk to me and tell me, "No, that's just the way it is and we all have to face it." She said that we would do it all right. And years later after my mother died I would talk about death with my wife. I still feared it. I didn't want it to come.
>
> But since this experience, I don't fear death. Those feelings vanished. I don't feel bad at funerals anymore. I kind of rejoice at them, because I know what the dead person has been through.
>
> I believe that the Lord may have sent this experience to me because of the way I felt about death. Of course my parents comforted me, but the Lord showed me, whereas they couldn't do that. Now, I don't talk about all this, but I know, and I am perfectly satisfied.

 Exercise
Questions

1. What two reasons does Dr. Moody give for the subject of death being taboo?

2. What analogies do people make to death?

3. How well do Dr. Moody's examples work? Are they convincing? Why?

4. Which of the death experiences had you heard of before? Which seemed the most unusual? Which, if any, seemed humorous?

5. What does the author say is the most common element of dying?

6. Overall, what feeling did people have while dying? Is this what you would expect? How do most people think death will feel?

7. What does the author say most people learned from this experience?

8. Why did education become so important to the people quoted in the essay?

9. Has the author convinced you that there is a life after life? Why?

10. How many other things do people pretend are not there as they do with death? What effect does this have on their lives?

 Exercise

Staying Alive Indefinitely

Scientists have been working for many years in the field of genetic engineering, searching for a substance that will stop the aging process. It has been predicted that within twenty years they will be able to completely stop or drastically slow it down. While considering that a drug were available to stop you from growing old, preserving you physically, at the age of twenty, answer the following questions in small groups.

1. Would you take a drug that would keep you from aging?

2. If this kind of drug were available, would most people take it? Why?

3. If the practice were acceptable, would a limit have to be placed on a person's life? If so, what limit would you choose?

4. Would some form of population control be necessary? How would you solve this problem?

5. What effect would this practice have on employment? Would people be able to work all their lives?

6. What effect would staying young indefinitely have on marriage? Would people still get married, or would they stay married longer? Would divorce become more prevalent?

7. If a limit on a person's life span were necessary, how would the person's life be terminated? Who would be in charge of such a task?

 Writing Exercise

Write a six-paragraph essay on one of the topics associated with death. Some alternatives you might use are: the advantages or disadvantages of staying alive indefinitely, euthanasia, mercy killing, suicide, death counseling, why people ignore or fear death, and the benefits of facing death. You may also use any other related topics.

Prewriting

Use brainstorming to compose a list of possible topics, and choose the most interesting one; then brainstorm several opinions related to the topic to explore the different approaches you may use in your essay. Pick one opinion and outline the paragraphs that will make up the body of the essay, limiting each to a reason, way, quality or cause-effect so that you can develop it in detail.

Writing

Use the technique of freewriting and emphasize the explanation of your reasoning in each of your paragraphs. Include detailed examples or descriptions to illustrate what you are saying in general. When you have finished writing the body of the essay, compose the introduction, including a limited thesis statement, and the conclusion.

Reading and Revising

Use the usual methods of reading and revising, and critically evaluate the primary and secondary support of your paragraphs. Check the paragraphs in the body of the essay to see that they are closely related to the thesis. Finally, write a second draft of the essay, using the notes you made on revisions.

PART 5

Review of Writing Mechanics

The Sentence Unit

To communicate ideas clearly, and to satisfy the expectations of educated readers, you must write in complete sentences. A complete sentence must have three elements: it must be about something (noun), it must make an assertion (verb), and it must express a complete idea.

> The baseball strike lasted three months.

This is a complete sentence because it has a subject (baseball strike) and a verb (lasted). The idea is completed by the phrase "three months."

> The committee reviewed the superintendent's complaint.

This is also a complete sentence, for it has a subject (committee) and a verb (reviewed); finally, it expresses a complete thought by telling *what* the committee reviewed.

SUBJECTS

The subject of a sentence is the topic about which the statement is being made. It may be a noun, pronoun, nominal (another part of speech functioning as a noun), or a noun clause (a clause functioning as a noun). The subject generally comes near the beginning of the sentence and is usually placed in front of the verb.

A noun is normally defined as a word representing a person, place, thing, or idea. Moreover, it is a word that will fit into this pattern:

(The) _____ is/are good (or bad).

A number of common word endings may help you identify nouns: -acy, -age, -ance or -ence, -ancy or -ency, -dom, -hood, -ity, -ment, -ness, -er or -or, -tion or -sion, -ist, -tude, and -ure.

Exercise
Identifying Nouns

Underline the words in the following list that are nouns.

N 1. freedom	N 11. resistance	21. if
2. jeopardize	12. advertise	N 22. prevention
3. convenient	N 13. happiness	N 23. artist
N 4. dependency	N 14. worker	N 24. mayor
5. because	N 15. establishment	25. omit
N 6. motherhood	16. teach	N 26. simplicity
7. humble	N 17. bondage	27. noisy
8. leisure	N 18. attendance	N 28. procedure
9. beautiful	19. possess	29. likable
N 10. attitude	N 20. composure	N 30. submission

VERBS

Verbs are words that show action, condition, state of being, or they can make an assertion about the subject. They can also ask a question or give a command or direction. Verbs usually come after the subject. One way to test a verb is to see if you can put it into the sentence pattern:

Let us _____.

Another way to test a verb is to see if you can form a past tense from the word; no other part of speech has a past tense. To test a word to see if it has a past tense, put it into the following pattern:

Yesterday we _____.

Most verbs have five principal parts or forms: infinitive (to sing), present (sing, sings), past (sang), present participle (singing), and past participle (sung). A participle must be accompanied by an auxiliary, or helping, verb in order to express a complete idea. The auxiliary may consist of a single word or several words; it always precedes the main verb, as illustrated below. Some auxiliary verbs are: is, was, shall, would, should, did, have, might, could, etc.

The children have eaten the pie.

The children are eating the pie.

The children might have been eaten by the witch.

Exercise

Identifying Verbs

Underline the verbs in the following list.

1. vitality	11. plant	21. bother
2. break	12. love	22. boredom
3. private	13. for	23. kiss
4. fool	14. authorize	24. affect
5. advise	15. inflation	25. incredible
6. report	16. butter	26. salvage
7. station	17. substantiate	27. project
8. severely	18. observation	28. penalty
9. dream	19. erase	29. frolic
10. waiter	20. vote	30. critical

SENTENCE PATTERNS

Although a complete sentence may consist of only a subject and verb ("Birds fly"), most often a writer wishes to convey more information than is possible in two words. Several sentence elements make it possible to add information about the subject or verb.

The *direct object* indicates what or who receives the action of the verb. It is always a noun or noun substitute.

George bought a *video camera.* (Noun)

We enjoyed *traveling* in France. (participle as noun)

The *indirect object,* likewise, is always a noun or noun substitute. Indicating the one to whom or for whom the action is taken, it is placed between the verb and the direct object.

My friend did *me* a favor. (Read *"for me"*)

The *object complement,* like the subject complement (see below), is always a noun or noun substitutes, or an adjective. You will understand its function most easily if you think of the words "to be" or "as" preceding the object complement.

The team elected Jim (as) *captain.* (Noun)
mary's parents consider her (to be) *brilliant.* (Adjective)

The *subject complement* is a noun or adjective that follows certain verbs and adds information about the subject. The verb in the Subject-Verb-Subject Complement pattern is a type that does not take an object, but functions rather like an "equals" sign between the subject and the following noun or adjective. These verbs, called *linking verbs,* usually express a state of being or becoming, rather than an action. The most common linking verbs are these:

be	The show was a success.
become	My uncle became a librarian.
get (meaning "become")	Joe's practical jokes are getting old.
feel*	Marian felt sorry for what she had done.
seem	This book seems interesting.
taste*	The freshly baked cake tasted delicious.

*These words, of course, also function as action verbs, verbs that take objects, as in these examples.

He tasted the freshly baked cake.
"Feel the material," the salesman said.

These sentence elements and their uses should not confuse you, once you realize that they combine to form only seven basic sentence patterns. The seven patterns are listed below, with examples.

1. N-V or Subject-Verb
    The child awoke.
    The rain stopped.

2. N-V-Adj. or Subject-Verb-Subject Complement

    I was astonished.
    My friend was skeptical.

3. N1-V-N1 or Subject-Verb-Subject Complement

    My cousin is a violinist.
    The politician is a pathological liar.

4. N1-V-N2 or Subject-Verb-Direct Object

    The car hit the divider.
    The people watched the accident.

5. N1-V-N2-N3 or Subject-Verb-Indirect Object-Direct Object

    The pitcher threw the second batter a spit ball.
    The nurse gave the patient a sedative.

6. N1-V-N2-Adj. or Subject-Verb-Direct Object-Object Complement

    We consider him creepy.
    The doctor pronounced the patient cured.

7. N1-V-N2-N2 or Subject-Verb-Direct Object-Object Complement

    We elected a fool president.
    They think him an intellectual.

 Writing Exercise
Using Sentence Patterns

Write three sentences to fit each of the seven basic sentence patterns that are repeated below.

1. N-V or Subject-Verb.

2. N-V-Adj. or Subject-Verb-Subject Complement.

3. N1-V-N1 or Subject-Verb-Subject Complement.

4. N1-V-N2 or Subject-Verb-Direct Object.

5. N1-V-N2-N3 or Subject-Verb-Indirect Object-Direct Object.

6. N1-V-N2-Adj. or Subject-Verb-Direct Object-Object Complement.

7. N1-V-N2-N2 or Subject-Verb-Direct Object-Object Complement.

Exercise

Identifying Subjects and Verbs

Underline the subject once and the verb twice in the following sentences, and note which rules the sentence breaks or whether it is a complete sentence.

1. The lobby of the Hallmark Hotel was filled with dignitaries from all over the world.

2. During the long winter in Idaho, the snow piling up in drifts as high as fifteen feet.

3. Mr. Kripes brought home the new sofa and showed it to his wife, who was quite alarmed at the color.

4. My next door neighbor's dog barks all night long at the sound of the wind.

5. Being a senior in high school and working part-time for my uncle as a flunky.

6. The bouncer implied that I was not dressed for the occasion.

7. Night fell.

8. The book explaining how to make sound investments.

9. I could not see him at the end of the pier, but he was there.

10. Alarmed by the late-night telephone call.

SENTENCE FRAGMENTS

As explained in the sentence unit, a complete sentence (independent clause) must have both a subject and a verb. If either the subject or the verb is missing, the sentence will express an incomplete idea, and it can be confusing to the reader.

Fragments occur often in writing, and one of the most common is a subordinate (adverb) clause that is not linked to an independent clause. In many cases the independent clause needed to complete the idea expressed comes either before or after the subordinate clause, and the writer simply needs to correct the punctuation.

Incorrect: If you hand in your tax return early. You are more likely to be audited by the I.R.S.

Correct: If you hand in your tax return early, you are more likely to be audited by the I.R.S.

Incorrect: We were completely exhausted. After we won the game and tore down the goal posts.

Correct: We were completely exhausted after we won the game and tore down the goal posts.

Another common sentence fragment is created when a Verb-ing or participle phrase is treated like a complete sentence.

Incorrect: Jacking up the car and changing the tire in the middle of the freeway. I was frightened by the oncoming traffic.

Correct: Jacking up the car and changing the tire in the middle of the freeway, I was frightened by the oncoming traffic.

Incorrect: Delighted by the long-distance phone call from her son in New Jersey. Mrs. Adams sent him another check.

Correct: Delighted by the long-distance phone call from her son in New Jersey, Mrs. Adams sent him another check.

Another common fragment is a prepositional phrase that stands by itself as though it were a complete sentence.

Incorrect: At the end of his performance at Carnegie Hall. Harry Belafonte was given a standing ovation.

Correct: At the end of his performance at Carnegie Hall, Harry Belafonte was given a standing ovation.

Incorrect: Along Pacific Coast Highway near Huntington Beach during rush hour. It is dangerous to ride a bicycle.

Correct: Along Pacific Coast Highway near Huntington Beach during rush hour, it is dangerous to ride a bicycle.

An additional frequent way of creating fragments occurs when a sentence has two verbs linked together by a coordinating conjunction, and the writer puts a period in front of the conjunction.

Incorrect: I enjoy playing poker with my friends. And winning all of their money.

Correct: I enjoy playing poker with my friends and winning all of their money.

Exercise I
Sentence Fragments

In the following exercises underline the part of the sentence that is a fragment and correct the punctuation so that each example is a complete sentence.

1. We were all greatly disappointed. When Gerald Ford lost the election. *NO COMMA*

2. Before the performance by the Grateful Dead at the Palladium, We waited patiently in line for two hours.

3. It took an hour to catch the dog. Running along the beach and playing in the surf at Point Mugu.

4. His engine stalled by a vapor lock in the middle of Nebraska, The young salesman walked to the nearest farm.

5. The air pollution which had covered Los Angeles for five weeks was cleared away. When it rained for three days straight. *NO comma*

6. Kathy's father was completely delighted with the court's decision. Concerning the accident that he had as a mechanic. *NO comma*

7. We all enjoyed going to the airport to meet the President. But not driving home through the weekend traffic.

8. The doctor continued to work at the hospital. Throughout the evening and well into the next morning. *NO COMMA*

9. The food at the restaurant was expensive. Yet was quite delicious despite the price.

10. My sister left the party early, Tired of all the loud music and pointless conversation.

Exercise II
Sentence Fragments

1. Gerald did not join us for the chamber music concert last night, Being a punk rock fan.

2. Stranded at the drive in theater with a dead battery, My date decided to go home with my best friend.

3. I bought a small economy car, Which cost only $7,000.

4. I won't be able to videotape the late movie on H.B.O. tomorrow night, Unless I pay an additional fee.

5. The trustees of Little Hills College provide as many free services as possible for their students, Whereas the trustees of Big River College have imposed a fifty dollar parking fee.

6. After I graduated from Harvard with honors, I was hired to manage a Burger King Restaurant.

7. Needles, California, can be a miserable place to visit, Especially in the summer when the temperature often reaches 110 degrees at night.

8. In the middle of the Alaskan tundra where it was − 30 degrees, Paul and Mary were playing frisbee dressed in jeans and tee shirts.

9. Driving through a downpour on my way to work, My car stalled in the middle of the Harbor Freeway.

10. In Glacier Park last spring when the wildflowers were blooming, My friends hiked up to Crater Lake. And went swimming near the waterfall.

Check Answer Key at the end of the book.

FUSED SENTENCES AND COMMA SPLICES

A *fused sentence* occurs when two independent clauses are joined with no punctuation, as in the following example:

> Professor Weber didn't just criticize my essay she showed me how to improve it.

If you analyze this sentence, you quickly see that there are two independent subject-verb groups; the first ends with the word "essay." This fused sentence (sometimes called a run-on sentence) can be corrected easily; place a period after "essay" and capitalize the first letter of "She." A better solution, since the two clauses are closely related, is to place a semicolon after "essay."

> Professor Weber didn't just criticize my essay; she showed me how to improve it.

Here are other ways of correcting the original fused sentence.

> Professor Weber didn't just criticize my essay. She also showed me how to improve it.

Professor Weber didn't just criticize my essay, but she also showed me how to improve it.

A *comma splice* is similar to a fused sentence in that it also joins two independent clauses with insufficient punctuation. Consider this example:

My instructor suggested a new thesis for my essay, he also helped me to construct an outline.

Again, analysis of the sentence indicates two independent subject-verb groups. The two sentences must be separated with a period, joined with a comma and a coordinating conjunction (in this case, "and"), or joined with a semicolon.

My instructor suggested a new thesis for my essay. He also helped me to construct an outline.

My instructor suggested a new thesis for my essay, and he also helped me to construct an outline.

My instructor suggested a new thesis for my essay; he also helped me to construct an outline.

One of the most common comma splices occurs in sentences beginning "Not only . . ."

Not only did I enjoy the concert, I got the piano player's autograph.

You will occasionally see this type of sentence in print, but it still is not considered acceptable in serious writing. Although the close relationship between the independent clauses invites you to join them with a comma, it is better to use a semicolon:

Not only did I enjoy the concert; I got the piano player's autograph.

You may also link the independent clauses together with a coordinating conjunction as in the following example.

Not only did I enjoy the concert, but I also got the piano player's autograph.

Exercise I

Fused Sentences and Comma Splices

Most of the following are either fused sentences or comma splices. If an item is a fused sentence, mark FS to the left of the number and then correct the punctuation; if it is a comma splice, mark CS and correct the punctuation. If the sentence is correct, simply write C in the margin.

1. Of course I'm going to the concert, I wouldn't miss it for anything. *CS*

2. When the phone rang, John dropped his cup, he was apprehensive. *F/S*

3. He wasn't merely worried; he was frightened half to death. *FS*

4. Penny's constant smile is not just a facade; it's a reflection of her cheerful outlook. *C*

5. Pay attention; this lecture is important. *FS*

6. One big advantage to owning a cassette deck is convenience; the cassettes are easy to handle and store. *FS*

7. David had been out of school for several years; however, he quickly adjusted to college life. *CS*

8. Although he missed going to concerts and parties on week nights, he was proud of being the best student in his physics class. *C*

9. This music sounds distorted I must have had the volume too high when I made the recording. *FS*

10. I don't usually make that kind of mistake; perhaps the tape deck needs repair. *C*

■ **Exercise II**

Fused Sentences and Comma Splices

Check the following sentences. If an item is a fused sentence, mark FS to the left of the number and then correct the punctuation; if it is a comma splice, mark CS and correct the punctuation.

1. I've always hated fused sentences I think it's because I've written so many of them.

2. I arrived at the party early I wanted to get a chance to talk to the host alone.

3. The high tides during the storm damaged the beach houses, many were washed out to sea.

4. Your tiny hands are frozen let me warm them for you.

5. I've told you a thousand times, always put the blade guard in place before using the power saw.

6. I don't like it I never have I never will.

7. George was driving down Main Street changing the cassette in his radio, he never saw the swerving truck.

8. *The Loved One* was a very entertaining book the movie was even better.

9. Hazing has always been a tradition with fraternities most colleges now forbid it.

10. We never heard the Steely Dan concert on Friday, it had been canceled for some reason.

Check Answer Key at the end of the book.

SOLVING PROBLEMS WITH VERBS

Verbs, those words that express action or a state of being, change their forms according to *tense* (time), *person* (I, you, he), and *number* (singular or plural). Errors with verbs are the result of failure to make the necessary changes in form. Let's begin with tense.

All verb tenses are based upon the following forms.

Infinitive (basic, "unlimited" form), usually the same as the present form; often preceded by *"to"*	to stand
Present:	stand
Past:	stood
Present Participle:	standing
Past Participle:	stood

Note that with *stand,* as with the majority of English verbs, the past and past participle are identical. The following list, however, includes some "irregular" verbs whose past and past participle forms differ.

Infinitive	Present	Past	Present Participle	Past Participle
to talk	talk(s)	talked	talking	talked
to see	see(s)	saw	seeing	seen
to tear	tear(s)	tore	tearing	torn
to sleep	sleep(s)	slept	sleeping	slept
to order	order(s)	ordered	ordering	ordered
to bring	bring(s)	brought	bringing	brought

Many problems with verbs can be avoided if the writer has a clear understanding of how verb tenses are formed. There are six basic tenses—present, past, future, present perfect, past perfect, future perfect—and each indicates a different time.

1. Present tense shows an action currently going on, or which usually goes on, or which continually goes on.

   I *see* my cousin Dave about once a year.
   I *notice* by your outfit that you are a cowboy!

2. Past tense shows action at a definite time prior to the time of speaking or writing.

   George *sold* his motorhome and *bought* a Mercedes.

3. Future tense shows action that is to come.

   Our group *will depart* for London next week.

   (As you are probably aware, English speakers often use the present tense to indicate future action—a practice that confuses most newcomers to the language: *We leave for San Francisco next Friday.*)

4. Present perfect tense shows action begun in the past and continuing to the present, or repeated past action.

   Santiago *has lived* in Arcadia for several years.
   My sister *has seen* the movie *Superman* seven times.

5. Past perfect tense shows a past action that preceded another past action.

   When Linda arrived home, the party *had begun.*

   (Note that if we use the past tense in both clauses, Linda's arrival and the start of the party are simultaneous; the meaning differs importantly from the first version.)

6. Future perfect tense shows a future action that will precede another future action. This tense is most often used along with the present tense, rather than the future (which would be more logical).

   By the time you arrive (rather than "will arrive"), my cousin *will have gone* home to New York.

Sequence of Tenses

Problems often occur when a writing situation calls for the use of more than one tense. This is especially true in *conditional* sentences, which take the form: If _____ then _____. (Most of the time the word *then* is omitted.)

   If you want me to do that, I *will do* it.

This sentence uses the present and future tenses and presents no problem. But when the conditional sentence refers to a past time, using such helping verbs as *could* and *would,* it can be tricky.

   If I *had known* your address, I *would have written* you.

Here, the second clause correctly uses *would have;* the *if* clause uses the past perfect tense. That is the standard arrangement (sequence) of tenses.

As a general rule, conditional sentences follow these two patterns.

1. *If* clause in present tense; *then* clause in future.

   (If you graduate from college with a 4.0 G.P.A., you will find a job easily.)

2. If clause in past perfect tense; *then* clause in past conditional (would have).

   (If you had arrived at the swap meet on time, you would have found the water bed you wanted.)

One word of caution: Do not write *could of, would of,* etc. These are incorrect because *of* is not a verb. The writing error is caused by confusing sound-alikes; the contractions *would've* (for *would have*), *could've* (for *could have*), etc., can sound like *would of* and *could of,* but must not be written that way.

Shifts in Verbs Tense

A major error in the use of verbs is an unnecessary shift from past to present tense, or vice versa. Such shifts distract and confuse the reader, who may wonder how many events are being discussed. This sentence demonstrates a common error.

When I *walked* into the room, everybody *looks* at me as if I'm crazy.

CORRECTED: When I *walked* into the room, everybody *looked* at me as if I *were* crazy.

or, possibly,

Whenever I *walk* into the room, everybody *looks* at me as if I were crazy.

I *rounded* the corner, dead tired and streaming with sweat, and there *stands* Jim looking relaxed and neat in his Brooks Brothers suit.

CORRECTED: I *rounded* the corner, dead tired and streaming with sweat, and there *stood* Jim looking relaxed and neat in his Brooks Brothers suit.

Exercise I

Verb Tense

Underline the verb that is in the improper tense, and write the proper tense above it.

1. If I knew when the test was going to be, I'd have been there on time.

2. Led Zeppelin was so exciting in concert I am standing in the aisle of the auditorium and dancing.

3. Billy Budd is summoned to the captain's quarters; he has been accused of mutiny.

4. If you look both ways, you wouldn't have hit that fire hydrant.

5. As I left her house, I think of all the good time we've had.

6. We hiked all the way up to Snyder Lake. It is raining there.

7. The commercials are always so boring I have stopped watching them.

8. Though the boxers were barely able to stand, they keep fighting as though they aren't tired.

9. I told her if she washes my car I'd have paid her five dollars.

10. When I walked into Saks Fifth Avenue, the sales people treat me like a king.

 Exercise II

Verb Tense

Underline the verb that is in the improper tense, and write its proper tense above.

1. If it wouldn't have rained all day Saturday, the swap meet in the parking lot would have been a big success.

2. The executive and his wife were leaving the Cafe Ritz after dinner, and they run into his old girlfriend.

3. The quarterback made a mistake. If he waits just one more second before throwing the pass, his receiver is open and they score a touchdown.

4. Jonathan Swart, the embezzler, would never be in prison if he hadn't grown so ambitious.

5. If I knew you were coming, I'd have baked a cake.

6. If you see Benny at the picnic tomorrow, you probably see his sidekick Joe.

7. Patrick says that he would not play the piano so well today if he didn't study with Mr. Bennett as a teenager.

8. I might have made it to class on time if there wasn't an accident on the freeway.

9. I would have stopped if I would have seen you.

10. By the time we got to David's house, the party ended an hour ago.

AGREEMENT OF SUBJECT AND VERB

When we say that the verb of a sentence must agree with its subject, we mean two things: (1) The subject and verb must be both singular or both plural, and (2) the verb must be in the proper form to correspond with the person of the subject.

> Marilyn is a dental technician.

In this sentence the verb is *be*. The form *is* appears because the subject, *Marilyn*, is singular and third person.

The "S" Rule

Correcting or avoiding errors in subject-verb agreement becomes fairly easy if you remember that these errors occur mainly in one situation: the third person singular, present tense. (The exception is the past tense of *be*.) Look at the verb *have*.

Present		Past	
I have	we have	I had	we had
you have	you have	you had	you had
he, she, it has	they have	he, she, it had	they had

Future	
I will have	we will have
you will have	you will have
he, she, it will have	they will have

Note that the form of the verb changes in only one position, the third person singular (he, she, it) in the present tense. We can, therefore, reduce subject-verb agreement problems to a basic rule, the "S" rule: In the present tense, if there is an *-s* (plural) ending on the noun, there is no *-s* ending on the verb; if there is no *-s* ending on the noun, there is an *-s* ending on the verb.

    0   S

The boy walks his dog.

    S   0

The boys walk their dogs.

    0   S

Richard sees Karen every week.

    S   0

The Taylors see Richard occasionally.

Singular nouns ending in -s (usually subject areas ending in -ics) are exceptions to the "S" rule.

Economics has been called "the dismal science."

When such nouns refer to an individual's behavior, however, they are treated as plural.

Mr. Snyder's politics *are* questionable at times.

Compound Subjects

Compound subjects, those consisting of more than one noun or pronoun, are usually treated as plural and used with plural verbs.

Suzanne and Mike often stop here in the morning.

Do not, however, use a plural verb with a singular subject followed by a connecting prepositional phrase such as *along with, in addition to, as well as,* and so on. These phrases do not make the subject plural.

Incorrect: My art teacher, as well as my mother, think I am a genius.

Correct: My art teacher, as well as my mother, *thinks* I am a genius.

Incorrect: In *Ten-Speed and Brown Shoe,* a whimsical young private detective, along with his devious partner, constantly *find* themselves in trouble.

Correct: In *Ten-Speed and Brown Shoe,* a whimsical young private detective, along with his devious partner, constantly *finds* himself in trouble.

Better: In *Ten-Speed and Brown Shoe,* a whimsical young private detective and his devious partner constantly find themselves in trouble.

Either . . . or and *Neither . . . nor*

These are two more expressions that do not compound subjects. If they connect two singular subjects, the verb must be singular.

Either Del Mar College or Cerritos College *offers* a major in prosthetics.
Professor Whitecastle says that neither *The Chairs* nor *The Cherry Orchard* *is* a true comedy.

When these two expressions (called disjunctives) link a singular subject with a plural one, the standard practice is to make the verb agree with the subject closer to it.

> Neither the committee chairman nor the members *know* what action to take.
>
> Neither the committee members nor the chairman *knows* what action to take.

The two preceding sentences are both grammatical, but a bit awkward. A better approach to the situation is to rewrite the sentence, using a few more words but achieving greater clarity:

> The committee members do not know what action to take; neither does the chairman.

Prepositional Phrases

Normally, prepositional phrases do not affect the number of the verb. Remember that the object of a preposition can serve no additional function in the sentence; do not, therefore, treat it as the subject of a verb, as in this sentence.

> Incorrect: The price of those cassette decks *are* too high.
>
> Correct: The price of those cassette decks *is* too high.
>
> The subject of the sentence is *price,* not *decks.*

An important exception to this rule involves prepositional phrases that modify indefinite pronouns such as *any, none, some, more, most,* and *all.* Consider these sentences:

> Some of our time *is* spent in reading. Some of the women *were* outraged by the performance. None of the students *are* political activists.

Because these pronouns do not specify number, it must be determined by the following prepositional phrases. The pronoun *none* is a special case. When its meaning is "not one," it takes a singular verb.

> None of my friends was available to play tennis.

Collective Nouns

Some nouns that refer to groups may be either singular or plural. The number of these collective nouns, words like *team, group, congregation,* is often determined by other information in the sentence. Consider this:

> The team *were* all hanging *their heads* after the loss.

Here the emphasis is on the individual members of the team. The emphasis is different in the next example.

Our team *is* playing at Long Beach this afternoon.

	Collective Nouns	
team	band	council
group	crew	jury
crowd	audience	middle class
congregation	pair	nation
couple	lot	family

Consistency is the key to using these nouns. If the noun—say, *committee*—is given a singular verb, then pronouns that refer to the noun must also be singular.

Incorrect: The band *was* picking up *their* instruments.

Correct: The band *were* picking up *their* instruments.

Correct: The band *was* rehearsing *its* routines.

Exercise I
Subject-Verb Agreement

If there is an error in subject-verb agreement, write the correct form of the verb at the end of the sentence. If there is no error, write "C" in the space to the left of the number.

1. The style and fit of a shirt is more important than the price.

2. Both my art teacher and my mother are encouraging me to continue my studies.

3. Neither the faculty nor the administration consider the plan worthwhile.

4. *The Times* and *The Herald-Examiner* have announced their ballot recommendations.

5. Neither *The Bee* nor *The Chronicle* are endorsing a candidate for governor.

6. Many students think that Bill's honesty and intelligence makes him a good candidate for the student court.

7. These open-toed sandals and this two-toned bolero blouse is just your style.

8. The white, sandy beach and the exiting night life attracts many visitors to the island.

9. Neither the writing nor the acting was particularly good.

10. Either the witnesses or the defendant are lying.

Exercise II
Subject-Verb Agreement

Choose the correct form of the verb.

1. A lot of the problems most people have (is/are) their own fault.

2. The committee (has/have) decided to cast their votes in secret.

3. Neither of the killers (show/shows) any remorse.

4. Each of the traffic tickets I have received (is/are) for parking illegally.

5. Neither Sam nor Jennifer (know/knows) the answer.

6. An angry mob (was/were) waving signs and shouting.

7. The singer's polished voice and distinctive style (is/are) the key to her success.

8. What sets Bill apart from the other candidates (is/are) his honesty and intelligence.

9. The crew of electricians (has/have) finished the job on my house in three days.

10. The team (want/wants) their helmets painted gold.

Exercise III
Subject-Verb Agreement

Choose the correct form of the verb in parentheses.

1. The men in the green sports car (look/looks) foolish.

2. My uncle's career in the armed forces (has/have) been spectacular.

3. George's boldness, as well as his persistence, (make/makes) him a good salesman.

4. The size of the wheels on those trucks (astound/astounds) me.

5. The police have concluded that the perpetrator of the many recent burglaries (is/are) still at large.

6. That singer's good looks, as much as his voice, (account/accounts) for his success.

7. Sam's writing instructor, as well as his mother, (think/thinks) he is a genius.

8. The wheels on that truck in the parking lot (is/are) enormous.

9. I think that the woman with the two Afghan hounds (look/looks) stunning.

10. The aroma of barbecued spare ribs (attract/attracts) many passing shoppers.

Check Answer Key at the end of the book.

PARALLEL STRUCTURE

The principle that "form follows function" applies in writing as well as in architecture. In writing it is referred to as the principle of parallel structure, and it means that when sentence elements are alike in function and content, they should be expressed in similar constructions.

>He asked me for my phone number and to tell him where I live.

Here, the elements joined by *and* are both objects of *asked,* but their expression is not parallel. Here are a couple of possible improvements;

>He asked me for my phone number and my address.
>He asked me to tell him my phone number and my address.

Faulty parallelism occurs most often when sentence elements are joined by coordinating conjunctions (*and, or*) or by correlatives (*not only . . . but also; neither- . . . nor; either . . . or*). Consider the following example:

>It's time officials get on board with efforts to develop realistic plans to relieve congestion which are infinitely less costly, environmentally accept-able and *can be accomplished in a fraction of the time.*

The first two elements relating to the verb *are* consist of adjectives: *costly, acceptable*; the third element is an independent clause. One alternative lengthens the sentence but makes the relationships clear:

>It's time officials get on board with efforts to develop realistic plans to relieve congestion which are infinitely less costly, environmentally accept-able, and *capable of being accomplished in a fraction of the time.*

Many times, problems with parallel structure are the result of a false series. Make certain that all the items in a series are related to the rest of the sentence in the same way. Study this example:

> He encouraged me to remain in business, assisted in counseling my two young daughters in their educational programs, and recently my youngest daughter was accepted at the Colorado School of Mines.

There is not a real series in this sentence. Two verbs (*encouraged, assisted*) are related to the subject, *he,* in the same way. The last part of the sentence, however, is an independent clause and is not governed by the subject of the sentence; it is not parallel in function to *encouraged* and *assisted,* and should not be placed in an apparent series with them. Here is a better version.

> He encouraged me to remain in business and assisted in counseling my two young daughters in their educational programs.

> As a result, my youngest daughter was recently accepted at the Colorado School of Mines.

Be careful, in editing your writing, to read slowly and carefully so that you may spot and correct instances of faulty parallelism, as well as any other errors.

 Exercise

Parallel Structure

Read the following sentences carefully and correct any errors in parallel structure. Do not make unnecessary changes.

1. At my high school there were very easy requirements, such as little class work, no homework, and watch films.

2. Janet was criticized both for her behavior and how she dressed.

3. When you revise your paragraphs, include coordination, subordination, and put in some simple sentences as well.

4. The candidate declared that he always has and always will believe in the right to free expression.

5. The passage will become clear after repeated readings or by underlining key words and phrases.

6. John poured syrup over his pancakes, his hash-brown potatoes, and even poured some over his eggs.

7. The telephone solicitor wanted to know not only my age and my address, but also how much money I make.

8. We wanted a house which could accommodate six children, which had a fireplace, and overlooking the ocean.

9. The director has augmented his storytelling with screen projections, a beautiful music score, and the lighting is fantastic.

10. I never saw a more moving production of *The Glass Menagerie*; nor has my wife.

PROBLEMS WITH PRONOUNS

Problems with Pronoun Case

Personal pronouns have three forms (cases). The subjective case (I, you, she, he, we, they) is used as the subject or subject complement in a sentence (refer to the sentence patterns near the beginning of the review of writing mechanics).

Incorrect: *Her* and *me* are going to the fun zone this afternoon.

Correct: *She* and *I* are going to the fun zone this afternoon.

Incorrect: The winner of the 500-mile marathon appears to be *him* (subject complement).

Correct: The winner of the 500-mile marathon appears to be *he.*

Incorrect: *Bob* and *me* are the best of friends.

Correct: *Bob* and *I* are the best of friends.

Incorrect: The woman who returned your wallet was *her.*

Correct: The woman who returned your wallet was *she.*

Incorrect: *Us* Democrats were overjoyed by the election.

Correct: *We* Democrats were overjoyed by the election.

The objective case of personal pronouns (me, you, her, him, us, them) is used as the direct or indirect object or the object of a preposition.

Incorrect: Mrs. Holmes accused Caroline and *she* of being out past curfew.

Correct: Mrs. Holmes accused Caroline and *her* of being out past curfew.

Incorrect: The letter addressed to *I* was left on the kitchen counter.

Correct: The letter addressed to *me* was left on the kitchen counter.

Incorrect: The plumber gave the estimate to my mother and *I*.

Correct: The plumber gave the estimate to my mother and *me*.

Incorrect: Running toward the farmer and *she,* the billy goat lowered his head.

Correct: Running toward the farmer and *her,* the billy goat lowered his head.

The third form of pronouns is the possessive case (my, you, her, his, our, their), which is used to show ownership. These pronouns must be followed by nouns in order for them to make sense in a sentence as in the following examples.

My car stalled in *their* driveway.

Her youngest sister sold *your* stamp books.

The most common errors in using pronouns occur with the subjective and objective forms; these errors happen most often when the pronoun is included as part of a compound subject or object.

Incorrect: Frank, Charles and *me* were up until two in the morning fixing the transmission.

Correct: Frank, Charles and *I* were up until two in the morning fixing the transmission.

Incorrect: The judges gave the grand prize to Marvin and *she*.

Correct: The judges gave the grand prize to Marvin and *her*.

Incorrect: *Her* and her family went to New Zealand for the Spring.

Correct: *She* and her family went to New Zealand for the Spring.

Incorrect: The package was sent to my girl friend and *I*.

Correct: The package was sent to my girl friend and *me*.

Problems with Pronoun Agreement

A pronoun has to agree in number with the noun or pronoun it refers to (the antecedent). If the noun is singular, the pronoun must be singular (*I, me, my, you, your, she, her, him, his*). Also, a plural noun must have a plural pronoun (*we, us, our, they, them, their*) referring to it. In addition, a number of indefinite pronouns are considered singular (*each, every, either, neither, any*), so they agree only with singular pronouns. Other indefinite pronouns are considered plural (*all, both*).

Incorrect: Each of the men finished *their* work.

Correct:　Each of the men finished *his* work.

Incorrect: Either Mary or Joan forgot *their* coat.

Correct:　Either Mary or Joan forgot *her* coat.

Incorrect: The committee gave *their* recommendation to the president of the company.

Correct:　The committee gave *its* recommendation to the president of the company.

Incorrect: All of my problems has *its* solution.

Correct:　All of my problems have *their* solutions.

Incorrect: Every man at the convention wore *their* ceremonial robes.

Correct:　Every man at the convention wore *his* ceremonial robes.

Problems with Who and Whom

Both of these are called relative pronouns. They, however, have only two forms or cases, the subjective and objective. *Who* is the subjective case, and it functions the same as *he* or *she* in a sentence (the subject or subject complement). *Who* takes the place of or refers to the subject or subject complement in a sentence. This is also true of the pronoun *whoever*.

Incorrect: Whom cleaned my car?

Correct:　Who cleaned my car?

　　　　　(He cleaned my car.)

Incorrect: I don't really know *whom* is running for the Senate.

Correct:　I don't really know *who* is running for the Senate.

　　　　　(*Who* is the subject of the sentence . . . is running for the Senate.)

Incorrect: Whom would you like to be?

Correct:　Who would you like to be?

(Who is the subject complement of the sentence.)

Incorrect: Mrs. Ford, whom donated a great deal of her time to charity, was a true friend to everyone.

Correct: Mrs. Ford, who donated a great deal of her time to charity, was
             a true friend to everyone.

             (Who is the subject of the adjective clause.)

Whom or *whomever* is the objective form of the pronoun; it functions as or
refers to the direct or indirect object or the object of a preposition like *him* or *her.*

Incorrect: *Who* were you standing with in the restaurant?

Correct: *Whom* were you standing with in the restaurant?

             (Whom is the object of the preposition *with.*)

Incorrect: This is the man *who* I admire.

Correct: This is the man *whom* I admire.

             (Whom is the direct object of *I admire.*)

Incorrect: *Who* are you inviting to the roller disco party?

Correct: *Whom* are you inviting to the roller disco party?

             (Whom is the direct object of *you are inviting.*)

Problems with Pronoun Reference

Another problem with pronoun reference occurs when an indefinite pronoun
(*someone, no one, everyone, etc.*) is used. These pronouns include both men and
women, so it is considered sexist to use *he, his,* or *him* for pronoun reference; for
example, study the following sentence.

Incorrect: Everyone gave me his address.

In order to solve this problem, you may at times use "he or she," but it is best not
to overuse this phrase. Whenever possible, eliminate the pronoun showing gender
as in the following example;

Correct: Everyone gave me his or her address.

Correct: Everyone gave me an address.

You can also avoid using indefinite pronouns as in this revision of the same
sentence.

Correct: All of the people gave me their addresses.

Consider the following example.

Incorrect: Someone left his raincoat on the porch.

Correct: Someone left a raincoat on the porch.

Correct: A raincoat was left on the porch.

AMBIGUOUS PRONOUN REFERENCE

When the reference of a pronoun is ambiguous—that is, when it could refer to more than one antecedent—the meaning will be unclear and likely to confuse the reader. Usually, a simple rewording of the sentence will clear up the problem.

John did not write a letter to his brother Bob the entire time he was in summer camp.

It is unclear who was in summer camp. The sentence must be revised so as to answer that question.

The entire time that John was in summer camp, he did not write a letter to his brother Bob.

The entire time that Bob was in summer camp, his brother John did not write him a letter.

Exercise I
Pronoun Problems

Make the necessary correction for pronoun use.

1. (I/Me) and Bill stacked the pots in the kiln Friday afternoon.

2. The League of Women Voters had (its/their) annual meeting at the Disneyland Hotel.

3. Neither of the contestants who won several events was able to attend the ceremony to receive (his/their) awards.

4. The Hari Krishnas had managed to pester everyone at the airport except (she/her).

5. The lady in the window smiling at us was (she/her).

6. I thought the bank promised to give a million dollar reward to both you and (I/me).

7. You and (I/me) should hot-wire this Rolls Royce and go for a spin.

8. The recipients of the sour apple award were (they/them).

9. Why do the people around here treat (we/us) men so coldly?

10. All of the men in the grandstand gave (his/their) opinion of the umpire's decision.

 Exercise II

Pronoun Problems

1. The jury finally convicted the burglar (who/whom) the witnesses identified.

2. (Who/Whom) did you take with you to the Mardi Gras?

3. e.e. cummings, (who/whom) the critics misunderstood, was a popular poet among college students.

4. (Who/Whom) did you invite to the dinner this evening?

5. My aunt entrusted her fortune to the attorney (who/whom) she had known for ten years.

6. (Who/Whom) did you want to be when you were a child?

7. No one sent his R.S.V.P. as we requested.

8. Everyone wanted his name included on the plaque.

9. Neither of our friends has any plans for a career.

10. The candidate (who/whom) the voters approved of failed to be nominated by the Republican party.

Check Answer Key at the end of the book.

Exercise III
Ambiguous Pronoun Reference

Revise the following sentences in order to clarify pronoun reference.

1. When the children gave their parents a hamster, they were delighted.

2. The family dog can no longer bring in the Sunday *Times*; it has grown too heavy.

3. My mother told my sister that she was an excellent photographer.

4. Fred unexpectedly ran into Chuck at the playhouse. He was delighted to see him after so many years.

5. I always look forward to the student paintings at these exhibits; they are always so unusual.

Solving Problems with Punctuation

THE COMMA

The comma must be the world's favorite piece of punctuation because people use it so often. Many people believe that when they hear a pause, they need to put in a comma, but this simply is not true. Commas do indicate a pause in the sentence, but *all* pauses are not represented by commas.

Independent Clauses

Two independent clauses (complete sentences) cannot be joined by only a comma. They must be separated by a semicolon, a period, or a conjunction.

Incorrect: I stopped at the market, I needed a bottle of milk.

Correct: I stopped at the market; I needed a bottle of milk.

Coordinating Conjunctions

A comma is needed when two independent clauses are linked together by a coordinating conjunction (for, and, nor, but, or, yet). Be sure to note that the comma comes *before* the conjunction; many people make the mistake of putting the comma after it.

Incorrect: The beach was covered with driftwood for a severe storm had struck San Diego during the week.

Correct: The beach was covered with driftwood, for a severe storm had struck San Diego during the week.

Incorrect: I had the entire summer so I went up to Wyoming.

Correct: I had the entire summer, so I went up to Wyoming.

If, however, there is only a phrase after the coordinating conjunction, then a comma is not necessary.

Incorrect: I enjoy going to the beach, and walking along the water's edge.

Correct: I enjoy going to the beach and walking along the water's edge.

Incorrect: When we were at the Huntington Library, we saw the art collection, but not the Japanese garden.

Correct: When we were at the Huntington Library, we saw the art collection but not the Japanese garden.

Subordinating Conjunctions

A comma is needed when an adverbial clause begins a sentence. An adverbial clause starts with a subordinating conjunction, and the comma is placed after the clause that is introduced. Below is a list of subordinating conjunctions.

after	because	in order that	than
although	even though	now that	though
as	every time	once	till
as if	how	since	unless
as long as	if	so that	until
when	where	why	

Consider the following examples.

Incorrect: If you will lend me your notes over the weekend I will be able to catch up with the class.

Correct: If you will lend me your notes over the weekend, I will be able to catch up with the class.

Incorrect: After we arrived at the party the band took a forty-five-minute break.

Correct: After we arrived at the party, the band took a forty-five-minute break.

If the adverbial clause comes after the main clause, a comma is not necessary. This is one of the most common places where people put unnecessary commas.

Incorrect: The teacher wanted to commend us, because we had all turned in our homework on time.

Correct: The teacher wanted to commend us because we had all turned in our homework on time.

Incorrect: We went to the Red Onion to dance, before we want to the midnight show at the Roxy.

Correct: We went to the Red Onion to dance before we went to the midnight show at the Roxy.

Introductory Phrases

When an introductory phrase is long (around six or more words in length), it must be set off by commas. This type of phrase is usually a participial or prepositional phrase.

Incorrect: At the end of her final performance Dolly Parton sang my favorite song.

Correct: At the end of her final performance, Dolly Parton sang my favorite song.

Incorrect: Showing that he was fair and impartial the judge withdrew himself from the trial.

Correct: Showing that he was fair and impartial, the judge withdrew himself from the trial.

Words, Phrases, and Clauses in a Series

When two or more adjectives are used to describe a noun, they must be separated by a comma.

Incorrect: Her beautiful long blonde hair made her stand out from the rest of the women.

Correct: Her beautiful, long, blonde hair made her stand out from the rest of the women.

Incorrect: My canoe trip down the Snake River was the most exhilarating strenuous and frightening experience I have ever had.

Correct: My canoe trip down the Snake River was the most exhilarating, strenuous(,) and frightening experience I have ever had. (The comma before the *and* is optional; you may or may not want to use one. Regardless of your choice, be consistent in your usage throughout your writing.)

If you are listing more than two nouns, they must also be separated by commas.

Incorrect: She wanted to take the radio the television the electric frying pan and her hair dryer on the camping trip.

Correct: She wanted to take the radio, the television, the electric frying pan(,) and her hair dryer on the camping trip.

Incorrect: Trees bushes scrap wood and litter washed ashore during the storm.

Correct: Trees, bushes, scrap wood(,) and litter washed ashore during the storm.

Phrases also should be set off by commas when they are listed in a series.

Incorrect: You should sell your old car buy a Honda and save yourself a lot of money on gasoline.

Correct: You should sell your old car, buy a Honda(,) and save yourself a lot of money on gasoline.

Incorrect: The man walked up to me apologized for his mistake asked for my forgiveness and gave me a hundred dollars.

Correct: The man walked up to me, apologized for his mistake, asked for my forgiveness(,) and gave me a hundred dollars.

Clauses, too, when listed in a series, must be separated by commas.

Incorrect: The country needs a President who is honest who is intelligent and who is strong enough to make unpopular decisions for the benefit of the people.

Correct: The country needs a President who is honest, who is intelligent(,) and who is strong enough to make unpopular decisions for the benefit of the people.

Incorrect: We wanted a house which could accommodate six children which had a fireplace and which overlooked the ocean.

Correct: We wanted a house which could accommodate six children, which had a fireplace(,) and which overlooked the ocean.

Transitional Devices

Transitional devices are phrases or conjunctive adverbs placed within or between sentences to add emphasis or indicate a kind of relationship.

Conjunctive Adverbs	Transitional Phrases
accordingly	after all
also	as a consequence
anyway	as a matter of fact
besides	as a result
consequently	as an illustration
finally	at any rate
furthermore	at least
hence	at the same time
however	by the way
indeed	for example
instead	for instance
later	in addition
likewise	in a like manner
meanwhile	in conclusion
moreover	in fact
namely	in other words
nevertheless	in the first place
next	of course
notwithstanding	on the contrary
otherwise	on the other hand
still	that is
then	to be sure
therefore	
thus	
truly	

These transitional devices should be enclosed in commas; this is especially important when they are placed between the major elements of a sentence.

I am, of course, confident we will be successful.

The ushers, however, thought we were being too noisy.

Note that in the first example the transitional phrase comes between the verb and its complement. In the second, the conjunctive adverb is placed between subject and verb. In both cases the paired commas are mandatory.

Incorrect: The other energy alternatives on the other hand are far more expensive.

Correct: The other energy alternatives, on the other hand, are far more expensive.

Interrupters can also be used to link two sentences together. When they do so, they function almost like conjunctions. Since they are not conjunctions, the two sentences must be separated by a semicolon or a period, and a comma must be placed after the interrupter.

Incorrect: I was tired of writing however I had to have my essay finished in an hour.

Correct: I was tired of writing; however, I had to have my essay finished in an hour.

Incorrect: I cannot afford to buy a house right now as a matter of fact I can barely afford to rent an apartment.

Correct: I cannot afford to buy a house right now; as a matter of fact, I can barely afford to rent an apartment.

There are short clauses that interrupt the sentence in much the same way as an interrupter. Because they are clauses, they have a subject and a verb such as: I suspect, we understand, they noticed.

Incorrect: His explanation I suspect is not altogether truthful.

Correct: His explanation, I suspect, is not altogether truthful.

Incorrect: Their decision we felt was unjustified.

Correct: Their decision, we felt, was unjustified.

Appositives

Appositives are nouns—or word groups functioning as nouns—that add further information about another noun in the sentence. In a sense they restate the other noun. Often the appositive follows the noun to which it refers, interrupting the flow of the sentence. In such cases the appositive must be set off by commas as in the following examples. (Note that the appositive noun is often followed by a descriptive phrase or clause that adds even more information.)

Incorrect: The Broadway a department store known throughout Southern California is having a year—end sale.

Correct: The Broadway, a department store known throughout South-ern California, is having a year—end sale.

Incorrect: My best friend a workaholic who spends all of his time at the office was unable to attend my wedding.

Correct: My best friend, a workaholic who spends all of his time at the office, was unable to attend my wedding.

Incorrect: The Lakers the team that won the Pacific Conference were defeated in the NBA finals.

Correct: The Lakers, the team that won the Pacific Conference, were defeated in the NBA finals.

Nonrestrictive Clauses and Phrases

These adjective clauses or participle phrases are not essential elements of the sentence. If they were left out, the sentence would still be grammatically complete. Nonrestrictive clauses usually insert additional information about the nouns they modify. Because they are not essential to the meaning of the sentence, they are set off by commas.

Incorrect: Gabriel's wife standing at the balcony reminded him of a Greek goddess.

Correct: Gabriel's wife, standing at the balcony, reminded him of a Greek goddess.

Incorrect: Our teacher who was always at class on time was accused of chronic tardiness.

Correct: Our teacher, who was always at class on time, was accused of chronic tardiness.

Incorrect: Muhammad Ali known for his success in boxing is a talented actor.

Correct: Muhammad Ali, known for his success in boxing, is a talented actor.

Incorrect: Superman who used to leap tall buildings with a single bound now lives in retirement on the planet Krypton.

Correct: Superman, who used to leap tall buildings with a single bound, now lives in retirement on the planet Krypton.

Restrictive Clauses and Phrases

These adjective clauses or participial phrases identify the noun that they refer to, and are essential to the meaning of the sentence. Without such a phrase or clause, the sentence would lose its meaning, so no commas are used to set it off.

Incorrect: The man, who robbed my apartment, lives one door away from me.

Correct: The man who robbed my apartment lives one door away from me.

Incorrect: The statements, expressed in the *New York Times,* were denied by the White House.

Correct: The statements expressed in the *New York Times* were denied by the White House.

Incorrect: The airplane, flying close to the beach, crashed near the break-water.

Correct: The airplane flying close to the beach crashed near the break-water.

Incorrect: We finally decided to buy the car, that got the best gas mileage.

Correct: We finally decided to by the car that got the best gas mileage.

Exercise I
Commas

Put commas where they are necessary in the following sentences.

#4 1. My brother was an excellent photographer, but he was also an accomplished musician.

#6 2. After the movie, we went to McDonalds, where we met Brenda and John.

#6 3. When Stevie Wonder finished his concert, the audience applauded him for two hours without stopping.

#1 correction 4. The accountant decided against the Cadillac and bought the Mercedes.

#4 5. I hadn't worked for six months, so I took the first job I was offered.

6. The students, who supported the faculty's demands, demonstrated at the Board of Trustees' meeting, where they insisted on the resignation of the president of the college.

7. As I hiked around Avalanche Lake, the sun was setting, making the water appear purple.   End modifier

8. Although the programs on public television are very good, most people rarely watch them.

9. During the first act of *King Richard II*, I fell asleep and didn't wake up until intermission.

10. I have planned to visit Alaska for years, yet I have never been there.

Exercise II
Commas and Semicolons

Place commas or semicolons where necessary in the following sentences.

1. The 35 mm color pictures which I had processed by Fotohut were not returned to me for over seven months.

2. The woman wanted us to cut the lawn pull the weeds and plant two trees in her large overgrown back yard.

3. We went tobogganing in the afternoon then we had a snowball fight.

4. In addition to the luncheon our guests were also treated to a tour of the art gallery.

5. They were of course astounded by my expensive private collection of master-pieces.

6. I took off my coat threw it on the floor and headed straight to the refrigerator.

7. George Benson a guitarist who has been acclaimed by professional musicians is a versatile singer however his albums do not sell as well as they should.

8. My two closest friends as a matter of fact moved to Idaho a state known mostly for its potatoes.

9. The Porsche speedster had a sleek aerodynamic shape in addition it had an economical air-cooled engine.

10. The man who stopped me in the parking lot wanted to sell me his watch his rings and his portable radio.

Exercise III
Commas

Place commas where they are necessary in the following sentences:

1. The sailboat which finished last in the race had a broken sail.

2. The Martians who had inhabited our planet for centuries were never discovered by the earthlings.

3. Leonardo da Vinci who painted the Mona Lisa is one of the world's most well-known artists.

4. My next-door neighbor gave me the puppy that cries all the time.

5. The carpenter's supervisor whom he had admired for years gave him an excellent recommendation.

6. The earthquake of 1972 which struck Southern California caused three million dollars worth of damage.

7. The Sherwood amplifier which I bought in 1970 has been an outstanding piece of audio equipment.

8. The advice given by the defendant's attorney was ignored by the judge.

9. We wanted to buy the house on the beach located near Malibu.

10. The cost of living which has gone up increasingly every year should be controlled more effectively by the government.

Check Answer Key at the end of the book.

THE SEMICOLON

The semicolon (;) is a stronger mark of separation than the comma. For that reason it can be used to separate two independent clauses, something the comma cannot do. Most often, the two sentences connected by a semicolon are closely related; the second clause explains the first.

> We decided to pack up our cameras; the sunlight had disappeared from Avalanche Lake.

> Do not remove the back from this appliance; you could receive a dangerous electrical shock.

In addition, the semicolon may be used together with a coordinating conjunction (*but, for, yet,* etc.) if one or both of the clauses contain commas within them.

The production of Leonard Bernstein's *Mass,* which opens next Friday on our campus, is attracting thousands of requests for tickets; but because the auditorium is quite small, many of the requests will be denied.

The semicolon is used in a series of paired or grouped items containing one or more commas, like cities and states or names and titles, to separate the pairs or groups.

The firm has offices in Boston, Massachusetts; Boca Raton, Florida; Missoula, Montana; and Fresno, California.

I sent copies of my report to Dr. Button, the college president; Mrs. Booker, the head librarian; and Mr. Lackman, the chairman of my department.

It is important to use a semicolon when two independent clauses are linked by a conjunctive adverb (*however, moreover,* etc.) or by a transitional phrase (*on the other hand; as a matter of fact,* etc.); otherwise, the connected clauses form a comma splice.

Incorrect: I sent in my payment before the tenth of the month, consequently, there should be no late charge.

Correct: I sent in my payment before the tenth of the month; consequently, there should be no late charge.

Incorrect: Susan is quite studious, her brother, on the other hand, enjoys only frivolous pursuits.

Correct: Susan is quite studious; her brother, on the other hand, enjoys only frivolous pursuits.

Incorrect: Don is a more versatile musician than you may think, as a matter of fact, he plays both trumpet and string bass quite well and is an excellent arranger.

Correct: Don is a more versatile musician than you may think; as a matter of fact, he plays both trumpet and string bass quite well and is an excellent arranger.

Unnecessary Semicolons

Do not overuse the semicolon. If two sentences are not very closely related (one explaining or clarifying the other), it is best to separate them with a period. It is even more important to avoid using a semicolon where a comma (or no punctuation at all) is called for.

Incorrect: Dana has moved to Philadelphia; but his parents still live in Tustin.

Correct: Dana has moved to Philadelphia, but his parents still live in Tustin.

Incorrect: I tell you; it can't be done.

Correct: I tell you it can't be done.

THE COLON

It may be useful to think of the colon, in its most common uses, as a sign pointing to something that follows. Most often, it will follow a grammatically complete sentence. In these cases what follows the colon is a restatement or illustration of what precedes it.

The terrorists made the usual demands: safe conduct out of the country, the release of their imprisoned comrades, and an enormous sum of money.

Note that the three phrases following the colon are like a restatement of the word "demands," immediately following the colon. Here is another example.

We have three choices: stay home and do our homework, go to the concert, or go to the concert and then spend the rest of the night doing our homework.

Again, a complete sentence precedes the colon, and a specific word, "choices," is restated or illustrated by the three phrases following the colon.

What follows the colon may be a single word, a phrase, a series of words or phrases, or even an independent clause.

I have only one thing to say: Good-bye.

For our outing at Hollywood Bowl, you will need to bring the following: a picnic lunch, sunglasses, a hat, and your concert ticket.

During the earthquake drill there are just three things to remember: duck, cover, and hold.

There was a simple reason why the radio would not play: It had been unplugged.

We have three choices: We can stay home and do our homework, we can go to the Herbie Hancock concert, or we can go to the concert and then stay awake the rest of the night doing our homework.

There is one common use of the colon in which it does not follow a complete sentence: the introduction of formal quotations. Usually this involves the quoting of written, rather than spoken, material.

Embarrassed at having publicly released secrets that helped *The Progressive* magazine explain how to make an H-bomb, a Department of Energy official in Washington, D. C., insisted: "We are not involved in a cover-up. We got caught between a rock and a hard place."

On that same day, in Boise, Idaho, the head of the Farm Bureau—who had arranged grain sales with Libya, a nation pressuring Idaho's Senator Frank Church into approving the sale of troop-transport planes—was quoted as saying: "Church is in between a rock and a hard place."

William Safire, On Language *(New York: Times Books, 1980), p. 27*

In each of these examples, the quoted material functions grammatically as the object of a verb form preceding the colon. Other uses of the colon include the salutations of formal letters, literary citations, footnotes, and bibliographies. For these you might consult the section on punctuation in a good handbook or an unabridged dictionary.

Exercise I

The Semicolon and the Colon

Insert punctuation marks in the following sentences as needed.

1. The St. Johns cannot come for dinner their automobile is being repaired.

2. The family dog can no longer bring in the Sunday *Times* it has grown too heavy.

3. The Oscar-winning actress thanked her director who had guided her performance her co-star who had made helpful suggestions and her mother who had encouraged her to pursue an acting career.

4. The jazz critic Leonard Feather writes approvingly of the music Miles Davis played in the 1950's and 1960's he doesn't seem to care for the electronic sounds of today's "fusion" groups.

5. Of course artists should strive for greater freedom of expression they must not however abandon discipline.

6. The roofers continued their work on the historic old mansion; even though the temperature was over 100 degrees.

7. My parents didn't believe the salesman; who told them the Renault was a reliable automobile.

8. The novelist Will Sindora maintains three residences a farm outside Bellingham Washington a cabin in Big Bear City California and a townhouse in Manhattan.

9. Instructional aides were given a choice either hand in their time cards by the 25th of the month or wait two additional weeks for their pay checks.

10. Expressing his attitude toward criticism, Samuel Johnson wrote "I would rather be attacked than unnoticed. For the worst thing you can do to an author is to be silent as to his works."

 Exercise II

The Semicolon and Colon

Correct the punctuation in the following sentences as necessary.

1. An eerie sound can be heard at night in Pasadena; when the coyotes howl in the Arroyo Seco.

2. We never go jogging at night in the arroyo, the coyotes there have been known to attack humans.

3. One statement in the auction booklet made some prospective buyers nervous "Although the information contained in the brochure was obtained from sources deemed reliable, it is not guaranteed and may be incomplete or in error."

4. The Westons have homes in Boulder, Colorado, Merced, California, and Flint, Michigan.

5. My friend in Alexandria Virginia amazes me he rides his bicycle to work even in snow storms.

6. I promise you this my report will be delivered on time.

7. The plumber told us this morning; the water heater must be replaced.

8. The woman wanted to find a new career; which would give her financial security.

9. The hummingbird flew around the backyard looking for the feeder I had moved it to the front of the house near the living room window.

10. If you don't pay the electric bill on time the Edison Company will shut off the power to your apartment, furthermore they will charge you twenty dollars to have it reconnected.

Check Answer Key at the end of the book.

PARENTHESES

Sentence elements enclosed in parentheses are generally considered nonessential to the meaning of the sentence. Usually these elements are less than complete sentences.

> The elevator's emergency button (the red one) is at the bottom of the control panel.
> Turn right at the second signal (just past the bank) and drive three blocks.

> Here are some common uses of parentheses.

To introduce or explain certain abbreviations:

> Mrs. Wagner has long been associated with the California Teachers Association (CTA); for ten years she has been president of the local CTA.
> A spokesperson for PSA (Pacific Southwest Airlines) has announced an increase in the fare from Los Angeles to San Francisco.

To enclose numerals or letters in a series:

> The terrorists made the usual demands: (1) that they be given safe conduct out of the country, (2) that their imprisoned comrades be set free, and (3) that the government give them an enormous sum of money.
> We have three choices: (a) we can stay home and do our homework; (b) we can go to the Herbie Hancock concert; or (c) we can go to the concert and then stay awake the rest of the night doing our homework.

To enclose other explanatory or identifying information:

> Senator Cranston (Dem., Calif.) voted for the bill.
> You can look it up in the Bible (Genesis 2:7).

In a sense, parentheses remove the enclosed element from the sentence. For that reason, they should not be used in place of italics or quotation marks to indicate emphasis or the idea "so-called."

Incorrect: Now in his forties, Melvin still likes to (soup-up) automobiles.

Correct: Now in his forties, Melvin still likes to "soup-up" automobiles.

Incorrect: Remember that this week's meeting will be on (Tuesday), not Thursday.

Correct: Remember that this week's meeting will be on *Tuesday*, not Thursday.

A word of caution about parentheses: Some student writers use parentheses to insert ironic comments, as in these examples;

All of the candidates assure us that they are honest (ha-ha).

When I opened the package, there was (would you believe?) the watch that I had wanted.

The cautionary advice concerns the elements enclosed in the parentheses. Most instructors discourage such playful, "cute" remarks; they are best omitted.

DASHES

Because some student writers use dashes indiscriminately, instructors often advise students not to use the dash at all. The suggestion is worth considering. Still, the dash can be a useful mark if its functions are understood. The most common uses of the dash are these.

1. Dashes are used in pairs to enclose parenthetical elements, often short sentences, that interrupt the flow of the main sentence.

   Bill's sister shares her apartment—I'm serious—with twelve cats.
   When you dine at The Right Track, try the hot beer-and-cheese soup—don't accept it cold—with your dinner.

2. A single dash may be used to mark a sudden turn in thought or change in tone, at the end of a sentence.

   The coastal commissioners insist that there was nothing irregular about their accepting large gifts of money from potential developers—what a joke.

3. Use a single dash also to emphasize an introductory series, especially when the main sentence contains a word that refers to the series.

   A concert grand piano, white plush carpet, expensive wall hangings, a Dali painting—all the furnishings in Miss Hughes's living room suggested wealth.

Dashes should be used sparingly, and should not substitute for orthodox punctuation. Overuse of dashes gives writing an unsure, somewhat hysterical quality.

Undesirable: In the middle of the San Joaquin Valley—of all places—a new Shakespearean theater company has sprung up—within the past year—and has won critical approval. I saw one of the first productions—it was *The Taming of the Shrew*—and was quite favorably impressed.

Better: A new Shakespearean theater company has sprung up in the middle of the San Joaquin Valley, of all places, within the past year and has won critical approval. I saw one of the first productions, *The Taming of the Shrew,* and was quite favorably impressed.

Exercise

Parentheses and Dashes

Insert parentheses and dashes as needed.

1. Push the emergency handle the red one to the "UP" position.

2. Many people were astonished when Senator Hayakawa Rep. Calif. suggested that all Iranians in the United States be placed in concentration camps.

3. Please note that my telephone number 415 573-2121 has been changed; the new one, 714 826-2525, is unlisted.

4. An A.A. degree in business administration, two years' experience, and a knack for dealing with the public these are my qualifications.

5. My mother's hair I was absolutely shocked had been dyed a light blue.

6. My brother was apprehended while driving across the desert at 110 miles per hour a serious mistake for anyone to make.

7. The likeliest candidate for the position is A. R. "Rob" Greene.

8. Bring me an order of French fries, two cheeseburgers don't forget onions and a tall Coke.

9. To get to the submarine races, take the Santa Monica Freeway to the Pacific Coast Highway exit the one after Atlantic Boulevard.

10. Jack Anderson reported that baby seals are being slaughtered by employees of the United States government, at a cost to taxpayers of 4.3 million dollars per year how senseless and wasteful!

Check Answer Key at the end of the book.

QUOTATION MARKS

Quotation marks, as the name implies, should be used to enclose quoted material such as another person's exact spoken or written words.

"If adults can be so accepting of the reality of television," the authors write, "imagine its effect on children."

Note that only the actual words of the authors are enclosed in quotation marks; the attributive phrase is not. When the attributive phrase is placed at the beginning of the sentence (its usual position), it is followed by a comma.

Gerbner and Gross state, "If adults can be so accepting of the reality of television, imagine its effect on children."

The quotation may also be preceded by a colon, most often when the quotation is introduced by a complete sentence.

They have this to say about television plots: "Unlike the real world, where personalities are complex, motives unclear, and outcomes ambiguous, television presents a world of clarity and simplicity."

Note that in every example, concluding periods and commas are placed *before* the closing quotation marks. Elements briefer than complete sentences are sometimes quoted, as in the following examples.

1. Individual words and phrases
    Answer all questions "Yes" or "No."
    It was clear to Dick Gregory that being called a "worthy boy" was not a compliment.

2. Titles of stories, articles, etc.
    Doris Lessing's "A Woman on a Roof" is a story about disillusionment and unwarranted assumptions.
    The Los Angeles Times reported the latest developments in an article titled "Mideast Peace Initiative in Sudden Crisis."

Special note: There are some situations in which it is important *not* to use quotation marks. One is with your own essay titles.

Incorrect: "Why I like Jazz Music"

Correct: Why I Like Jazz Music

Incorrect: "Three Types of College Students"

Correct: Three Types of College Students

Do not use quotation marks with nicknames or slang expressions. If a person is generally known by a nickname, there is no need to suggest that there is something unusual or substandard about it (which is what quotation marks imply in that situation). In a formal letter of recommendation, it is common to enclose a nickname in quotation marks the first time it is used; thereafter, the marks are omitted.

> Robert T. ("Toby") Shepard has been employed by this department for the past two years. In all his assignments, Toby has demonstrated a thorough grasp of subject matter.

Slang expressions are best avoided altogether. If, however, you feel it necessary to use one, use it forthrightly; forget the quotation marks.

Not Good: Bob was so "up-tight" that it was impossible to talk to him.

Better: Bob was so up-tight that it was impossible to talk to him.

Better Yet: Bob was so agitated (nervous, excited, angry, frightened) that it was impossible to talk to him.

Remember to use quotation marks only when the exact words of the original source are being reproduced. When a statement has been recast in your own words, it is an indirect quotation and should not be enclosed in quotation marks.

Incorrect: Arnold Cooper asked me "When I was coming to Fresno."

Correct: Arnold Cooper asked me when I was coming to Fresno.

Correct: Arnold Cooper asked me, "When are you coming to Fresno?"

Quotations within Quotations

When quoting a passage that contains a quotation, use normal, double marks (") for the entire passage and single marks (on a typewriter, the apostrophe) for the internal quotation. "Sadly," writes Patti, "the only conclusion I can come to is that, as long as we continue to live with the so-called 'right to bear arms attitude,' there will be no effective gun control laws."

Exercise

Quotation Marks

Copy the following sentences and insert quotation marks where they are needed. Remember to place commas and periods correctly in relation to closing quotation marks.

1. I was reading Ray Bradbury's The Pedestrian when the phone rang.

2. It was David. What are you doing? he asked. I'd like to come over and play you my new Hubert Laws album.

3. I'd like to hear it, I said, but I'm busy; I have to finish The Pedestrian and two other stories tonight.

4. Can't you put the reading off until tomorrow? David asked. I know you'll enjoy this record.

5. I told him that was impossible; Professor Belroy had said that anyone who was unprepared for class discussion would be in trouble.

6. What did he mean by in trouble? David asked.

7. I explained that my grade in Professor Belroy's course would be partly based on my participation in class discussion. So far, I haven't said much in class.

8. If you cut class tomorrow, you won't have to say anything, David insisted.

9. That would be a good idea if I hadn't cut last Friday, I reminded him, to go skiing with you.

10. Finally David said that he understood, but before hanging up he said I was turning into a bibliomaniac.

Check Answer Key at the end of the book.

THE APOSTROPHE

Apostrophes can be used for two purposes: to make contractions of two words or to show possession.

Contraction

A contraction consists of two words joined together to make a shortened form leaving out one or more letters. The apostrophe (') is put in place of the missing letter(s). For instance:

could not	couldn't
I am	I'm
she is	she's
he would	he'd
they will	they'll
will not	won't
who is	who's

Possession

The apostrophe can also show ownership. You add an apostrophe and s ('s) for singular words or plural nouns that do not end in s. For instance:

Bob's car
men's clothing
people's ideas
Charles's recorder
audience's response

You add only an apostrophe (') to plural nouns ending in s.

Students' center
Attorneys' fees
Senators' opinions
Disk jockeys' prattle
Teachers' absences

You must add an apostrophe and s ('s) to the last word in a compound subject and object to show joint ownership.

Ralph and Harold's apartment
Joyce and Carol's hair dryer

The mayor and governor's decision

You need to add an apostrophe and s ('s) to each modifier of a plural subject or object to show individual ownership.

Ron's and Dave's homes
Rhonda's and Loraine's mothers
The car's and motorcycle's damages

You also need an apostrophe and s ('s) when you make a plural out of a number, symbol, or word.

There are four S's in Mississippi.
The class should count off by 4's.
I received three B's on my report card.
Don't give me any more but's.
I don't want to hear any additional No's.

You should never add an apostrophe and s to possessive pronouns (his, hers, ours, theirs, its, yours, whose).

his bike
its paw
Whose hat is this?
The error is theirs.

Exercise
Apostrophes

Put an apostrophe or apostrophe and s where they are needed in the following sentences.

1. Our teachers wont accept any more maybes.

2. I found Toms books in the girls gym.

3. Bob (or Bobs) and Carols report cards show straight Ds.

4. Dont hide the clowns rubber nose in the womens lounge; hell suspect its there.

5. Well never get the cars engines started in time to get to the doctors convention.

6. Theyre not going to listen to any more of Jeans whys.

7. My aunt (or aunts) and uncles present was in my parents bedroom.

8. The contestants figures were all 10s.

9. Theyd assumed that youd go to the party if Norma wont be there.

10. Its apparent the governments spending isn't being reduced.

Check Answer Key at the end of the book.

SEXIST LANGUAGE

Sexist language involves the use of words that in most cases refer to men only. This usage indicates a bias against women and is considered unacceptable to many readers because it shows favoritism for one sex. As a result, a writer should avoid sexist terms. Most often this language includes compound nouns that have "man" or "men" as part of them. A good example is the word mailman that excludes women who deliver the mail. It is preferable to use another term that is all-inclusive such as mail carrier or letter carrier. Another example is the word chairman for which the word chairperson is preferable.

By using nonsexist language a writer appears to be more objective and, thereby, more credible to the reader than a writer who uses sexist language.

Exercise

Sexist Language

Consider the following sentences and replace any words that are sexist.

1. When we visit the movie set, you will be amazed at how much work the cameraman has to do to prepare a scene.

2. To be effective a congressman must communicate frequently with his constituents.

3. The salesman who sells you a computer may guarantee its performance, but he may be difficult to find when you have a problem with it.

4. When you take the car to the garage, tell the serviceman that the air conditioner is not working properly.

5. All of mankind would benefit from a peace agreement among nations.

EDITING

Through much of the text of *Getting Down to Specifics* and in this review, we have discussed numerous mechanical aspects of writing. These are matters you should concern yourself with after finishing the brainstorming, prewriting, and writing stages. To deal with them during the writing process would most likely interrupt your thinking and weaken the writing. You cannot forget about mechanical matters altogether, though, because educated readers—and these are the people you are addressing—expect you to observe certain conventions. An essay or letter full of ungrammatical sentences, misspellings, and so on can offend readers and cause you to lose their interest and sympathy.

Reading over a piece of writing to improve mechanical and other aspects is called *editing (or proofreading)*. So far you have dealt with various parts of editing in reading and revising your own writing. Editing your writing requires many separate readings, for it is difficult to see the errors you make. You must develop skill, therefore, at recognizing and correcting errors.

You should either memorize the checklist below or refer to it when editing your paragraphs and essays.

Editing Checklist

1. *Content.* Clear main and supporting ideas; adequately detailed support.

2. *Organization.* Paragraphs and sentences arranged in the most logical and climactic order.

3. *Unity.* All main ideas and supporting statements clearly refer to thesis and topic sentences; no off-the-topic ideas.

4. *Coherence.* Flow of ideas is smooth and uninterrupted; transitions indicate relationship between ideas.

5. *Language detail.* Most appropriate choice of words; no wordiness or avoidable jargon; correct spelling.

6. *Grammar and usage.* Writing is in edited American English (sometimes called "Standard").

 Exercise

Editing

The following sample paragraphs will give you practice in using the editing checklist. Read each paragraph carefully, noting whatever problems you encounter; your instructor's marking symbols should be useful to you. Then complete the exercise by solving the problems; in addition to correcting mechanical errors, feel free to rewrite as necessary (but make no unnecessary changes).

1. Beauty is not all you need in a woman. Beauty is important to today's women; in the sense that they are spending all kinds of money on themselves for that reason. Women may be beautiful but do they have the specific qualities that would make her a real human being in the sense of feelings and kindness? You may see a very beautiful woman and say to yourself "She is all I need" but is it? A woman must have feeling for you and in addition for herself, otherwise she would not care for you and help you in time of need.

2. When Abe Fonseca was only 14 he was not only drinking beer, he was conceited about how much he could drink. He would get involved in contests with his friends to see who can drink the fastest. And the most. One night him and his friends went to a party where there was all kinds of older people and some heavy drinkers; who were amazed at how much the youngsters could drink. There was a fast-drinking contest and the older people jokingly asked Abe if him and his friends wanted to take part. They did. It was a big mistake for

Abe he became sick and was sick for days. Later, one of his friends asked Abe how he felt. All he could say was Never again.

3. One condition of attending a college is that the student must pay for their own cost of books and supplies. I can understand this. It would get too expensive for the government to buy thousands of people books and supplies each semester. Anyway, there would be much more of a hassle each term with computing every single student's spendings on books and supplies. This way, the student can sell the books after the semester and use that money to purchase the new books and supplies he/she needs for the upcoming semester. Another aspect, which I will not go into completely, of attending a community college is the transportation costs. There are no dorm's to live in so everyone must commute. I have to fill my gas tank 2–3 times a week because I live about a half-hour away. But then again, it was my choice to attend here so I cannot charge the government with that.

4. Installing a mandatory student-body fee at Clay College could have an effect on attendance. Clay College has always been inexpensive, thats why its been so successful. Paying more for materials is out of the question, we pay enough now for books. The parking fee isn't so bad, we need more security patrolling the parking lots.

Check Answer Key at the end of the book.

Answer Key for Review

of Writing Mechanics

Identifying Nouns (page 230)

1, 4, 6, 8, 10, 11, 13, 14, 15, 17, 18, 20, 22, 23, 24, 26, 28, 30.

Identifying Verbs (page 231)

2 (also a noun), 4 (also a noun), 5, 6 (also a noun), 7 (also a noun), 9 (also a noun), 11 (also a noun), 12 (also a noun), 14, 16 (also a noun), 17, 19, 20 (also a noun), 21 (also a noun), 23 (also a noun), 24, 26 (also an adjective), 27 (also a noun), 29.

Using Sentence Patterns (page 233)

Have your instructor, a tutor, or writing workshop instructor or aide check the sentences you have written for this exercise.

Identifying Subjects and Verbs (page 234)

1. The *lobby* of the Hallmark Hotel *was filled* with dignitaries from all over the world. (Complete sentence.)

2. During the long winter in Idaho, the *snow piling* up in drifts as high as fifteen feet. (No main verb.)

3. *Mr. Kripes brought* home the new sofa and showed it to his wife, who was quite alarmed at the color. (Complete sentence.)

4. *My next door neighbor's dog barks* all night long at the sound of the wind.

5. Being a senior in high school and working part time for my uncle as a flunky. (Incomplete sentence, two present participle phrases.)

6. The *bouncer implied* that I was not dressed for the occasion. (Complete sentence.)

7. *Night fell.* (Complete sentence.)

8. The *book explaining* how to make sound investments. (No main verb.)

9. *I could not see* him at the end of the pier, but he was there. (Complete sentence)

10. Alarmed by the late-night telephone call. (Incomplete sentence, past participle phrase.)

I. Sentence Fragments (page 236)

1. We were all greatly disappointed *when Gerald Ford lost the election.*

2. *Before the performance by the Grateful Dead at the Palladium,* we waited patiently in line for two hours.

3. It took an hour to catch the dog *running along the beach and playing in the surf at Point Magu.*

4. *His engine stalled by a vapor lock in the middle of Nebraska,* the young salesman walked to the nearest farm.

5. The air pollution which had covered Los Angeles for five weeks was cleared away *when it rained for three days straight.*

6. Kathy's father was completely delighted with the court's decision *concerning the accident that he had as a mechanic.*

7. We all enjoyed going to the airport to meet the President, *but not driving home through the weekend traffic.*

8. The doctor continued to work at the hospital *throughout the evening and well into the next morning.*

9. The food at the restaurant was expensive *yet was quite delicious despite the price.*

10. My sister left the party early, *tired of all the loud music and pointless conversation.*

II. Sentence Fragments (page 236)

1. Gerald did not join us for the chamber music concert last night, *being a punk rock fan.*

2. *Stranded at the drive in theater with a vapor lock,* my date decided to go home with my best friend.

3. I bought a small economy car *which cost only $7,000.*

4. I won't be able to videotape the late movie on TV tomorrow night *unless I pay an additional fee.*

5. The trustees of Little Hills College provide as many free services as possible for their students *whereas the trustees of Big River College imposed a fifty dollar parking fee.*

6. *After I graduated from Harvard with honors,* I was hired to manage a Burger King restaurant.

7. Needles, California, can be a miserable place to visit, *especially in the summer when the temperature often reaches 110 degrees at night.*

8. *In the middle of the Alaskan tundra where it was − 30 degrees,* Paul and Mary were playing Frisbee dressed in jeans and tee shirts.

9. *Driving through a downpour on my way to work,* my car stalled in the middle of the Harbor Freeway.

10. *In Glacier Park last spring when the wildflowers were blooming,* my friends hiked up to Crater Lake *and went swimming near the waterfall.*

I. Fused Sentences and Comma Splices (page 238)

1. Of course I'm going to the concert; I wouldn't miss it for anything.

2. When the phone rang, John dropped his cup. He was apprehensive. (or "cup; he")

3. He wasn't merely worried; he was frightened half to death.

4. Penny's constant smile is not just a façade; it's a reflection of her cheerful outlook.

5. Pay attention; this lecture is important. (or "attention. This")

6. One big advantage to owning a cassette deck is convenience; the cassettes are easy to handle and store. (or "convenience. The")

7. David had been out of school for several years; however, he quickly adjusted to college life.

8. Although he missed going to concerts and parties on weeknights, he was proud of being the best student in his physics class.

9. This music sounds distorted; I must have had the volume too high when I made the recording. (or "distorted. I")

10. I don't usually make that kind of mistake; perhaps the tape deck needs repair.

II. Fused Sentences and Comma Splices (page 239)

1. I've always hated fused sentences; I think it's because I've written so many of them. (or "sentences. I")

2. I arrived at the party early. I wanted to get a chance to talk to the host alone. (or "early; I")

3. The high tides during the storm damaged the beach houses; many were washed out to sea. (or "houses. Many")

4. Your tiny hands are frozen. Let me warm them for you. (or "frozen; let")

5. I've told you a thousand times. Always put the blade guard in place before using the power saw. (or "times; always")

6. I don't like it; I never have; I never will. (or "it. I" "have. I")

7. George was driving down Main Street; changing the cassette in his radio, he never saw the swerving truck. (or "street. Changing")

8. *The Loved One* was a very entertaining book. The movie was even better. (or "book; the")

9. Hazing has always been a tradition with fraternities. Most colleges now forbid it. (or "fraternities; most")

10. We never heard the Steely Dan concert on Friday; it had been canceled for some reason. (or "Friday. It")

I. Verb Tense (page 242)

1. If I had known

2. was standing

3. Correct, or was summoned . . . he had been accused

4. had looked

5. thought, we'd had (or had had)

6. was raining

7. Correct

8. kept fighting, weren't tired

9. had washed

10. walked, treated (or walk, treat)

II. Verb Tense (page 243)

1. If it hadn't rained
2. they ran into his old girlfriend.
3. If he had waited just one more second, his receiver would have been open, and they would have scored a touchdown.
4. Correct, or would never have been in prison.
5. If I had known
6. probably will see, or will probably see
7. if he hadn't studied
8. if there hadn't been
9. If I had seen
10. the party had ended

I. Subject-Verb Agreement (page 247)

1. are
2. C
3. considers
4. C
5. is endorsing
6. make
7. are
8. attract
9. C
10. is.

II. Subject-Verb Agreement (page 248)

1. are
2. have
3. shows
4. is

5. knows

6. was

7. are

8. is (noun clause subject is singular)

9. has

10. want (collective noun with plural pronoun)

III. Subject-Verb Agreement (page 248)

1. look

2. has

3. makes

4. astounds

5. is

6. account

7. thinks

8. are

9. looks

10. attracts

Parallel Structure (page 250)

1. At my high school there were very easy requirements, such as little class work, no homework, and much film watching.

2. Janet was criticized both for her behavior and for her attire.

3. When you revise your paragraphs, include coordination, subordination, and simple sentences as well.

4. The candidate declared that he always has believed in the right to free expression, and always will.

5. The passage will become clear after you read it repeatedly or underline key words and phrases.

6. John poured syrup over his pancakes, his hash-brown potatoes, and even his eggs.

7. The telephone solicitor wanted to know not only my age and address, but also my income.

8. We wanted a house which could accommodate six children, which had a fireplace, and which overlooked the ocean.

9. The director has augmented his storytelling with screen projections, a beautiful music score, and fantastic lighting.

10. I never saw a more moving production of *The Glass Menagerie;* nor did my wife. (Or: I have never seen . . . nor has)

I. Pronoun Problems (page 255)

1. I

2. its

3. his

4. her

5. she

6. me

7. I

8. they

9. us

10. their

II. Pronoun Problems (page 256)

1. Whom.

2. Whom.

3. Whom.

4. Whom.

5. Whom.

6. Who.

7. No one sent a R.S.V.P. as we requested.

8. Everyone wanted his or her name included on the plaque.
   All of the people wanted their names included on the plaque.

9. Neither of our friends has any plans for his or her career.
   Neither of our friends has any plans for a career.

10. Whom.

III. Ambiguous Pronoun Reference (page 257)

1. The parents were delighted when their children gave them a hamster.

2. The Sunday *Times* has grown so heavy that the family dog can no longer carry it.

3. My mother told my sister, "You are an excellent photographer."

4. Fred unexpectedly ran into Chuck at the playhouse and was delighted to see him after so many years.

5. I always look forward to these exhibits; the student paintings are always so unusual.

I. Commas (page 265)

1. My brother was an excellent photographer, but he was also an accomplished musician.

2. After the movie we went to McDonalds, where we met Brenda and John.

3. When Stevie Wonder finished his concert, the audience applauded him for two hours without stopping.

4. The accountant decided against the Cadillac and bought the Mercedes.

5. I hadn't worked for six months, so I took the first job I was offered.

6. The students who supported the faculty's demands demonstrated at the Board of Trustees' meeting, where they insisted on the resignation of the President of the college.

7. As I hiked around Avalanche Lake, the sun was setting, which made the water appear purple.

8. Although the programs on public television are very good, most people rarely watch them.

9. During the first act of *King Richard II,* I fell asleep and didn't wake up until intermission.

10. I have planned to visit Alaska for years, yet I have never been there.

II. Commas and Semicolons (page 266)

1. The 35 mm color pictures which I had processed by Fotohut were not returned to me for over seven months.

2. The woman wanted us to cut the lawn, pull the weeds(,) and plant two trees in her large, overgrown back yard.

3. We went tobogganing in the afternoon; then, we had a snowball fight.

4. In addition to the luncheon, our guests were also treated to a tour of the gallery.

5. They were, of course, astounded by my expensive, private collection of master-pieces.

6. I took off my coat, threw it on the floor(,) and headed straight to the refrigerator.

7. George Benson, a guitarist who has been acclaimed by professional musicians, is a versatile singer; however, his albums do not sell as well as they should.

8. My two closest friends, as a matter of fact, moved to Idaho, a state known mostly for its potatoes.

9. The Porsche speedster had a sleek, aerodynamic shape; in addition, it had an economical, air-cooled engine.

10. The man who stopped me in the parking lot wanted to sell me his watch, his rings(,) and his portable radio.

III. Commas (page 267)

1. The sailboat which finished last in the race had a broken sail.

2. The Martians, who had inhabited our planet for centuries, were never discovered by the earthlings.

3. Leonardo da Vinci, who painted the Mona Lisa, is one of the world's most well-known artists.

4. My next-door neighbor gave me the puppy that cries all the time.

5. The carpenter's supervisor, whom he had admired for years, gave him an excellent recommendation.

6. The earthquake of 1972 which struck Southern California caused three million dollars worth of damage.

7. The Sherwood amplifier which I bought in 1970 has been an outstanding piece of audio equipment.

8. The advice given by the defendant's attorney was ignored by the judge.

9. We wanted to buy the house on the beach located near Malibu.

10. The cost of living, which has gone up increasingly every year, should be controlled more effectively by the government.

I. The Semicolon and the Colon (page 270)

1. The St. Johns cannot come for dinner; their automobile is being repaired.

2. The family dog can no longer bring in the Sunday *Times;* the paper has grown too heavy. (Indefinite pronoun reference corrected)

3. The Oscar-winning actress thanked her director, who had guided her performance; her co-star, who had made helpful suggestions; and her mother, who had encouraged her to pursue an acting career.

4. The jazz critic Leonard Feather writes approvingly of the music Miles Davis played in the 1950's and 1960's. He doesn't seem to care for the electronic sounds of today's "fusion" groups. (The relationship doesn't seem close enough to call for a semicolon.)

5. Of course, artists should strive for greater freedom of expression; they must not, however, abandon discipline.

6. The roofers continued their work on the historic old mansion even though the temperature was over 100 degrees.

7. My parents didn't believe the salesman who told them the Renault was a reliable automobile.

8. The novelist Will Sindora maintains three residences: a farm outside Bellingham, Washington; a cabin in Big Bear City, California; and a townhouse in Manhattan.

9. Instructional aides were given a choice: either hand in their time cards by the 25th of the month or wait two additional weeks for their pay checks.

10. Expressing his attitude toward criticism, Samuel Johnson wrote: "I would rather be attacked than unnoticed. For the worst thing you can do to an author is to be silent as to his works."

II. The Semicolon and the Colon (page 271)

1. An eerie sound can be heard at night in Pasadena when the coyotes howl in the Arroyo Seco.

2. We never go jogging at night in the arroyo; the coyotes there have been known to attack humans.

3. One statement in the auction booklet made some prospective buyers nervous: "Although the information contained in the brochure was obtained from sources deemed reliable, it is not guaranteed and may be incomplete or in error."

4. The Westons have homes in Boulder, Colorado; Merced, California; and Flint, Michigan.

5. My friend in Alexandria, Virginia, amazes me; he rides his bicycle to work even in snow storms.

6. I promise you this: my report will be delivered on time.

7. The plumber told us this morning the water heater must be replaced.

8. The woman wanted to find a new career which would give her financial security.

9. The hummingbird flew around the backyard looking for the feeder; I had moved it to the front of the house near the living room window.

10. If you don't pay the electric bill on time, the Edison Company will shut off the power to your apartment; furthermore, they will charge you twenty dollars to have it reconnected.

Parentheses and Dashes (page 274)

1. handle (the red one)

2. Hayakawa (Rep., Calif.)

3. number, (415) 573-2121, ... one, (714) 826-2525,

4. public—these

5. hair—I was absolutely shocked—had

6. per hour—a serious

7. A. R. ("Rob") Greene.

8. cheeseburgers—don't forget the onions—and

9. exit (the one after Atlantic Boulevard).

10. per year—how senseless and wasteful!

Quotation Marks (page 276)

1. I was reading Ray Bradbury's "The Pedestrian" when the phone rang.

2. It was David. "What are you doing?" he asked. "I'd like to come over and play you my new Hubert Laws album."

3. "I'd like to hear it," I said, "but I'm busy; I have to finish 'The Pedestrian' and two other stories tonight."

4. "Can't you put the reading off until tomorrow?" he asked. "I know you'll enjoy this record."

5. I told him that was impossible; Professor Belroy had said that anyone who was unprepared for class discussion would be in trouble.

6. "What did he mean by 'in trouble'?" David asked.

7. I explained that my grade in Professor Belroy's course would be partly based on my participation in class discussion. "So far, I haven't said much in class."

8. "If you cut class tomorrow, you won't have to say anything," David insisted.

9. "That would be a good idea if I hadn't cut last Friday," I reminded him, "to go skiing with you."

10. Finally, David said that he understood, but before hanging up he said I was turning into a bibliomaniac. (or "bibliomaniac." This would seem to have been the word David used.)

Apostrophes (page 279)

1. Our teachers won't accept anymore maybe's.

2. I found Tom's books in the girls' gym.

3. Bob's and Carol's report cards show straight D's.

4. Don't hide the clown's rubber nose in the women's lounge; he'll suspect it's there.

5. We'll never get the cars' engines started in time to get to the doctors' convention.

6. They're not going to listen to anymore of Jean's why's.

7. My aunt and uncle's present was in my parent's bedroom.

8. The contestants' figures were all 10's.

9. They'd assumed that you'd go to the party if Norma won't be there.

10. It's apparent the government's spending isn't being reduced.

Sexist Language (page 280)

1. Camera operator

2. Representative, member of congress, congressperson

3. Sales person, sales manager, sales clerk

4. Service technician, mechanic

5. Humanity

Editing (page 281)

In each instance there are several possible revisions. We have chosen to deal with the mechanical problems in the original paragraphs and otherwise change the originals as little as possible.

1. Beauty is not all you need in a woman. Beauty is important to today's women in the sense that they are spending all kinds of money on themselves for that reason. Women may be beautiful, but do they have the specific qualities that would make them real human beings in the sense of feelings and kindness? You may see a very beautiful woman and say to yourself, "She is all I need," but is she? A woman must have feeling for you and, in addition, for herself; otherwise, she will not care for you and help you in time of need.

2. When Abe Fonseca was only 14, he was not only drinking; he was conceited about how much he could drink. He would get involved in contests with his friends to see who could drink the fastest—and the most. One night he and his friends went to a party where there were all kinds of older people, some of them heavy drinkers who were amazed at how much the youngsters could drink. There was a fast-drinking contest, and the older people jokingly asked Abe if he and his friends wanted to take part. They did. It was a big mistake for Abe; he became sick and was sick for days. Later, one of his friends asked Abe how he felt. All he could say was, "Never again."

3. One condition of attending a college is that the student must pay for his or her own books and supplies. I can understand this. It would be too expensive for the government to buy thousands of people's books and supplies. In addition, computing every student's allowance would be tremendously complicated and difficult. Although students have to buy their own books, they get some relief by being able to resell the books at the end of the semester. (The original paragraph suffers from a lack of unity, among other problems. We have rewritten only the part that seemed most unified.)

4. I am opposed to most of the fees that have been proposed for Clay College. A mandatory student-body fee could have an adverse effect on attendance. Clay College has always been inexpensive; that's why it has been so successful. Increased materials fees are also out of the question. We pay enough now for books, along with lab fees in chemistry and photography and some other classes. The parking fee isn't so bad; it will pay for more security patrolling in the parking lots, which we need. (The original paragraph lacked a clear main idea; therefore, it seemed unorganized and incoherent. We have supplied a topic sentence and a few details.)

Credits

Text

Pages 16–17 and 25–27: Success Sharing and Two Guided Fantasies are adapted from exercises by Jack Canfield. Page 99, "New Health Hazard: Being Out of Work" by Abigail Trafford, © June 14, 1982, reprinted by permission of *U.S. News & World Report*. Page 103, "Why Work?" an excerpt from Bill Moyers' Journal by Bill Moyers, © 1976, reprinted by permission of *Bill Moyers' Journal*, WNET-13. Pages 107–108 and 114–115: "Top Problems" and "Opinionnaire on Womanhood" adapted from J. W. Pfeiffer and J. E. Jones (Eds.), *A Handbook of Structured Experiences for Human Relations Training*, Vol. I (revised), San Diego, CA: University Associates, 1974. Used by permission. Page 149, "The Myths of Competition" by Alfie Kohn, © January 1988, reprinted by permission of *The Rotarian*. Page 155, "Competition as a Mixed Good" by Richard W. Eggerman, © July/August 1982, reprinted by permission of *The Humanist*. Page 160, "Winning—an Ancient Tradition" by James G. Thompson, © August 1985, reprinted by permission of *Journal of Physical Education and Dance*. Page 164, "Football Breaks More Than Bones" by Ellen Goodman, © October 28, 1989, reprinted by permission of *The Los Angeles Times*. Page 168, "Shame" from *Nigger* by Dick Gregory, © 1964 by Dick Gregory Enterprises, Inc., reprinted by permission of E. P. Dutton. Page 171, "Margaret" from *I Know Why the Caged Bird Sings* by Maya Angelou, © 1969, reprinted by permission of Random House. Page 176, "The Physical Miseducation of a Former Fat Boy" by Louie Crew, © February 1973, reprinted by permission of *The Saturday Review of Education*. Page 181, "Fear and Reality in the Los Angeles Melting Pot" by Joel Kotkin, © November 5, 1989, reprinted by permission of *The Los Angeles Times*. Page 189, "Prejudice in Intercultural Communication" by Richard W. Brislin, © December 1979, reprinted by permission of *Intercultural Theory and Practice: Perspectives on Education, Training and Research*. Page 196, "Communication in a Global Village" by Dean C. Barnlund from *Public and Private Self in Japan and the United States*, © 1975, reprinted by permission of Tokyo Simul Press, Inc.

Photos

Index

Index for Review
of Writing Mechanics